VALUE PLURALISM
AND ETHICAL CHOICE

DAVID COOPER
Northern Michigan University

ST. MARTIN'S PRESS   NEW YORK

Senior editor: Don Reisman
Manager, publishing services: Emily Berleth
Project management: Beckwith-Clark, Inc.
Cover design: Judy Forster

For information, write:
St. Martin's Press, Inc.
175 Fifth Avenue
New York, NY 10010

ISBN: 0-312-06843-3

Acknowledgments
Material on the Zimbardo Prison Experiment in Chapter One copyright © 1971 Philip G.
Zimbardo, Inc., and reproduced by permission.

Preface

This text is an argument for a philosophically favored point of view from which to view ethical conflicts in a pluralistic world. Throughout, there is a continuous emphasis on clarifying the virtues one needs to function as a responsible moral agent who adopts the recommended point of view. I attempt to ensure philosophical integrity by giving opposing positions proper recognition, or by acknowledging their omission when requirements of space dictate brevity.

Because this book reflects personal conviction, it in no way pretends to be a value-neutral study. The text is animated by my own beliefs about moral agency and professional life. The guiding assumption is that everyone can benefit from learning to use a theoretical perspective to judge practical value conflicts, especially in those contexts where our stations require us to intervene in the lives of "dependent" others in medicine, law, engineering, research on human subjects, social work, teaching, parenting, and so forth. My faith in theory is based in part on personal experience. My own grasp of theory, and my attempts to master the virtues that can help me integrate it into my life, continue to shape my behavior and add to the feeling of awe I have for the moral world. A theoretical orientation to values, of course, will not eliminate immorality from life, guarantee that we will always make the right decisions, or replace the importance of personal moral experience. But, it can help diminish our human propensity to be ethically careless when we confront ethical dilemmas in our rapidly evolving pluralistic culture.

Twenty-five years of teaching students who will take only one philosophy course has convinced me that it is a mistake to begin an introduction to applied ethics with a supposedly value-neutral historical survey that emphasizes esoteric philosophical differences between competing theories. While this approach provides a good foundation for philosophy majors, for the average career-oriented student it is more likely to teach a hidden curriculum of value relativism that may simply reinforce what Sabini and Silver refer to as the modern tendency to be "ethically muddled."[1]

R. S. Peters argues that before people can choose a rule they must first learn, from the inside, what it means to follow a rule.[2] The same can be said for choosing a position from which to evaluate moral conflicts. Before people can adequately choose between competing abstract ethical theories, they must first come to understand, from the inside, what it means to value a theoretical perspective. This text uses developmental research to explain the point of using theory in applied ethics. We begin on a concrete level with a psychological experiment—The Zimbardo

Prison Experiment. Reading the experiment provides us with a common experience upon which to ground later abstract discussions. To find adequate answers to the ethical questions raised by the experiment, we need to transcend the local context of the experiment and enter into theoretical speculation about how one ought to design institutions to protect proper human relationships. A developmental explanation for why we must move up to such an abstract level of discussion clarifies the practical rationality behind taking a theoretical approach to concrete problems.

A developmental approach also helps us see why a theory does not have to be invulnerable to criticism to provide a rational foundation for ethical judgments. It only needs to be one of the best positions so far developed. The fact that we do not have final solutions for all ethical questions does not mean that there has not been ethical progress. Ethics, like science, is a developing discipline, so ethical theories evolve and change. Most of the changes are not arbitrary; they represent conceptual progress that has immediate practical implications for decision makers. Once a person learns to appreciate the reasons for using a theoretical perspective, she* will be in a better position to critically judge the adequacy of competing theories as well as the attempts to apply the theories to practical problems.

Since ethics raises questions about how one ought to live, by its nature it leads a person to reflect on his personal style of relating to others. In this regard, I have consciously tried to adopt the same personal style that informs my conversations with friends and students. The text strives for traditional academic rigor, but also uses personal anecdotes to facilitate discussion. In addition, since an introduction to a field should not contain unnecessary academic jargon, there is a judicious balance between professional vocabulary and ordinary English. Because I assume there will be readers who would like to move on to additional professional literature, the text introduces some of the technical vocabulary used in philosophical ethics. The terms are introduced gradually, however, so as not to interfere with the emphasis on ordinary language.

The overall goal is to rather quickly sketch a picture of the mainstream theoretical perspective found in Western philosophy (adjusted to accommodate contemporary metaethical criticisms). The writing style is narrative rather than overly argumentative, but it becomes increasingly sophisticated as the text develops. I assume an instructor will use the text for about four to six weeks to teach students the background information that will help them philosophically analyze cases in applied ethics. The text can also accommodate instructors who need to cover ethical theory in a shorter span of time. The fastest theoretical reading would focus on Chapters One, Two, Four, Seven, Nine, and Ten.

The second chapter introduces a version of a standard decision procedure from applied ethics that recommends solving conflicts in three stages: first, clarify the background context for the conflict; second, clarify the ideal theory and principles that will be used; and third, implement a practical strategy to solve the

---

*Rather than use "his or her" every time I need to use a gender-neutral pronoun, I prefer to randomly switch back and forth between using masculine and feminine pronouns.

conflict. This text follows the same format, since the first six chapters focus on background metaethical descriptions and conceptual and empirical material from the social sciences and psychology, the next four chapters discuss ideal theory, and the final chapter discusses a theory of implementation.

In particular, Chapters One through Four explain why philosophy is different from science; discuss the special cross-disciplinary nature of applied ethics; survey attempts to make sense of values under conditions of cultural pluralism; explain how taking a rational approach to cultural pluralism can help us avoid muddled thinking, moral drift, and the banality of evil; contrast relativism with absolutist approaches to ethical values; clarify the difference between relativism and theoretical pluralism; and offer a brief discussion of the hermeneutic attempt to transcend the debate between relativists and absolutists. Chapters Five and Six place philosophy on the cognitive, emotive developmental map and discuss the significance of gender differences in ethics. Chapters Seven and Eight address the question "What ethical theory would a morally autonomous person choose to help her establish ethical priorities in a pluralistic culture?" I analyze the concepts of moral autonomy and moral accountability in detail, then discuss the practical and conceptual problems that surround these concepts. Chapter Nine covers consequentialist theories, focusing on ethical egoism and utilitarianism. Chapter Ten covers three nonconsequentialist theories: natural rights, social contract, and Kant's duty ethics. Finally, Chapter Eleven applies theory to practice by developing a theory of implementation that places professional codes of ethics in philosophical context, and then illustrates how to use the decision procedure in Chapter Two to solve a conflict: a contractual dispute from business ethics.

As every instructor knows, personal education accelerates once one begins to teach. I will end this lengthy preface by acknowledging my debt to all my students. Trying to teach them has taught me much more than I ever learned as a student, and, equally important, each semester their infectious enthusiasm adds to the quality of my life.

I would also like to thank Northern Michigan University for the institutional support for this project, as well as my extremely competent assistant and ever-patient typist Colleen Lerret. I'd like to thank the following reviewers for St. Martin's Press: Donald N. Blakeley, California State University—Fresno; Michael S. Pritchard, Western Michigan University; Kevin W. Saunders, The University of Oklahoma; S. N. Tagore, The University of Texas at San Antonio; Stephen C. Taylor, Delaware State College; Jeffrey Tlumak, Vanderbilt University; and Burleigh Wilkins, University of California—Santa Barbara.

I dedicate the text to the people who taught me about love and commitment, especially my children Katherine and Brian.

■ NOTES

1. For the sociological study of the morality of muddle, see John Sabini and Maury Silver, *Moralities of Everyday Life* (Oxford: Oxford University Press, 1982).

2. R. S. Peters, *Reason and Compassion* (London: Routledge & Kegan Paul, 1977), pp. 45–46.

Contents

NINE ■ Ideal Theory: A Consequentialist Background   148

TEN ■ Ideal Theory: A Nonconsequentialist Background   168

ELEVEN ■ Theory of Implementation: The Best Means   191

Note to Students

There are certain reasoning strategies and conceptual tools that are not always explicitly taught but that are vital for success in the culture of higher education. Studies show that even though good students use the strategies, they cannot necessarily pass them on to other students because they are not always explicitly aware of their own skills.[1] This makes learning seem mysterious to those who have not learned the strategies. But there is no mystery here; strategies can be mastered, and once acquired they increase general competence. If you will make use of them, I can guarantee that your journey into the culture of academic philosophy not only will be interesting but will also broaden your repertoire of skills for solving problems in general.

There are many ways to get to the same place. If you have a system that works for you, continue to use it. What I am going to suggest is that you broaden your skills by adding some new strategies. Experience will teach you which tools are most useful for different contexts. One of the best learning strategies is *active reading*. Too often students say, "I read this chapter six times and it still makes no sense." The problem is often *passive reading*. They start with the first word and read to the last word and do very little in the middle. If you are doing something wrong, doing it six times will not make it better. Remember, reading academic material is not like reading a story. It requires thought and reflection. I have been reading philosophy for 30 years. I still read new material at a rate of about 15 pages an hour. You have to give yourself time to reflect while you read.

Enter into a dialogue with the text. Ask questions about every paragraph. "What is this paragraph supposed to tell me?" "If I was going to be asked a question about this paragraph, what question would I be asked?" "Do I know the answer?" At the top of each page, write out questions that the page can answer. At the end of each section, write out the questions that the information in that section can answer. And always keep a "global" perspective. "What are the questions that this discipline tries to answer?" "How does this particular bit of material contribute to that overall task?"

There are several steps to active reading. First, don't keep reading when you get confused. Stop. Then try to explicitly identify *where* you got confused. Second, try to *formulate a question* directed at your confusion; that is, a question that, when answered, will clear up your confusion or at least lead the way toward an investigation that will clear it up. Third, try to *specify some plans* for getting rid of the confusion. Take an active role in trying to generate a number of solutions to your question. Fourth, try to *evaluate which possible solution is the best* and pay attention to how you came to your conclusion. Finally, *internalize the whole process* so you will remember it. Make it part of you. Write it down or visualize it in a context.

This is the ideal time to think of questions that you can ask in class. Asking questions is crucial in becoming an active philosophy student. If students don't ask questions, the instructor is not getting feedback and has no idea if the students are understanding the material. An academic blunder is apparent when the first test shows both the instructor and students that they have not been communicating.

One strategy for remembering new material is to make maps. Create charts that show how concepts are related. Keep the concepts from different theories on different maps so that you will not confuse the theories with one another. Then draw a master map that brings the smaller maps together so that you can compare theories. For example, you might draw a map for each social contract theory, and then a larger one that highlights conceptual similarities and differences between the theories.

It is very hard to remember abstract terms because they are not usually tied to specific visual events. Maps can help us begin to visualize. Why bother? Well, because visual memory seems to be almost inexhaustible. If you can attach abstract concepts to a visual image, you are far less likely to forget the terms. For example, "justice" is a very abstract concept often defined as "getting one's due" or "having one's rights respected." Students often have trouble remembering the definition (along with the hundred or so other abstract concepts they must remember). But when they visualize the definition, they report that it is much easier to remember. It does not matter how they visualize it, so long as they use their own memory system.

Some students find it useful to *visualize* different rooms in their house, and then keep each philosophical theory in a different room. The individual terms of each theory can be attached to different objects in the room. For example, you could remember "utility" by placing utilitarianism in the kitchen and associating "utility" with useful cooking utensils.

The strategies listed above are useful in any academic discipline. There are also strategies that have to be mastered in individual disciplines. Since each discipline focuses on questions and problems that are special to it, each has developed its own methods for solving its problems. You increase your own ability to cope with the world when you master the problem-solving strategies of several different disciplines.

■ NOTE

1. David B. Ellis, *On Becoming a Master Student* (Rapid City, South Dakota: College Survival, Inc., 1984).

■ CHAPTER ONE

Introduction to Philosophical Ethics

■ PHILOSOPHY AS AN ACADEMIC CULTURE

You are about to undertake a journey, perhaps over unexplored academic terrain. In fact, you are about to enter an intellectual subculture called philosophical ethics. Since the best way to understand a culture is to live it rather than passively view it from the outside, I invite you to enter into the spirit of this text and live within it. If you actively participate in the academic philosophical way of life by using its special vocabulary and style of thought to reflect on ethical questions, you will begin to see why this special kind of intellectual culture is useful.

Teachers learn very early in their careers that students do not necessarily appreciate the academic perspective that the teachers have learned to take for granted. If we stop to think about it, this makes complete sense. How well we can "see" a figure will depend on the type of background against which it is presented (e.g., it may be difficult to see the boundaries of a red patch against a background that is a slightly different shade of red, but it will be easy to see the figure's boundaries against a white background). The background that influences how we perceive events can be both external (environmental factors) and internal (beliefs, desires, previous perceptions, etc.). We are predisposed by these factors to see certain figures clearly and to ignore others. Teachers who are sensitive to the "ground" of the student/teacher relationship accept the fact that students will not initially focus on the same figures as teachers. Nonetheless, the extent of the differences can be startling.

For example, I like to show my students a film called "The Death of Socrates" from the old CBS TV series "You Are There." The film reenacts the events surrounding the execution in Athens, Greece of the famous philosopher in 304 B.C.E. The gimmick behind the film is to have modern CBS reporters interview key historical figures and then film the philosophical discussion between Socrates and his friends just before his execution. I show the film so that students can "see" for themselves how inspiring a person's life can become when it is governed by a sophisticated philosophical theory. I am assuming, of course, that students will "see" something inspiring in Socrates' life.

I have shown the film hundreds of times, and it continues to teach me about the importance of the figure/ground phenomenon. Often students share enough of my background that they "see" what I hope they will see. But just as often I am startled by comments like "What is a Socrates, anyway?" or "Well, that was dumb. Why didn't he escape?" The reaction that startled me the most occurred when I showed the film to student inmates behind the walls of a maximum security prison. This was my first experience with teaching at the prison. I did not pay enough attention to the prisoner's "ground," thus I was not at all prepared for how they would see the "figures" in the film. The opening interview is with Aristophanes, a famous Greek poet and writer of comedies. At the end of the interview, Aristophanes is asked if he thinks Socrates "might yet be saved?" He replies, "I hope that he will, I think that he will not. But, valuing what is most precious to me, my greatest concern at the moment is to protect myself." While students at the university have never openly reacted to Aristophanes' comment, a number of students at the prison spontaneously shouted out, "Right on!" "All right! That dude knows where it's at." Later, some of these same students expressed contempt for Socrates. They thought he was a "chump." They were seeing the film from a background that was radically different from my own. It had never occurred to me that students would see Aristophanes, rather than Socrates, as the hero of the film. I was in for an interesting semester. It takes time to master the boundaries that define a different culture.

To understand the culture of mainstream Western philosophy we will need to focus continually on the "ground" that shapes its intellectual boundaries. Contemporary philosophers are aware of how *the background shapes the foreground.* As a discipline, philosophy has become increasingly concerned about its background presuppositions; thus it has become increasingly SELF-REFLECTIVE. This means it 'critically evaluates its background assumptions at the same time that it uses them to analyze and judge all the other various grounds or belief systems that define and give meaning to human experience'. It seems paradoxical to use one's background to evaluate one's background, and yet this task also appears to be unavoidable (the nature of the paradox will be explored in detail in Chapters Four through Eight). Because it is confusing to try to understand how we understand things, and because it is so important in philosophy to understand the background presuppositions behind our understandings, most forms of Western philosophy have chosen to make self-critical rationality their ultimate standard. Other values (like self-preservation, power, tradition, wealth, prestige) are treated as subservient to the task of trying to reach greater understanding through a process of self-critical rational debate. This book will help you participate in a philosophical culture and should, therefore, help you develop: logical skills that facilitate rational debate and self-analysis; an attitude that welcomes rational criticism; a broad base of knowledge upon which to anchor your judgments about theories; and a keen appreciation for the importance of historical and personal background context in a fully rational investigation. You will also learn about historical traditions and develop a technical vocabulary (each technical term will be shown in boldface small capital letters the first time it is used). Initial definitions in the text will often be quite broad, so as not to exclude subject matter before discussing it. As we proceed, definitions can be refined and appropriately narrowed.

■ *Conceptual Context*

I will define ETHICS as 'a discipline that tries to understand rationally (as opposed to understanding in ways that are aesthetic, religious, economic, patriotic, etc.) how we ought to resolve various kinds of value conflicts'. Value conflicts in ethics may occur on many different levels, and they may involve people, animals, the environment, spiritual beings, and so forth. As a way of getting started, I will narrow the focus and only discuss value conflicts that occur between two or more people. This move will simplify our task, but it will not make the task simple. In the first place, to make sense of a value conflict we will need to understand the background or context within which the conflict occurs. This is sometimes expressed by saying that any event must be "historically" or "conceptually" situated before its full meaning can be understood. (We will explore various ways of being "situated" throughout the text.)

To get a feel for this concept, consider the following question: "What does it mean to place a value conflict in a philosophical context?" The easiest way to answer this question is to start with a simple, concrete conflict familiar to each of us, then see what we will have to do to make its philosophical context clear. For example, suppose I am driving down the street, when suddenly I say, "Nuts!" and stop my car. Without an explanation of context this apparent action is no more than a meaningless physical event. Suppose my young and inexperienced daughter is present. She may ask, "What's wrong? Why did the car stop?" The simplest explanation would draw her attention to the fact that the car didn't just stop; I stopped it on purpose. So I will clarify the context by saying, "I didn't want to stop now, but the light turned red, so I had to stop the car." This explanation reveals

> ACTIONS AND JUDGMENTS
>
> NEED TO BE
>
> HISTORICALLY SITUATED

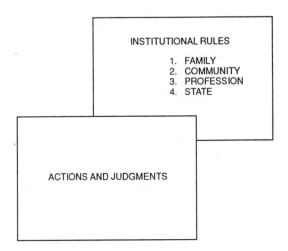

that there is a conflict behind my action. Although I stopped on purpose, I wanted to continue in spite of the community's decision to have cars occasionally stop at this spot on the street.

But suppose my daughter does not understand the rules of the road. She might ask, "If you don't want to stop, then why did you stop?" She is asking why I did not choose to act on my own preference and keep going. To satisfy her, I will have to move up to another level of abstraction and point out that there is a background rule for driving that demands I override my own preferences. I could say, "The rule for driving is, you can go only if the light is green. You must stop when it is red."

This explanation may satisfy those who understand the social context for traffic laws, but suppose my son is in the back seat, and he is a simple anarchist who resents all rules (or is a budding philosopher who craves deeper explanations). He may challenge the rules themselves by asking, "But why do we have to have rules anyway?" From his perspective, traffic lights seem to be arbitrary commands. If I want him to see that the rules might make sense, I will need to explain that there is a more abstract background that explains and justifies the rules of the road. So I would argue:

> Since people who drive have a right to share the highway, it is only fair that they should get their turn to cross this busy intersection. If the rules let everyone cross whenever they want to, they may crash into each other. To reduce the possibility for harm while people are taking their turn, we need some way to coordinate their timing. A traffic light is useful in busy spots. It makes sure everyone has a turn, and it also prevents harm by telling us when it is our turn to go.

I have clarified and justified not only the rule but also the device for implementing the rule by tracing them back to a principle of justice and a principle of harm.

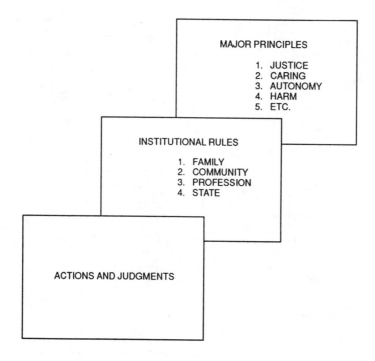

MAJOR PRINCIPLES

1. JUSTICE
2. CARING
3. AUTONOMY
4. HARM
5. ETC.

INSTITUTIONAL RULES

1. FAMILY
2. COMMUNITY
3. PROFESSION
4. STATE

ACTIONS AND JUDGMENTS

■ *Levels of Justification*

Notice the form of the discussion so far. To answer the "why" question about a simple concrete action, we had to refer to increasingly abstract background concepts to justify the behavior. In ordinary circumstances, basic principles usually have a fairly universal appeal, so most people would stop asking questions at this point. How soon a person stops asking "why" questions will, of course, depend on the personal historical background of the person. There will always be some people who will not be satisfied by an appeal to common principles. Perhaps they won't agree with the principles used, or perhaps they will disagree about the best way to interpret the principles, or perhaps they just want to see where they will go if they keep asking "Why?" For whatever reason, if people keep asking, they will eventually have to go behind principles to explore the background context that justifies them. When we challenge principles, we are asking for a justification that is so abstract it can only be answered by grounding the principles in some theoretical framework. The justification will refer to the belief system or theory that is being used to give meaning to our way of life. This is the ultimate background conceptual context in ethical justifications.

One aim of philosophy is to study all the fundamental theories that are used to give this kind of foundational conceptual grounding for major principles. But, there is yet another level of consideration that can arise. A normative philosophy that is self-reflective will also try to go behind theories themselves,

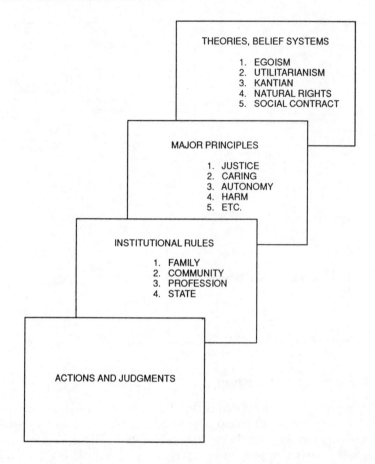

THEORIES, BELIEF SYSTEMS

1. EGOISM
2. UTILITARIANISM
3. KANTIAN
4. NATURAL RIGHTS
5. SOCIAL CONTRACT

MAJOR PRINCIPLES

1. JUSTICE
2. CARING
3. AUTONOMY
4. HARM
5. ETC.

INSTITUTIONAL RULES

1. FAMILY
2. COMMUNITY
3. PROFESSION
4. STATE

ACTIONS AND JUDGMENTS

in an attempt to pinpoint "what it means to have a theory." This level of reflection leads to theories about theories. It also leads to attempts to discover criteria that can be used to recommend some theories over others. 'Attempts to answer questions about the nature of an ethical point of view, the nature of ethical theories, the meaning of ethical terms, and the types of reasons that can serve as justifications in ethics' make up a field of study called METAETHICS. This level of ethical consideration is about as abstract as ethics can get.

Obviously, value conflicts can arise on any of these conceptual levels. To avoid confusion, then, when trying to resolve value conflicts it is important to be clear about the level at which the conflict occurs, because a different type of justification is appropriate at each level. We need to know whether a disagreement involves different desires, judgments, intentions, rules, principles, or theories. For example, a conflict over rules may be settled by appealing to shared principles, but a conflict over principles cannot be settled by appealing to rules.

When we begin to reflect on the importance of levels, new questions begin to emerge. If we agree at a higher level of generality (e.g., on theory or principles), why can't we get agreement at the lower levels (e.g., agreement on rules or

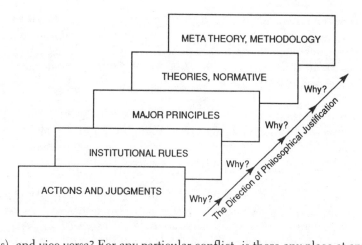

actions), and vice versa? For any particular conflict, is there any place at any level at which agreement can be reached? One concern in ethics is to find rational answers for all the questions that come up when we begin to reflect about types of disputes and how best to situate them at a proper level.

Discussions in philosophical ethics often begin with the most abstract background considerations. Abstract terms are, of course, very useful. They help us to communicate about "kinds" of things even though we have not directly experienced all members of the kind. IDEALS are abstract in this sense. They are 'conceptions of perfect states of affairs that we think should exist, but which may exist only in our thoughts'. Ethical theories organize such abstract concepts into frameworks that provide the broad intellectual and value contexts we use when we judge concrete ethical experiences.

Since people find it easier to learn about abstract concepts when they can relate them to the kinds of concrete events the abstractions were designed to explain, it will be useful if you begin by reading about a complex concrete event before we start to discuss the details of abstract ethical theories. While you read the following account of a social psychology experiment, do not focus exclusively on the fact that it involves a pseudo prison environment. If you focus exclusively on this aspect of the experiment you will miss the main point, which is: "This experiment created a small ethical community that cannot be adequately evaluated without the use of ethical theory." As a minicommunity, the experiment serves as a rich pedagogical tool for clarifying the practical use of ethical theories. To get the full impact of the experiment you should read it without interruption, so wait until you have thirty minutes free before you begin.

■ THE ZIMBARDO PRISON EXPERIMENT

In 1971, the social psychologist Dr. Philip Zimbardo conducted a fascinating experiment in the basement of a Stanford University dorm. He converted the rooms in the basement into a miniature prison environment. The goal was to see how living in a prison would affect a group of average, normal, healthy men who had never been in trouble with authority. He randomly assigned paid volunteers to be either guards or prisoners and then sat back to watch what happened (the material that follows is taken from the transcript of Zimbardo's slide/tape presentation of his experiment).[1]

> Each prisoner, . . . blindfolded and still in a state of mild shock over the surprise arrest by the city police, is put into the car of one of our men and driven to the Stanford County Jail for further processing. The prisoners are brought into the jail one at a time and greeted by the warden.
>
>> Warden: "As you probably already know, I'm your Warden. All of you have shown that you are unable to function outside in the real world for one reason or another—that somehow you lack a responsibility of good citizens of this great country. We, of this prison, your correctional staff, are going to help you learn what your responsibilities as citizens of this country are. You have heard the rules. Some time in the very near future there will be a copy of the rules posted in each of the cells. We expect you to know them and to be able to recite them by number. If you follow all of these rules and keep your hands clean, you repent for your misdeeds and show a proper attitude of penitence, you and I will get along just fine."[2]
>>
>> [Examples of rules][3] Rule number 1: Prisoners must remain silent during rest periods, after lights are out, during meals, and whenever they are outside the prison yard. 2: Prisoners must eat at mealtimes and only at mealtimes. 3: Prisoners must not move, tamper, deface, or damage walls, ceilings, windows, doors, or other prison property. . . . 7: Prisoners must address each other by their ID number only. . . . 8: Prisoners must address the guards as "Mr. Correctional Officer.". . . 16: Failure to obey any of the above rules may result in punishment.
>
> Each prisoner is searched and then systematically stripped naked. He is then deloused, a procedure designed in part to humiliate him and in part to be sure he isn't bringing in any germs to contaminate our jail.
>
> The prisoner is then issued his uniform. It consists of five parts. The main part is a dress which each prisoner wears at all times with no underclothes. On the dress, in front and in back, is his prison number. On each prisoner's right ankle is a heavy chain, bolted on and worn at all times. Loosely fitting rubber sandals are on their feet, and on their heads, to cover their long hair, stocking caps, a woman's nylon stocking made into a cap which also had to be kept on day and night. . . . [R]eal male prisoners . . . feel emasculated . . . [and] we thought we could produce the same effects very quickly by putting men in a dress without underclothes. . . . The chain on their foot . . . was used in order that the prisoner always would be aware of the oppressiveness of his environment. So even when a prisoner was asleep he could not escape the atmosphere of oppression. When a prisoner turned over,

the chain would hit his other foot, waking him up and reminding him that he was still in prison, unable to escape even in his dreams.

His prison number was one way of making the prisoner feel anonymous. Each prisoner had to be called only by his number and could refer to himself and the other prisoners only by number. The stocking cap on the head was a substitute for having the prisoner's hair shaved off. This process of having one's head shaved, which takes place in most prisons as well as in the military, is designed in part to minimize each human being's individuality, since some people express their individuality through hair style or length. It is also a way of getting each person to begin to comply with the arbitrary, coercive rule of the institution.

. . . The guards were given no specific instruction or training on how to be guards. Instead they were free, within limits, to do whatever they thought was necessary to maintain law and order in the prison and to command the respect of the prisoners. The guards made up their own set of rules which they then carried into effect under the general supervision of Warden David Jaffe, also an undergraduate student. They were warned, however, of the potential seriousness of their mission and of the possible dangers in the situation they were about to enter, as of course are real guards who voluntarily take such a job. As with real prisoners, our prisoners expected some harassment and to have privacy and some of their other civil rights violated while they were in prison. . . . All the guards were dressed in identical uniforms of khaki, they carried a big billy club borrowed from the police, a whistle around their neck, and they all wore special . . . reflecting sunglasses [which] prevented anyone from seeing their eyes or reading their emotions, and thus helped to further promote their anonymity. We were, of course, studying not only the prisoners who were made to feel anonymous but the guards as well.

We began with nine guards and nine prisoners in our jail. Three guards worked each of three eight-hour shifts, three prisoners occupied each of the three cells all the time. . . . The cells were so small that there was room for only three cots on which the prisoners slept or sat.

At 2:30 A.M. the prisoners were rudely awakened from sleep for their count. The count served the function of familiarizing the prisoners with their numbers. But more importantly, it provided a regular occasion for the guards to interact with and exercise control over the prisoners. There were several counts every day and night. As you can hear in this first count, the prisoners were not yet completely into their roles and were not taking it too seriously. They were still trying to assert their independence. The guards, on the other hand, were also feeling out their new roles of asserting some authority over their prisoners.

> Guard: "No talking. Do you want this to last all night? First we're going to count off by ones, beginning down here with 1037. We're gonna do it till we do it right, till we're satisfied with it." Guard: "And I want you to do it fast, and I

want you to do it loud." Guard: "Let's start with 1037. What's your number?"
Prisoners: "One . . . . two . . . three . . . four . . five, six, seven, eight, nine."
(Everyone talking at the same time) "Oh, that was not bad (Babble, etc., some
laughing) . . . didn't do very well." Guard or Prisoner: "Oh, we'll have to do that
again. OK, 1037." Prisoners: "One . . . two, three, four, five, six, seven, eight,
nine." (Laughing) Prisoner: "Oh, that was real bad, slow." (Laughter) Guard:
"Hey!!!" (Sudden silence) "I don't want anybody laughing." Guard: "Let's have
no laughing now. This is no laughing matter. You guys'll be out here all night
if you don't get it right. Let's get it right! Huh?" Prisoner: "Yes sir, Mr. Correctional Officer." Guard: "All right. You're not going to like it very much if you
have to stand out here for a long time." Prisoners: (Sound of suppressed laughter)
Guard: "Hey!! Hey! Did I say you could laugh, 819? Didn't I tell you that you
could not laugh? 819, maybe you didn't hear me right!" Guard: "819, how'd you
like to step out of line and do 23 push-ups for us, huh?"

Push-ups were a common form of physical punishment imposed by the
guards to punish infractions of the rules or displays of improper attitudes
toward the guards or toward the institution. When we saw the guards doing
this, we thought this was an inappropriate kind of punishment in a prison.
However, we later became aware of the fact that in concentration camps in
Nazi Germany, push-ups were often used as a form of punishment. . . . It's
curious that one of our guards also stepped on the prisoners' backs while they
did enforced push-ups toward the end of our experiment.

Because the first day passed without incident, we were surprised and
totally unprepared for the rebellion which broke out on the morning of the
second day. The prisoners removed their stocking caps, ripped off their
numbers and barricaded themselves inside the cells by putting their beds
against the door. And now the problem was, what were we going to do about
this rebellion? The guards were very much upset because the prisoners also
began to taunt and curse them to their faces. When the morning shift of
guards came on, they too were upset at the night shift who, they felt, must
have been too permissive and too lenient or else this rebellion would not have
taken place. The guards had to handle the rebellion themselves, and what
they did was fascinating to behold.

At first they insisted that reinforcements be called in. The three guards
who were waiting on stand-by call at home came in and the night shift of
guards voluntarily remained on duty to bolster the morning shift. The guards
met and decided to treat force with force. They got a fire extinguisher which
shot a stream of skin-chilling carbon dioxide and forced the prisoners away
from the doors; they broke into each cell, stripped the prisoners naked, took
the beds out, forced some of the prisoners who were then the ringleaders
into solitary confinement, and generally began to harass and intimidate the
prisoners.

(Noises of the prison riot; the sound of the fire extinguisher) Prisoner: "NO! NO! NO! NO!" (The fire extinguisher) "NO! NO!" Guard: "Put handcuffs on him." Prisoner: "NO!" (Chaotic random noise) Prisoner: "They're gonna take our beds!" (Noise and shouting) Guard: "Against the wall." Prisoner: "Don't let 'em in!" Prisoner shouting: "They took our clothes! They took our beds! They took our clothes!" Guard: "Hands off the door! Off the Bed!" (Chaotic noise) Prisoner: (Shouting) "Fuck this experiment! Fuck Dr. Zimbardo!" Prisoner: "Fucking simulation!" Prisoner: (Shouting) "Fucking simulation! Fucking simulation! Fucking simulation! It's a fucking simulated experiment. . . ."

The rebellion had been temporarily crushed, but now a new problem faced the guards. . . . [w]hat were they going to do? One of the guards then came up with an ingenious solution. "Let's use psychological tactics instead of physical ones." Psychological tactics amounted to setting up a privilege cell. . . . The three prisoners least involved in the rebellion were given special privileges. They got their uniforms back, they got their beds back, they were allowed to wash and brush their teeth. The others were not. They also got to eat special food in the presence of the other prisoners who lost the privilege of eating. What this amounted to was breaking the solidarity among the prisoners.

After half a day of this treatment, the guards then took some of these "good" prisoners and put them into the "bad" cells, and took some of the "bad" prisoners and put them into the "good" cell, thoroughly confusing all the prisoners. Some of the prisoners who were the ringleaders now thought that the prisoners from the privileged cell must be informers, and suddenly, at a psychological level, there could no longer be any trust or solidarity within each cell.

. . . In contrast, the prisoners' rebellion played an important role in producing greater solidarity among the guards. Because now, suddenly, it was no longer just an experiment, no longer just a simple simulation for the guards. Indeed, here were some troublemakers who were out to get them, who might really cause them some harm, who had, previously, humiliated them publicly. They were taunting them, teasing, cursing, and the guards were not going to have any more of that shit. Now the guards began to step up even more their control, authority, surveillance, and aggression.

Every aspect of the prisoners' behavior fell under the total and arbitrary control of the guards who were on any given shift. To go to the toilet became a privilege which the guard could grant or deny at his whim. Indeed, quite often, as the days wore on, a guard might refuse the request of a prisoner to go to the toilet, and after our 10:00 P.M. lockup when lights were out, the prisoners had to go to urinate or defecate in a bucket which was left in their cell, and on occasion the guard would refuse to allow the prisoners even to empty that bucket. And soon the prison began to smell of urine and feces.

Also, while escorting a prisoner to the toilet, the guard who was alone with the prisoner, not under the surveillance of the prison superintendent, or anyone else, was free to push, trip, or do anything else he thought necessary to keep the prisoner in line, and also to get back at him personally for having been a troublemaker.

The guards were especially tough on the ringleader of the rebellion, prisoner #5401. We learned later, when we were censoring the prisoners' mail, that he was also a self-styled radical activist. He had volunteered with the idea of exposing our study which he had mistakenly thought was an establishment tool to find ways to control student radicals. In fact, he had planned to sell the story to Berkeley's underground newspapers, *The Barb* and *The Tribe*, when the experiment was over. However, even he fell so completely into the role of prisoner that he was proud to be elected leader of the Stanford County Jail Grievance Committee as revealed in this letter to his girl friend.

> Dear Dot, Needless to say things didn't work out as planned. I have wound up as a prisoner here. C'est la guerre. Have made arrangements with the Tribe and the Barb to carry the article after I get out. Should get out on the 29th, as that's when the 2 weeks is up. I organized a hunger strike on the 2nd day. It was a stand off. Today I've gotten together a Stanford County Prisoner Inmates Grievance Committee, of which I am the Chairman. Today we see the Superintendent to present our Grievances. The guards are really harassing me now, but you just can't keep the old _____ morale down. I really don't think anybody will crack before this thing is over. A few of the prisoners are starting to get servile, but they exert no influence on the rest of us. Well, got to go. Love, _____

Most of the grievances of the Grievance Committee which pertained to recreation and rehabilitation activities had to be ignored, of course, until the staff was satisfied that the internal threat to prison security was no longer a menace. On Monday night, in less than 36 hours, we were forced to release our first prisoner. Prisoner #8612 was suffering from acute emotional disturbance, disorganized thinking, uncontrollable crying, screaming, and rage. In spite of all of this we had already come to think so much like prison authorities that we thought he was fooling, so to say, trying to "con" us. It took quite a while before we could be convinced that he was really suffering, and then we released him.

> Prisoner 8612: "Now! I gotta go. I just, ah, to a doctor, anything. I can't seem to, ah . . . I'm fucked up. I don't know how to explain it." (Shouts) "I'm all fucked up inside! and I want out! and I want out now! God damn it! . . ." (Quieter) "You don't know. You don't know. I mean God, I . . . Solitary, that doesn't bug me. It's just the whole thing. I . . . jeez," (Pleading voice) "call my lawyer. This is really serious. I . . . I gotta have my lawyer now. No . . . No more

fucking around. I gotta have a lawyer. I mean, I just can't take it. I've gotta have a lawyer. I haven't a lawyer or anything. . . ." Guard: "You will . . . you will wait until the counselor comes back. He'll be back this evening and you can talk to him about. . . ." Prisoner 8612: (Quietly) " . . . Can't sit here or anything. I'm sorry, I can't, listen. I, I, I promise, I'll, I'll, stay chained to the damn chair . . . or ceiling . . ." (Shouts) "I mean Jesus Christ, I'm burning up inside don't you know!!!!"

There were two events which highlighted Tuesday. The first was visiting hour by parents and friends. . . . We were worried that when the parents saw the state of our jail and of their children, they might insist on taking them home. To counter this, we first grossly manipulated the situation, and then we subtly manipulated the visitors. . . . We washed, shaved, and groomed the prisoners, had them clean and polish their cells; we removed all the signs, fed them a big dinner, played music on the intercom, and even had an attractive coed, Susie Phillips, greet the visitors at our registration desk. When the dozen or so visitors came, full of good humor at what seemed to be a novel, fun experience, we systematically brought their behavior under situational control. They had to be taught that they were our guests whom we were allowing the privilege of visiting their sons, brothers, and lovers. They had to register, were made to wait half an hour, were told that only two visitors could see any one prisoner, the total visiting time was cut to only ten minutes, they had to be under the surveillance of a guard, and before any parents could enter the visiting area, they had to discuss their son's case with the warden. Of course they complained about these arbitrary rules, but remarkably, they did nothing but comply with them. And so they, too, became part of the prison drama we were playing. Indeed, some of the parents got upset when they saw how fatigued and distressed their boy was. But their reaction was to work within the system to appeal privately to the superintendent to make conditions better for their little prisoner. When I said to one mother, "What's the matter with your boy? Doesn't he sleep well?" this complaining mother said, "I'm sorry; I don't want to make any trouble, but he seems so tired." She was reacting to the authority that I was unconsciously becoming—as superintendent of the Stanford County Jail.

The second major event we had to contend with on Tuesday was a rumor of a mass escape plot. One of the guards overheard the prisoners talking about an escape that would take place immediately after visiting hours. The rumor went as follows: Prisoner #8612, whom we had released the night before, was really only faking. What he was going to do was go out, round up a bunch of his friends, and they were going to break in right after visiting hours. How do you think we reacted to this rumor? Do you think we recorded a pattern of rumor transmission during the day and waited for the impending escape, and then observed what happened? That was what we should have done, of course, if we were all acting like experimental social psychologists, which is our usual role. Instead, by Tuesday our main concern was to maintain the security of our prison. So what we did in fact was for the warden, the superintendent, and one of the chief lieutenants, Craig Haney, to meet and plan our strategy.

First we put an informer in the cell that #8612 occupied. He was a confederate who would give us information about the escape plot. Then I went back to the Palo Alto Police Department and asked if we could have all our prisoners transferred to their jail. My impassioned request was turned down only because the City Manager notified the Chief of Police that they would not be covered by their insurance if we moved our prisoners into their jail. Angry and disgusted at this lack of cooperation, I left, and we formulated a second plan. The plan was to dismantle our jail immediately after the visitors left, call in our reinforcements, take all of our prisoners, chain them, put bags over their heads, put them in an elevator, bring the prisoners up to a fifth floor storage room that we had spent several hours cleaning out, and leave all the prisoners in there with the guards until after their friends broke into the basement. When the conspirators came, I would be sitting there alone. I would tell them simply that the experiment was over and we had sent all of their friends home, that there was nothing left to liberate. After they left, we'd bring our prisoners back and redouble the security of our prison. We even thought of luring #8612 back on some pretext and then imprisoning him again because he was released on false pretenses.

. . . The rumor of the prison break turned out to be just a rumor. It never materialized. Imagine our reaction. We had spent one entire day planning to foil the escape, went begging to the Police Department, cleaned up the storeroom, moved our prisoners, dismantled most of the prison—we didn't even collect any data during the entire day, . . . [and] guess who was going to pay for this? The guards again escalated very noticeably their level of harassment, to the point of increasing the humiliation that they made the prisoners suffer, even to cleaning out toilet bowls with their bare hands, having the prisoners do push-ups, and increasing the length of the counts to several hours each.

> Guard: "416, you stand up, everybody else down in push-up position. 416, while they do push-ups you sing 'Amazing Grace.' Ready? Down!" (416 begins to sing) "Amazing grace how sweet the sound. . . ." Guard: "Keep going. Once I was blind but now I see." Prisoner 416 continues to sing: "Once I was blind. . . ." Guard: "Come on, 5714." (Song ends) Guard: "Not bad. Everybody over on their backs on the floor."

On Wednesday a strange event occurred which added a Kafkaesque element to our prison. A Catholic priest who had been a prison chaplain in Washington, DC was invited down to give me an evaluation of how valid our prison situation was, and also because the Grievance Committee had requested church services. He interviewed each of the prisoners individually and I watched in amazement as half the prisoners he spoke to, when he introduced himself, responded by giving their numbers rather than their name. After some small talk he popped the key question: "Son, what are you doing to get out of here?". . . . Each prisoner, as well as I, responded with puzzlement. And he proceeded to tell each of them that if they didn't help themselves, nobody else would, that they were college students; they were bright enough to realize that they were in prison and that the only way to get out of prison was with a lawyer. If they couldn't afford one, they had to get a public defender. He then volunteered to contact their parents if they wanted him to, in order to get some legal aid. Some of them asked him to do so.

The priest's visit highlights the growing confusion between reality and illusion, between role-playing and self-identity that was gradually taking place in all of us within this prison which we had created, but which now was absorbing us as creatures of its own reality. In real life this man was a real priest. . . . [and] this added to the general level of confusion we were all beginning to feel about our own roles, and where role ends and identity begins. The prisoners who were most disturbed by the priest's visit were those few who had been able to convince themselves, up to this time, that this was not a real prison.

The only prisoner who did not want to speak to the priest was prisoner #819 who was feeling sick and refusing to eat and wanted to see a doctor, not a priest. He was convinced to come out and talk to the priest and the superintendent so that we could diagnose what his problem was and what kind of doctor he needed. While talking to us he broke down and began to cry hysterically, just as had [another] two boys we had released with the same symptoms. I took the chain off his foot, the cap off his head, told him to go and rest in the rest and relaxation room we had adjacent to the prison yard; that I would get him some food and then go with him to see a doctor. While I was doing this, one of the guards lined up all of the prisoners and had them chant aloud.

> Prisoners chanting: "Prisoner 819 damaged, defaced, and tampered with prison property. Prisoner 819 damaged, defaced, and tampered with prison property. Prisoner 819 did a bad thing. Prisoner 819 did a bad thing. Prisoner 819 did a bad thing. Prisoner 819 did a bad thing. Prisoner 819 did a bad thing. . . ."

As soon as I realized that #819 was hearing all this, I raced into the room where I had left him, and what I found was a boy crying hysterically while in the background his fellow prisoners were yelling and chanting that he was a bad prisoner, that they were being punished because of him. No longer was this a chant or a count, disorganized and full of fun, as we saw on the first day. It was marked by its conformity, by its compliance, by its absolute unison. It was as if a single voice was saying, "819 is bad." Or like a million Hitler

Jugend chanting, "Heil Hitler" in a torchlight rally. Imagine how he felt! I said, "Okay, let's leave." Through his tears he said to me, "No, I can't leave." He could not leave because the others had labeled him a bad prisoner. Even though he was feeling sick, he was willing to go back into that prison to prove that he was not a bad prisoner. At that point I said, "Listen, you are not #819. My name is Dr. Zimbardo. I am a psychologist, and this is not a prison. This is just an experiment and those are students, just like you. Let's go." He stopped crying suddenly and looked up at me just like a small child awakened from a nightmare and said, "Okay, let's go." It was also clear that what I was doing was convincing myself of the statement that I had just made.

On Thursday morning the parole board met. All prisoners who thought they had a legitimate reason for being paroled could file an appeal for a parole hearing. The prisoners were chained together and brought to the parole board meeting with bags over their heads so that they could not see or talk. They were ushered into the room one at a time. The parole board was composed largely of people who were strangers to the prisoners and was headed by our prison consultant, Carlo Prescott. Three remarkable things occurred at this parole board meeting. The first was, we asked each prisoner if he would forfeit all the money [volunteer pay] he had earned up to that time if we were to parole him. All but two of them said yes, they would forfeit all the money they had made if we would parole them. This is dramatic in itself, but less so than the next event. At the end of the parole board meeting we told each person to go back to his cell and we would consider his request. Each one of them did so docilely. Now, realize that what we had made salient to them was the contract, that is, they had agreed voluntarily to be prisoners only because they needed the money they would receive for being experimental subjects. If they now no longer wanted the money, then naturally there was no reason or motivation to continue being a subject in this experiment. No one can be imprisoned against his will in an experiment, can he? What they should have said at this point is, "I quit this experiment, and no longer choose to be a subject for money, science, or any other reason." But they did not. They could not because their sense of reality had undergone a transformation. They did not have the power to choose to leave the experiment because it was no longer an experiment to them. They were in a prison where the verbal reality was parole, and forfeiting of wages earned for prison work. In this prison only the correctional authority had the power to grant paroles.

The third significant event of the day was the unexpected way in which our prison consultant went through a complete metamorphosis as head of the parole board. He literally became the most hated authoritarian official imaginable, so much so that when it was over he felt sick at what he had observed himself becoming: his own tormentor who had rejected his parole requests year after year.

Parole Officer: "You come into this room, and you ask for a parole. I assume you . . . you definitely want to be released?" Prisoner: "Uh huh." (Yes) Officer: "And yet, everything about you, your whole behavior pattern here, has continuously been one of rebellion and disregard of the rules from the moment you arrived. I . . . . don't imagine that you think you can come in here and in a few minutes, . . . because you are willing to be contrite . . . you can say some of the things that will eventually move us to parole you. Let me tell you something. You've neither shown the slightest indication of contrition for your act, you have no regard for society, or anyone else around you, you have no social consciousness, and if we can't produce those traits here, by the methods that we have in our control, while we have you! . . . then what indication is there that we can possibly expect you to even begin to behave by any decent standards. As far as I'm concerned, you're impossible, there's no reason to assume that you are in any way rehabilitated. Understand. Nothing personal in this. If it was left up to me personally, I'd see to it that you rotted here. Officer. Take him out."

What vicarious learning takes place in prisons where power, authority, and control are the chief virtues to be modeled by prisoners? By the fifth day a new relationship had emerged between prisoners and guards. . . . The guards could be characterized as falling into one of three groupings. There were the tough but fair guards whose orders were always within the prescribed rules of prison operation. Then there were several guards who were the good guys according to the prisoners, who felt genuinely sorry for the prisoners, who did little favors for them and never punished them. And finally, about a third of the guards were extremely hostile, arbitrary, inventive in their forms of degradation and humiliation, and appeared to thoroughly enjoy the power they wielded when they put on the guard uniform and stepped out into the yard, big stick in hand. None of our personality test scores predicted these extreme differences between the prisoners or guards and their reactions to imprisonment.

Each prisoner coped with the frustration, absolute sense of power-lessness, and growing sense of helplessness and hopelessness in his own way. In the beginning some prisoners coped by being rebellious, even fighting with the guards. One prisoner developed a psychosomatic rash over his entire body when he learned that his parole request had been turned down and we had to bring him to Student Health where he was treated and then released. Four of the prisoners reacted emotionally, breaking down as a legitimate way of passively escaping by having us release them. Some tried to cope with it by being good prisoners, doing everything the guards wanted them to do. One of them was even nicknamed by the other prisoners and guards "Sarge," because he was so military in his execution of all commands. By the end of the study, the prisoners were disintegrated, both as a group and slowly even as individuals. There was no longer any group unity, just a bunch of iso-lated individuals hanging on, much as we saw in the American prisoners of war in the Korean War, or in hospitalized mental patients. It was clear that the guards had won total control of this prison, that they commanded the respect of each prisoner, or more accurately, the obedience of each prisoner.

We did see one final act of rebellion. Prisoner #416 was newly admitted on Wednesday as one of our standbys. He tried to cope with the situation by refusing to eat, by going on an eating strike. Here was a last futile attempt of a prisoner to assert his individuality by refusing to eat. The guards tried, but they couldn't get him to do so. Here was a chance for the other prisoners to reorganize and solidify behind this new act of rebellion. What did they do? How did the guards handle this? Well, the guards did everything they could to try to force-feed him.

> Guard (Shouting): "You say you don't want to eat two stinking sausages. Maybe if you don't want to eat them, you want us to take them and cram 'em up your ass. Is that what you want? Want me to take that and cram it up your ass?"

They even tried to get the other prisoners to feed him. They began to punish his cellmates if he wouldn't eat, and finally they even threatened to cut off Thursday night visiting hours, an hour before the visitors came, if #416 didn't eat. The prisoners then exploded, not against the guards for this arbitrary rule, but against #416, screaming at him, cursing him, telling him he had to eat, that they weren't going to be inconvenienced by his stupid act of defiance. The guards then took #416 and put him in the hole, solitary, for three hours, although their own rule stated one hour was the limit. Still he refused. At this point he should have become a hero to the other prisoners. But what was he? He had become a troublemaker. And so, the head guard on that shift gave the prisoners a choice. They could have #416 come out of solitary if they were willing to give up some little thing of their own—their blanket. Or, if they refused to give that up, #416 would be left in solitary all night. What do you think they chose?

> Guard: "Now if 416 does not want to eat his sausages, then you can give me your blankets and sleep on the bare mattress, or you can keep your blankets and 416 will stay in another day. Now what'll it be?" Sound of several Prisoners: "We gotta sleep . . . keep the blankets." Guard: "Keep the blankets. 416, you're gonna be in there for a while, so just get used to it."

This guard, who was the most brutal of all the guards according to the prisoners, was nicknamed by them "John Wayne." It was curious that several months later we learned from a former Nazi concentration camp inmate, Professor Steiner of Sonoma State College in California, that the most notorious guard in the prison near Buchenwald was named Tom Mix, the John Wayne of 30 or 40 years ago.

Well, the guards in the camps were all anonymous to us. We called them Herr Leutnent or Mr. SS Officer. But they had no name, no identity. However, one of the guards, who was the most vicious of all, we gave him a nickname too. He was shooting the people, for no reason. Killing them, pushing them into the electric fence. His violence was like a Wild West cowboy, so we called him Tom Mix. But only behind his back.

Where had our "John Wayne" learned to become such a guard? How could he and others move so readily into that role? These were questions we were beginning to ask ourselves. On Thursday night when the visitors arrived, some parents asked me to contact a lawyer in order to get their son out of prison. They said some Catholic priest had called to tell them their son was in the Stanford County Jail, that they should get a lawyer or public defender if they wanted to bail him out. Now our play was being written by Pirandello and we were all trapped in our roles. I called the lawyer that they had requested and indeed the lawyer came down and interviewed each of the prisoners. At this point it became clear that we had to end this experiment. We had to do so because it was no longer an experiment. We had indeed created a prison in which people were suffering, in which some boys called prisoners were withdrawing, becoming isolated and behaving in pathological ways. On the other hand, some of the guards were behaving sadistically, delighting in what could be called the "ultimate aphrodisiac of power," and many of the guards who were not behaving that way felt helpless to do anything about it. In fact, they allowed it to go on, never once interfering with an order by one of the cruel guards. It might even be said that it was the good guards who helped maintain the prison, although the bad guards set the tone.

At this point we said, "Enough, we have to end this." And so our two-week simulation was called off after only six days. On Friday, the last thing we did was to have a series of encounter groups, first with all the guards, then with all the prisoners, including those who had been released and had been invited to come back, and then finally we had a meeting for all the guards and prisoners and staff together. We did this in order to get their feelings out in the open, to recount what we had all observed in each other and in ourselves, and to share the experiences which to each of us were very profound.

Finally, we tried to make this a time for moral reeducation by discussing the moral conflicts posed by the simulation and how we behaved and what were the moral alternatives available to us, so that hopefully we would all behave more morally in future real-life situations.

One of the good guards: The experience became more than just participating in an experiment. What I mean to say is that if this was an experiment, the results and products were almost too real. When a prisoner gives you a glassy stare and mumbles inaudibly, you just almost have to perceive the worst. It's almost because you fear that the worst will happen. It's almost as if I'd . . . I'd accepted that it would happen, and that the slightest indication of . . . indication of anxiety or breakdown is the beginning of all this worst possible effects. Specifically it . . . the experience became more than just an experiment when 1037 started acting as though he was breaking down. At this time I was afraid and apprehensive and thought of quitting, and I also was thinking of asking to become a prisoner. I felt as though I didn't want to become a part of a machine that . . . that beats down other men, and forces them to conform, and continually harasses them. I'd almost wished I was being harassed, rather than having to be the harasser.

Here is the reaction of prisoner #416, our would-be hero who had been left in solitary for a considerable time, a middle-class boy who had suffered in our jail for only a few days:

Prisoner 416: I forgot my reasons for being there. I had come there with reasons, like it'll make me money. You know. Things like that. But I found that . . . as I found after 25 hours, I really had no life of, of my own, except what happened to me in that small white room, and umm, what happened to me as I followed people's orders and, umm, was shoved around with a paper bag over my head— whatever. I began to feel that I was losing my identity, that . . . that the person that I call Clay, the person who . . . who put me in this place, the person who volunteered to . . . to go into this prison, 'cause it was a prison to me; it still is a prison to me, I . . . I don't look on it as an experiment or a simulation. It's just a prison that was run by psychologists instead of run by the state. I began to feel that . . . that, that identity, that the person that I was, that had decided to go to prison, was distant from me, was, was remote, until finally, I wasn't that, I was . . . I was 416. I was really my number.

. . . As a consequence of the time we spent in our simulated prison, we could understand how prison, indeed how any total institution, could dehumanize people, could turn them into objects and make them feel helpless and hopeless, and we realized how people could do this to each other. The question now is, how can we begin to change our real institutions so that they promote human values rather than destroy them?

■ APPLIED PHILOSOPHICAL ETHICS

The Zimbardo Prison Experiment is filled with concrete examples of value conflict—prisoners against guards, visitors against the institution, prisoners against prisoners. How should we settle all these conflicts? Which side is right? Would the conflicts even arise if the people were in a different kind of institution? The entire event should remind us that there is an important relationship between individual moral agents and institutional roles or stations. To understand individual actions, we must also understand institutional contexts, since most conflicts occur in institutional settings.

What is an institutional context? Anytime we occupy a station in a marriage, family, job, friendship, school, or church, we are being governed by the rules of an institution. Since I am interested in all contexts that generate concrete rules, I am defining an **INSTITUTION** as 'any rule-governed relationship'. Institutional rules tell us in an immediate concrete way how we ought to behave. After witnessing the Zimbardo experiment it seems appropriate to ask: "Should individual moral agents be held responsible for what they do or should we blame the background institutional rules that defined what was expected of the individuals?" How we answer this important question will reflect our background assumptions about how to apply ethical theory.

As we saw earlier, the direction of investigation in philosophy generally moves from the concrete level toward increasingly abstract background considerations, that is, it moves beyond individuals to rules, then to principles, and finally to the level of theory. Applied philosophy reverses this direction. Thus, a course in applied ethics investigates how abstract theories can be used to help resolve the kinds of value conflicts encountered on the concrete level. For instance, in the conflict between prisoner 416 and the John Wayne guard, we would use theoretical ideals to construct a background context that explains why it is wrong for the John Wayne guard to abuse prisoner 416. The same ideals would explain why it was wrong for the institution to treat the visitors in such an arbitrary fashion. Before we can understand how to solve the concrete conflicts in Zimbardo's experiment, then, we need to be clear about the appropriate background theory we should use to frame and give meaning to the actions and rules we see in the experiment (we will return to this issue throughout the text).

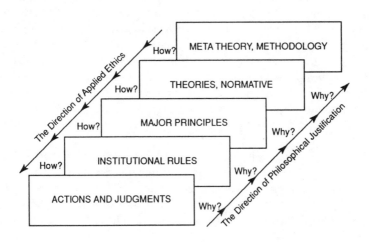

■ Philosophical Theories

Over the centuries philosophers have developed a number of different theories to serve as a background to help guide their judgments about concrete value conflicts. In debates about the theories, a general metaethical consensus has been developed among Western philosophers about a background MORAL POINT OF VIEW that is appropriate for grounding philosophical theories. This text clarifies why this mainstream background is favored. Many philosophers claim that this background "ought" to be adopted by all serious moral agents, which is, of course, an ethical judgment that needs to be judged in its own turn. As one would expect, there are metaethical theories that challenge the idea that there is or ever could be a philosophical consensus about a favored moral point of view for ethical inquiry (there are also those who would challenge most of the other philosophical distinctions that are developed in this text). As we shall see, continual reassessment of the basis for judgment is an essential part of self-reflective philosophical ethics. Such skepticism is welcome and healthy in philosophy, but since it is itself part of the philosophical story, the details of the skeptical metaethical debates can be set aside for now. They will be discussed in Chapters Three, Four, and Six as they naturally arise during our ethical investigations.

■ Prescriptive Principles

When it comes to resolving value conflicts, every theory of ethics assumes that some background features are more relevant than others. Theories try to draw our attention to these relevant features by formulating *foundational principles*, which command us to give certain values top priority in all our ethical decisions. Because these foundational principles give commands, the ethical theories that justify them are said to be NORMATIVE or PRESCRIPTIVE in nature. That is, they do more than describe the rules of a particular society, they also prescribe what ought to be. Ethical prescriptions have a special normative force, since they entail that agents are obligated to obey whether they want to or not. For example, "You ought to tell Jane the truth" refers to your possible conversations with Jane. The statement is prescribing an ideal state of affairs that ought to exist after you do your duty. The implication is that you ought to tell the truth even if you do not prefer that state of affairs. This is an interesting feature about ethics. In the end, even though it is about ideals, it is inherently *practical*, since the abstract, morally binding "ought" statements are supposed to lead to action that will change the concrete world.

Each of the five principles listed below draws our attention to some values that are of foundational concern to at least one major normative Western theory. Standard courses in philosophical ethics often do no more than focus exclusively on clarifying the background theoretical assumptions that are needed to understand and justify principles such as these (an approach that we will use in Chapters Nine and Ten).

1. *Ethical Egoism:* Everyone ought to act so as to promote their own best interest.
2. *Utilitarianism:* Everyone ought to act so as to promote the greatest amount of happiness for everyone.
3. *Natural Rights Theory:* Everyone ought to act in accordance with everyone's inalienable, indefeasible natural rights.
4. *Social Contract Theory:* Everyone ought to act in accordance with the principles of justice that would be chosen by free and equal rational people who come together to form a social contract.
5. *Duty Ethics:* Everyone ought to always treat people as ends unto themselves and never use them as a means only.

■ Virtue Ethics

These five principles do not exhaust the list of possible approaches to ethical inquiry. One might wonder, for instance, why I have not added to the list a principle that would represent VIRTUE* ethics by explicitly prescribing common virtues like honesty, courage, prudence, justice, charity, and so forth. Virtue ethics does not focus on guiding principles but on traits of character that help moral agents function well in situations calling for ethical judgment. It would be virtually impossible to summarize this approach to ethics in a single foundational principle. This difficulty can be illustrated with a simple summary of Aristotle's theory of virtue ethics.

Aristotle focused on clarifying the concept of virtue itself. He argued that it was virtuous to choose the proper amount of emotion and/or action called for in a particular situation and that extremes of emotions and action were vices (his theory of the golden mean). In all communities there are some men of practical wisdom who have the capacity to judge wisely. Aristotle argued that they have the capacity to follow the "right rule"[5] whatever the situation. This means they know how to balance all relevant variables in any circumstance so as to avoid extremes.

It is difficult to disagree with Aristotle. Of course, we should strive to be virtuous and avoid vices. But, exactly how are those of us who are not yet men of practical wisdom supposed to calculate the proportionate amount of emotion and action on all occasions? Advocates of the five theories listed above would say, "Wise men ought to always use our principle when they search for the 'right rule' in every situation." Aristotle did not give a major principle that we should use all the time; whatever the "right rule" is on a given occasion, it is not a universal determinate principle. It appears instead to be a practical capacity to act appropriately in different contexts. So, rather than follow the dictates of a major principle, Aristotle advises beginners in ethics to focus on imitating the behavior of obviously virtuous men.

---

* A virtue may be considered a human strength, since it helps us live as we "ought to." Since the skills that make us stronger moral agents are virtues, if nothing else, surely socialization procedures should enhance these virtues rather than destroy them. Of course, as MacIntyre[†] points out, virtues need to be situated. We can call a capacity a virtue only when there is a social context that requires us to develop the particular skill. *Cardinal virtues* represent the highest ideals or forms of conduct in a particular way of life. For example, with their background emphasis on leading a rational life, the classical Greeks chose as their cardinal virtues wisdom, justice, courage, and temperance.

In this way, beginners would themselves develop the habits of virtuous action. Wisdom in practical affairs must be learned on the job, so to speak, since it is not easy to summarize the virtues needed for an ethical life in a single principle.

Although I have not tried to formulate a principle that will summarize virtue ethics, the reader should not assume that I am trying to deemphasize this approach to ethics. On the contrary, I believe that to properly use the five principles listed above, one must first master certain common human virtues. Thus, this entire book is itself a study of how important certain virtues are to philosophical ethical deliberation. Considerable space has been devoted to discussing how these virtues develop and ought to function in ethics. In particular, the discussions in Chapters Four, Five, and Six of a philosophically favored moral point of view properly blends a concern for the virtues needed for practical wisdom (as they appear in both genders) with the consequentialist and nonconsequentialist concerns embodied in the five principles listed above (consequentialism and nonconsequentialism will be clarified in Chapters Nine and Ten).

One of the primary tasks of this text, then, is to clarify the ways in which philosophical theory can serve us on practical levels. When properly constructed, theoretically based applied ethics courses ought to increase our sensitivity to the kinds of ethical conflicts that exist in pluralistic cultures, clarify the skills or virtues needed for resolving ethical conflicts, clarify the value of using a theoretical perspective to shape concrete judgments, and introduce us to the major theoretical options. This text will primarily contribute to these goals by explaining why mainstream philosophy has found it necessary to situate concrete value conflicts in a theoretical context. As we shall see, in pluralistic cultures everyone can benefit from developing a theoretical perspective that can provide a background for judging concrete conflicts.

■ STUDY QUESTIONS

1. Why has philosophy become such a self-reflective discipline?
2. What does it mean to historically or conceptually situate a conflict?
3. Why is it important to pay attention to levels of justification?
4. Assume there is a common "moral point of view" in Western ethics. At which level of consideration would this point of view be discussed?
5. What is the purpose of foundational principles? What does it mean to say that they are "prescriptive"?
6. Why does the text leave "virtue ethics" off the list of initial principles?
7. What is a virtue?

■ NOTES

1. This narrative with dialogue comes primarily from a 50-minute taped slideshow presentation of the Zimbardo Prison Experiment. For information about the slideshow with

its synchronized taped narration and sound effects portraying the dramatic features of the experiment, write to: P. G. Zimbardo Inc., P.O. Box 4395, Stanford University, Stanford, CA 94305. The study was funded by an Office of Naval Research contract (N00014-67-A-0112-0041) to Philip G. Zimbardo and carried out in 1971. A 20-minute videotape of the study with some post-experiment interviews is also available at the same address.

2. Throughout the dialogue I have inserted the sound effects from the original sound tape. The precise words of the guards and prisoners were not always clear, especially during the prison riot on the second day. However, a research assistant and I listened carefully to each segment at least fifteen times to check for errors, so the typed dramatic effects that we added are quite accurate overall.

3. These rules were listed in a 1975 discussion of the experiment. See Philip G. Zimbardo, "Transforming Experimental Research into Advocacy for Social Change," in M. Deutsch and H. A. Hornstein, eds., *Applying Social Psychology* (Hillsdale, NJ: Lawrence Erlbaum Associates, 1975), p. 34.

4. Alasdair MacIntyre, *After Virtue* (Notre Dame, IN: University of Notre Dame Press, 1984), pp. 186–188.

5. Aristotle, *Nicomachean Ethics*, in Richard McKean, ed., *The Basic Works of Aristotle* (New York: Random House, 1941), pp. 957–959, 1022–1029.

■ CHAPTER TWO

Moral Agency in Applied Ethics

■ MORAL AGENTS AND SITUATIONAL CONTROL

Commonsense morality assumes individual moral agents are responsible for their actions. At this point, let us define a MORAL AGENT as 'someone who is held responsible because he knows the difference between commonsense notions of right and wrong and has the capacity to intentionally act on this knowledge'. People who lack the capacity for moral agency (e.g., the retarded, the insane, babies) are called AMORAL* to contrast their status with moral agents. For example, we do not hold babies ethically responsible even when their actions cause harm. A one-year-old boy can pull a trigger and kill someone, but because he lacks knowledge of cause and effect his motive is neither moral nor immoral. If we punish him, it is to educate rather than to seek retribution or justice. As children gradually learn to understand right from wrong, grasp the consequences of behavior, and control their emotional impulses, we also gradually recategorize their status in the moral community to welcome them in as moral agents. Commonsense morality recognizes the increasing responsibility of developing children by escalating the explicitness of the moral praise and blame given for their individual actions.

■ Situational Control

Many psychological experiments seem to challenge our commonsense beliefs about moral agents, because they cast doubt on the ability of agents to take responsibility for their own moral behavior. For instance, Zimbardo found his students taking on radically new behavior patterns in just a matter of days. Although the extent of the change seems shocking to most of us, social scientists are familiar with the phenomenon. They use the term SITUATIONAL CONTROL to

---

* "Amoral" should not be confused with NONMORAL. Something is nonmoral when moral categories are not needed to discuss it; for example, choosing the color of a necktie would generally not require us to use any ethical terms, so even though it involves a value choice it is a nonmoral activity.

refer to any situation 'where features of the environment shape and control individual behavior to such an extent that the individual does not appear to be acting in the usual voluntary or free manner we would expect from good moral agents'. Some psychologists go so far as to assert that all of our actions result from situational control. For instance, B. F. Skinner argued that individual freedom is an illusion.[1] He said since environmental contingencies of reinforcement are responsible for all behavior, we should stop using the language of freedom and dignity since it implies people are free agents. We should focus instead on explaining how the environment controls behavior.

Skinner's theory creates a paradox for most ethical theories—if people are exclusively controlled by environment, they are not free. But if they are not free, then they are not responsible for what they do. This implies that adults are more like amoral children than moral agents. If we can only blame the environment for what happens, the student subjects in Zimbardo's experiment cannot be conceived of as moral agents in a traditional sense. This seems odd, since they were chosen precisely because they were assumed to be good moral agents.

Rather than give up our beliefs about the strong connection between individual freedom, moral agency, and responsibility, it is tempting to try and avoid this entire issue by casting doubt on the moral significance of psychological research. For instance, one might try to argue that the subjects in the Zimbardo experiment were so atypical that there isn't a universal lesson to be learned from this experiment about the rest of humanity's capacity for moral agency. Although it may be tempting to dismiss data in this way, there are good reasons not to succumb to this line of thought. In the first place, what happened in the Zimbardo experiment is not unique or even uncommon. Similar experiments, as well as real-life situations, have shown again and again that ordinary moral agents when put under institutional pressure will often behave just as the subjects did in the Zimbardo experiment. Consider the similarity between what Zimbardo discovered and the following summary of an event that occurred in a high school history class.

All page references in the following account of the Third Wave Experiment are to the description of the experience written by the teacher, Ron Jones.[2] One of Jones's students asked him how so many German people could deny they knew about the Nazi holocaust (where millions of people were exterminated). Jones decided to take a week of class time to investigate the question. On Monday, he lectured his class on the virtue of "Discipline." He had the class adopt a set of new classroom behaviors that emphasized personal discipline and obedience to authority. On Tuesday, he talked about the virtue of "Community," the joy of fitting in with a group and of working with others toward common goals. To illustrate group boundaries he created a salute for classroom members only. He called it the Third Wave Salute, because they were to raise their cupped hand toward the right shoulder in such a way that the hand resembled a wave about to topple over. On Wednesday, he talked about the virtue of "Action." He gave them specific tasks to perform and handed out membership cards. He told the class that three cards were marked with a red "x," and whoever got the "x" would have the special duty to report those who failed to comply with class "rules." Although the three recipients of the "x" were the only ones who were secret agents, Jones found that over half the class began to inform on other class members. Students also began to show loyalty to the "movement" by bullying anyone who didn't fall into line and obey the rules. Students from other classes began to cut their classes to join the Third Wave Experiment. One student, Robert, assigned himself the role of bodyguard. He followed Jones around all day, opening and closing doors for him and so forth. When a faculty member told Robert students were not allowed to be in the faculty lounge (Robert was there standing at attention next to Jones's chair), Robert replied, "I'm not a student, I'm a bodyguard."

On Thursday, Jones talked about the virtue of "Pride." By now, the class had swollen to 80 students. Eventually, more than 200 students accepted membership cards and pledged obedience to the rules. Jones was amazed to find the students embracing the discipline and order he was imposing on them. He wanted to stop the experiment, but was not sure how to call a halt. If he stopped immediately, he would leave committed students like Robert hanging there, embarrassed in front of their peers. His solution was to tell all the Third Wave members that this was not just a game, that they were involved in the real thing. He announced that at noon on Friday a candidate for President of the United States would go on national TV and declare a Third Wave Movement for the entire nation. Thousands of youth groups across the country would stand up and declare their allegiance. Together, they would bring a new order of discipline, community, pride, and action to the entire nation. He invited all members to attend a special Friday noon rally for members only. When the candidate for president spoke, they would all pledge their obedience to him.

As a result of this deception, on Friday, Jones had the opportunity to intro-duce over 200 students to the virtue of "Understanding." After the students were seated and silent, he turned off the lights, turned on a TV set and let them sit there and stare at the blank TV screen. Tension and anxiety mounted. Eventually, someone came to his senses and shouted, "There isn't any leader, is there?!" Jones reports that the students gasped in shock, but remained silent.

He then showed them a film about Nazi Germany to help them understand where they had all been heading. It began with the promise of the super-race, then community, discipline, order, pride, and finally the big lie about the persecution of dissenters, terror, and the final stench of death camps. He told them that in a small way, "We learned what it felt like to create a disciplined social environment, pledge allegiance to that society, replace reason with rules" (p. 26). He pointed out how he had manipulated and controlled them, and how they were no better but also no worse than the people who lived in Nazi Germany. He predicted that they would continue to imitate the experience of many of the German people because probably they too would blank out the fact that they had been controlled and manipulated into participating in the noon rally. He said he believed that not one of them would want to face the fact that they were willing to give up "individual freedom to the dictates of order and unseen leaders" (p. 26).

Like Zimbardo, Jones stumbled across the common phenomenon of situational control. To review how situational control works, consider the following three examples.

1. Zimbardo and Jones both discovered that they were personally vulnerable to situational control, when they gave themselves roles in their experiments. Slowly, as their new roles began to dominate their behavior, they lost sight of the original purpose of their experiments. In 1975 Zimbardo reported:

   > . . . I and my research associates . . . were as much "subjects" imprisoned in our roles of prison staff as we were experimenters directing the events of the study. With each passing day, the immediacy of the demands and urgency of mundane decisions forced upon me as "superintendent" of the Stanford County Prison made me ever more remote from the reality of the detached, intellectual stance of "experimenter" (p. 35).[3]

   In a similar manner, Jones said:

   > I played the role [of benevolent dictator] more and more, and had trouble remembering its pedagogic origin and purpose. I wondered if this happens to many people. We get or take a role and then bend our lives to fit it. Soon the role is the only identity other people will accept (Jones, p. 23).

2. Zimbardo (1975) also reported that one of the guards said: "As I am a pacifist and nonaggressive individual, I cannot see a time when I might guard and/or maltreat other living things." Yet, in spite of this pacifist self-image, within six days this person became the brutal guard who said:

   > "The new prisoner (416) refuses to eat his sausages . . . I am very angry at this prisoner for causing discomfort and trouble for the others. I decided to force-feed him, but he wouldn't eat. I let the food slide down his face. I didn't believe it was me doing it. I hated myself for making him eat but I hated him more for not eating" (p. 49).

3. And as we saw in Chapter One, Prisoner 416 clearly showed he recognized that the institution had the power to control him when he reported:

   > "I began to feel that I was losing my identity, that the person I call Clay, the person who put me in this place, the person who volunteered to go into this prison . . . the person that I was . . . was distant from me, was remote, until finally, I wasn't that, I was 416. I was really my number."

In each of these cases, individuals were surprised to find themselves being controlled by pressures from an institution. Rather than being responsible agents, they seem to have become mirror images of their roles, shaped by the demands of the role rather than by their own beliefs. Although we have to think of them as adult moral agents, they do not appear to be responsible in the way that common sense says good moral agents ought to be.

It should not really surprise us when experimental subjects, who are suddenly placed in an entirely new institutional setting, begin to behave in radically new ways. However, while they are adapting to a new role it is not unreasonable to expect a certain amount of moral courage and wisdom on the part of individuals. Remember, all the guards were apparently under the same situational control, yet only about a third of them became sadistic. Obviously, individual differences do count. If there are alternatives from which to choose (even in closed institutions), then perhaps individuals can still be held responsible for how they choose to adapt to the institution.

As is often the case in ethics, the problem is to find a proper balance between the "poles" of a dimension. One pole would be absolute individual freedom and responsibility, and the other pole would be complete situational control with no moral agency. Most adult behavior falls somewhere between these extremes. Braybrooke calls the attempt to find a proper balance between two extremes the TRIPLET PRINCIPLE.[4] The third, or middle, position usually represents a proper compromise between the extremes. So, using the triplet principle we should not assume individuals are always totally responsible, nor should we assume that institutions always control all behavior. We must consider both extremes and then analyze the relationships involved to be sure that institutions are placing the proper kinds of pressures on individuals who are trying to accept responsibility within the institutions.

■ SOCIALIZATION AS SITUATIONAL CONTROL

To see how, in a proper context, individual agency and situational control form a natural partnership, we only need to consider the process of socialization that is used by all social groups to create new members. Over 2,000 years ago, Aristotle pointed out that human beings are social animals. To be human is to live in society and be socialized. SOCIALIZATION is 'a process in which one becomes accustomed to an institution'. Once we begin to habitually obey the norms of an institution, we have been successfully socialized into it. Since situational control is a necessary part of normal socialization into a way of life, this kind of situational control is not only not wrong, it is in fact required by morality itself.

■ *Level I: Childhood Socialization*

While growing up, children are socialized to have cultural values. The psychological term for this kind of socialization is INTROJECTION, which means 'to unconsciously internalize values that originated externally'. Introjection "happens to us"; we do not choose either the process or the content that gets internalized. Thus, many of our values about culture, love, sex, food, and lifestyle are all chosen for us, either by our genetic endowment or by those who introject values into us. Because childhood socialization is a clear case of complete situational control, it is more appropriate to hold institutions responsible for the value content introjected than to hold individuals responsible. As a general rule, then, we can say that institutions ought to socialize children to have introjected values that will not turn out to be dysfunctional from an acceptable moral point of view (we will explore this idea further in Chapter Seven).

■ Level II: Adult Socialization

Adults are comfortable with the idea that children are socialized, but some people find it difficult to believe a similar process can happen rapidly to them. The events we have been considering, however, are not unusual. We are all familiar with stories about how basic training shapes the beliefs of young men, and how prisoners of war in Korea were "brainwashed." The evidence is overwhelming. Socialization procedures are used not only to civilize each new generation, but also to initiate new adult members into social groups. Adults can be socialized to adapt to new institutions, often very rapidly. Teaching, parenting, IBM's year-long orientation program, indoctrination, and brainwashing are all instances of socialization. Although the focus so far has been on situations where adult socialization has led to harmful results, socialization of adults is not *per se* an evil activity. But because some methods of socialization can lead to harm, socialization techniques need to be ethically judged. Some forms are defensible, some not.

But, how can we judge socialization? Won't any judgment simply be a mirror of the judge's own previous form of socialization? To get insight into how to judge socialization we need to study the process itself. Let's begin with a type of socialization that is often used to train people to do the "dirty work" in institutions. Haney and Zimbardo discuss five common features that facilitate this kind of socialization.[5]

■ The Six Steps of Socialization

1. To increase its effectiveness, a process of socialization often requires people to make behavioral adjustments slowly, in a series of small steps over time. Little things we are asked to do often seem unimportant, so there is a slow unreflective accommodation to the demands of the institution. We make small compromises until the series of small compromises wears us down, and we find ourselves acting in ways that are radically different from what we would have expected at the start. Sometimes all the little steps add up to a big compromise we never explicitly chose. What would have happened if Jones had held the Friday rally on the first day? Would the students have been as likely to commit themselves to what would then appear to be the big step of joining the Third Wave?

2. There is typically a lack of awareness of the causal factors that control behavior, and a corresponding obliviousness to one's own vulnerability to situational control. One of the brutal guards in the Zimbardo experiment said he could not even

imagine "a time when I might maltreat other living things." He was so confident of his goodness that he seemed unaware he might be vulnerable to those situational role pressures that can tempt any person who is not careful.

3. There is a strong focus on the present, that is, there is no historical perspective to help us critically judge the context of our current role. Institutions need to be historically situated before they can be evaluated, but when they dominate our landscape it is hard to see past them to get a historical perspective. What might be the affect on the John Wayne guard if he were shown historical precedents that could clarify the choices available to guards? Would he have been as likely to follow the path of brutality?

4. There is an emphasis upon a narrow perspective. Some form of "centricism" gets emphasized. (EGOCENTRIC means to only be capable of understanding one's own point of view. ETHNOCENTRIC means one is only able to focus on the point of view of one's own group.) Notice how both Zimbardo and Jones report that they became so deeply involved in the narrow demands of their new roles that they forgot about the broader context within which these new roles should be judged. It often happens in decision making that duties on the institutional level become so important to us that we forget to coordinate them with the broader background ethical demands that were supposed to justify the institutions in the first place.

5. A person often has a sense of perceived freedom of choice, even in contexts where choice did not actually exist. When a person is unaware of situational control, she may feel free even in situations where she is nonetheless being controlled (as in cases where people are manipulated). After a time, her sense of freedom leads her to identify with behavior she would have rejected if she had adequate information about what was really happening to her. "It must be okay," she thinks, "because I have been doing it voluntarily." Creating this sense of perceived freedom is crucial if we want people to develop a sense of loyalty to the institutions that socialize them.

I would like to add a sixth factor to this list. It seems to me that because we are social animals, there is a natural tendency to give institutions the benefit of the doubt. Both the content introjected and the socialization process itself are less likely to be challenged when they occur in familiar institutions. People need to be pushed quite far before they will challenge an institution seen as part of a larger social system that seems rational. As Thomas Jefferson stated in the Declaration of Independence, " . . . All experience hath shown that mankind are more disposed to suffer while evils are sufferable than to right themselves by abolishing the forms to which they are accustomed."

Thus, to make their plans appear legitimate, people often try to associate their socialization activities with a well-known institution's value framework—religious, educational, scientific, patriotic. For example, recall Zimbardo's statement that "we systematically brought their [the visitors'] behavior under situational control." He said that the parents complained, but "their reaction was to work within the system." What system? Zimbardo's strategy was to alter appearances to remind the visitors that they were witnessing something that was sanctioned by a prestigious university. Stanford's educational prestige and the "official authoritative" structure of a well-run experimental prison combined to intimidate the visitors.

■ The Micro and Macro Level in Ethics

Because both individual agents and socialization practices in institutions need to be judged, the discipline of ethics must focus on at least two different levels. There is a MICRO LEVEL at which questions can be asked about individuals. What did prisoner #416 do? What was his motive? What did he hope to accomplish? Was he being ethical? We should, however, also ask questions about the MACRO LEVEL by focusing on the structure of the institution and the network of relationships created by its roles. What are the rules? Are they justifiable? What relationship ought to exist between the social environment and members of the group? Which duties ought to have priority when the demands of different roles conflict? To understand the ethical responsibilities at both levels, we will need to understand not only the phenomenon of situational control, but also how people develop the moral virtues that help them resist ethically inappropriate institutional control.

The micro and macro interrelationships in the Zimbardo experiment draw our attention to three important issues in applied ethics. First, as already discussed, we see the importance of the close connection between individual behavior and institutional roles. In this particular experiment the institution's negative impact was very dramatic, because we saw on a concrete level how an institution can "dehumanize people, turn them into objects, and make them feel helpless and hopeless." But, don't let the power of this negative example overwhelm you. The point of studying this kind of closed institution is to learn how to avoid such negative effects in the future. As Zimbardo says, we have to "begin to change our real institutions so that they promote human values rather than destroy them."

We also saw that each person responds to institutional roles in his own way. Individuals count; they are not just institutional pawns. Moral agents contribute something to the unfolding events. By studying different capacities for moral agency, we can learn about the different kinds of virtues that institutions ought to be promoting in individuals.

The second issue arises from Zimbardo's talk about reform. He is assuming that there are background ideal "human values" that ought to be promoted by institutions. We will need to study normative theories to be clear about which human values ought to be foundational.

The third issue raised by this experiment involves methods of reform. We need to pick the best means for promoting the ideal human values prescribed by the normative theories. To talk intelligently about means to reform, we need to assume we can combine normative ideals and empirical research. This assumption should be explored in detail.

■ NORMATIVE AND DESCRIPTIVE DATA IN APPLIED ETHICS

Empirical research is used to discover facts about how people behave in social settings. Thus, psychologists and social scientists begin by asking questions like: What values *are* promoted by various types of institutions? How *do* institutions influence individual choice? They formulate a hypothesis, gather data, formulate hypothetical explanations to account for the data, and then set up empirical tests to confirm or refute their hypotheses. Their aim is to generate value-neutral, causal explanations that can both describe "what is the case" and clarify how the observed events occurred. Scientific investigations lead to increasingly abstract,

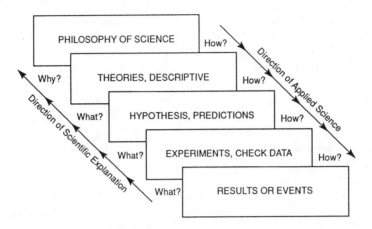

although empirically grounded, descriptions and theories, which enable scientists to predict events and eventually control them. Since the entire enterprise attempts to be value-neutral, it is quite appropriate to ask: "If ethics is concerned with prescriptions about *what ought to be*, then why do we need to study empirical research that is designed to test descriptions about *the way it is*? An adequate answer is complex, but for now we only need to point out that the results of empirical research can alter the background against which we see ethical "oughts."

■ Combining the Empirical and the Prescriptive

For instance, a famous motto in ethics, OUGHT IMPLIES CAN, draws attention to the logical connection between an agent's responsibility and her capacity to act. The motto reminds us that it is not logical to tell people they ought to do something if, because they lack knowledge or capacity or are externally constrained, they can't do it. For instance, it would be absurd to tell prisoner 8612 (who was screaming to get out of the Zimbardo prison) that he ought to just ignore his prison environment and stop complaining. At that moment, he can't ignore it. Without training, there is no reason to expect people to have the capacity to ignore intense institutional pressures. As we shall see in Chapters Five and Seven, extensive research data being collected suggests that the capacity to withstand institutional pressure develops rather slowly. The extent of our knowledge about this data will influence what we think people ought to do. Thus, it influences where we place blame and how we build institutions. For example, notice that in spite of the individual differences that showed up in his experiment, Haney and Zimbardo do not focus on blaming individuals for what happened. As social psychologists, they have seen so much situational control that they no longer adopt the commonsense approach that holds individuals responsible for every event. They say:

History has surely established the futility of seeking the sources of evil deeds exclusively in the nature of its performers. Even the greatest iniquity and inhumanity generally have been the products of unsettlingly "normal," average persons whose commonplace motives and relative naivete were perverted in the service of evil purpose.[6]

Typically, people assume they can blame evil deeds on "bad" agents; for example, "Of course prisons are bad places, the people in them are evil." A commonsense background that assumes individuals are always responsible for human evil draws attention away from the need to reform institutional structures. As we have seen, by designing innovative empirical experiments (e.g., filling a pseudo prison with "good" people to see what will happen), social psychologists have shown us again and again that some of our commonsense intuitions about individual moral responsibility seem to be in conflict with research data. Ethical behavior is complex, and good people placed in bad institutions will often do evil things.

Ethical theory, then, if it is going to be practically useful, must take into consideration the empirical research that reveals what ordinary good people can and cannot do. In response to empirical research, writers in applied ethics have been devoting more and more attention to discussing the significance of institutional roles. Although individuals are still being held accountable, there are now many people who would argue that institutions also ought to be held accountable, that is, they should be given many of the same responsibilities that we give to human moral agents.[7]

These considerations help us see why the idea of "applied philosophy" is controversial. It will only make sense if it is possible to cross back and forth between the borders of traditional normative (philosophical) and descriptive (scientific) disciplines. But, the logical structure of explanations in science are different from the logical structure of normative justifications. If we place the chart for scientific explanations next to the chart for normative justifications, we can see the differences. Explanations in the social and natural sciences are causal accounts that describe what has happened and clarify how events occur. Scientific practice moves back and forth between observation and abstract theory, always trying to keep theories in touch with something called "facts" or "the way it is." Scientists presuppose that facts are value-neutral in some significant sense, and they attempt to continually ground their descriptions with empirical investigations of these neutral facts.

Philosophical justifications, on the other hand, are concerned with motives rather than causes. They explain *why* people act as they do. They look behind the action to see what background normative prescriptions about "the way it ought to be" can justify the actions. Applied ethics then reverses the process and studies how these background norms ought to be implemented.

Since science tries to stay grounded in empirical fact, it is easy for applied scientists to come back to the concrete level and apply their theories. But, there are those who think that philosophical theories cannot be so easily applied. They argue that the understanding one gains by analyzing abstract background theories does not automatically translate into insights about what to do in concrete situations.

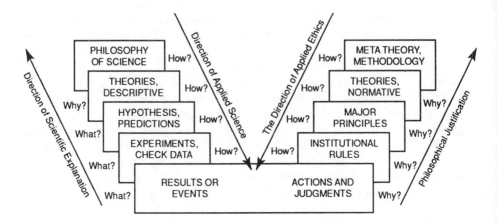

The goal of theory has always been to offer background explanations for principles; thus, theories have never been primarily policy-oriented. They argue that since policy is derived at the levels below principles, it is quite possible for a theoretician to have considerable background understanding of theory but lack practical wisdom. So, if applied ethics is concerned with cases at the lower levels, why bother to investigate theories in applied ethics?

■ Blending the Concrete and the Abstract

If only things were this simple. In a complex pluralistic world we cannot have an adequate understanding of ethical life if we do not also develop an understanding of the background theories used to justify our concrete ethical norms. Policy decisions presuppose ethical ideals, and "concrete focus" on practical issues can deflect our attention away from these ideals. For example, some time ago in a letter to the nationally syndicated advice columnist, Ann Landers, someone pointed out that the Declaration of Independence states: "We hold these truths to be self-evident. All men are created equal. . . ." The writer then said that he did not believe this was true and asked Ann Landers for her opinion. She responded that she also did not believe it, because many people are born handicapped in many ways and need special help.*

While it was probably useful to point out that many people are in need of help because of physical disabilities, I was nonetheless surprised by her response to the writer's overly concrete interpretation of the ideal of moral equality. I assumed that she would take the opportunity to point out that the Declaration of Independence addresses several different conceptual levels in morality. The Founding Fathers were not fools; they were all well aware of the day-to-day concrete inequalities

---

* As we shall see in Chapter Six, Ann Landers's reply may have been an expression of what has been called the women's voice in ethics, with its special emphasis on caring for unequals who are in need of our help.

among men, yet they ratified the Declaration of Independence with its claim that all men are created equal. Why? Jefferson (the primary author) believed that regardless of their obvious material inequalities, all men were in fact equal in that they shared a "moral sense" and human dignity. Moral equality and inalienable rights provide the theoretical moral background against which we are supposed to see the concrete conflicts in the foreground. The theory explains why the complaints against the King of England were justified. Jefferson was not claiming that all men were equal in concrete physical terms; he was talking about a different conceptual level where moral equality makes sense. So long as we focus exclusively on the concrete or practical (the immediate foreground), we will continue to fall short in our attempts to reform institutions so that they implement ideals that are derived from background moral beliefs. This example helps us see how important it is to stay focused on the proper level of ethical consideration when interpreting ethical situations.

Once we do reverse directions in ethics to start applying ideals to practice, the data from the empirically based social sciences become very important in ethics. The empirical nature of scientific methodology gives social sciences considerable practical authority, because it keeps them focused on what works. When members of these disciplines become experts in the application of their research, they often work as consultants who give concrete advice about how to achieve goals. (Since graduates of professional schools claim they have expertise in how to solve problems, many universities now house their professional schools in buildings with names tied to science; for example, the Department of Social Work at Case Western Reserve University is called the School of Applied Sciences.)

When questions are raised about fundamental values, however, empirical data and/or technological skills cannot answer the questions. Ideals involve value judgments about what "ought" to be the case; they are not simply reflections of what "is" already the case. Value judgments are prescriptive, not descriptive. They cannot be validated by empirical research; they can only be justified with rational arguments that are grounded in background normative theories.

But, since expertise in normative theory does not translate automatically into expertise on the practical level, in applied ethics we will need to cross back and forth between descriptive and normative disciplines to integrate the information from both. The "how to do it" data from the social sciences helps us make decisions about proper means for achieving our goals, while the insights from normative philosophy helps us to be clear about which human values we ought to be pursuing in the first place. Thus, if we create a time line to chart all the concepts needed in applied ethics, we see it is a very complex discipline. We must look at background ethical and scientific theories to get a perspective on where we are, and we must use this information to set future long-range goals and speculate on the best intermediate steps for achieving them.

To help people avoid being either overwhelmed or overly simplistic in their attempts to resolve conflicts, many applied ethicists recommend that people use decision procedures to help them focus on all the factual and ethical variables. The

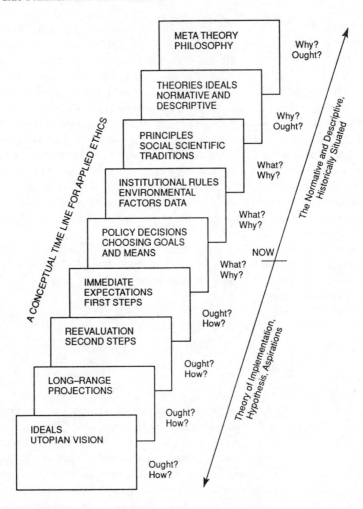

seven-step procedure on the following pages is typical of the kinds of devices that are recommended. Since decision making is a process, we will need to go back and forth between the steps of the procedure to make adjustments as the ethical deliberation progresses (e.g., in order to add an important fact or an additional ethical assumption or principle that was not emphasized the first time through).

■ *A Model Decision Procedure*[8]

■ BACKGROUND

I. What is the historical context?
   A. Determine the empirical facts: who, what, where, when, how? What do we know now? What do we still need to know that would help define the problem? Are there major assumptions about how to interpret data?

    B. List the significant stakeholders. (A stakeholder is a 'person (or institution) whose interests will be affected by a decision that is going to be made'.) When trying to identify stakeholders it is useful to think of things like goods, rights, claims, duties, interests, and so forth.

■ IDEAL THEORY

  II. Define the ethical aspects of the issue.
    A. What kind of ethical conflict is involved? For example, is it a conflict between interests only, or does it involve principles, obligations, or duties of station?
    B. What level of justification is needed to resolve the conflict? For example, do we need to appeal to rules only or do we also need to clarify principles and theories?
  III. Identify the major rules, values, principles, and theoretical assumptions that will be used.
    A. Name all values and principles. For example, list principles such as integrity, beneficence, rights, respect for persons, profit, and justice, but also be sure to name any personal values involved.
    B. Acknowledge your major ethical orientation if you have one. For example, are you a utilitarian, natural rights theorist, or social contractarian? Think about your ideal goals. What would an ideal state of affairs look like to you? In what direction should current policies be moving us? How far off from the ideal are current arrangements? Would the same conflict arise in an ideal state of affairs or would it be different?

■ IMPLEMENTATION

  IV. Specify the possible alternatives. All major alternatives should be listed, including those that represent some form of compromise between extremes (recall the triplet principle discussed on page 30).
  V. Determine whether there are any boundaries or side-constraints on the kinds of strategies that can be used.
    A. Are there limits on how one should make profit/loss calculations? Are both quantitative and qualitative variables being considered?
    B. What are the short-term and long-term positive and negative consequences of the major alternatives? Have they been measured against each other?
  VI. Compare the values and possible alternatives to see if a clear decision emerges. That is, see if there is one principle or value, or combination, that stands out as being so compelling that the proper alternative suddenly seems clear, for example, correcting a simple defect in a product that is almost certain to cause loss of life.
  VII. Make your decision. Select the best alternative according to your ethical framework. Ask yourself: "Would others be willing to go public and defend this choice?"

We will return to this decision model in Chapter Eleven, when we discuss professional ethics and how to implement theories. It is presented here to give us a general idea about how complex the interrelationships become in applied ethics when we shift back and forth between levels of abstraction and between descriptive and normative considerations. This text has been organized to emphasize the three dimensions of applied ethics that appear in this decision model. Thus, to develop background information upon which to ground later abstract discussions, Chapters Three through Six review ethically relevant empirical research from social science and psychology. This kind of investigation is called DESCRIPTIVE ETHICS, since it 'attempts to describe (rather than prescribe) how people in fact develop values and make value decisions'. This information will be helpful when we get to Chapters Eight and Eleven, which explore the applied question about *how* we ought to reform institutions and individuals.

One of the key questions in applied ethics is: How can we institutionalize the human values prescribed by normative theories? The third step in the decision model focuses on this question. To effectively answer it, we must develop a THEORY OF IMPLEMENTATION that will give 'practical recommendations about the best way to make ideals become real in concrete cases'. At the very least, the rules of our institutions ought to be designed so that they support the proper values in ways that are ethically appropriate. Since societies often use professions to implement values that are especially important, Chapter Eleven also has a section on the role that professional codes of ethics play in a theory of implementation.

Finally, Zimbardo's reference to promoting human values draws attention to the background moral theories that prescribe ideals. NORMATIVE or PRESCRIPTIVE ETHICS 'involves a search for the best ideals and principles for guiding human behavior'. In Chapter Seven we will analyze the foundational concepts of MORAL AUTONOMY and MORAL ACCOUNTABILITY. They play a crucial role in characterizing the moral point of view that underlies the five prescriptive theories discussed in Chapters Nine and Ten.

■ STUDY QUESTIONS

1. What is the difference between an amoral agent and a moral agent?
2. Why is situational control incompatible with moral agency?
3. In what sense does socialization bring institutions and individuals together in a natural relationship?
4. What features of the socialization process can be used to judge methods of socialization?
5. What is the difference between a micro and a macro focus in ethics?
6. What is the difference between a normative justification and an empirical description?
7. Why does the principle of "ought implies can" entail that ethical theory should also be grounded in some empirical research?
8. Why does the interdisciplinary nature of applied ethics make it a controversial discipline?
9. What are the three dimensions to ethical reflection that need to be considered when trying to solve a concrete moral conflict?

■ NOTES

1. B. F. Skinner, *Beyond Freedom and Dignity* (New York: Bantam Books, 1971); see Chaps. 2 and 3.

2. Ron Jones, "You Will do as Directed," *Learning*, May/June 1976, pp. 22–26.

3. Philip G. Zimbardo, "Transforming Experimental Research into Advocacy for Social Change," in M. Deutsch and H. A. Hornstein, eds., *Applying Social Psychology* (Hillsdale, NJ: Lawrence Erlbaum Associates, 1975).

4. David Braybrooke, *Ethics in the World of Business* (Totowa, Nova Scotia: Rowman and Allanheld, 1983), p. 19f.

5. Craig Haney and Philip G. Zimbardo, "The Socialization into Criminality: On Becoming a Prisoner and a Guard," in Jane Lovin Tapp and Felice J. Levine, eds., *Law, Justice, and the Individual in Society* (New York: Holt, Rinehart and Winston, 1977), pp. 203–204.

6. Ibid., p. 201.

7. See Kenneth E. Goodpaster, "The Concept of Corporate Responsibility," in Tom Regan, ed., *Just Business: New Introductory Essays in Business Ethics* (New York: Random House, 1984), pp. 306–311.

8. This decision model is similar to a version presented in William W. May, ed., *Ethics in the Accounting Curriculum: Cases & Readings* (Sarasota: American Accounting Association, 1990) pp. 1–2. Their version modified a model presented in Howard Brody, *Ethical Decisions in Medicine*, 2nd ed. (Boston: Little, Brown, 1981).

CHAPTER THREE

Descriptive Ethics and Metaethics

■ TRIBALISM VERSUS PLURALISM IN ETHICS

Throughout most of history, people living in fairly stable and isolated tribal communities had little reason to ask questions about either the socialization process or the nature of the values that were introjected into tribal members. Since everyone in a tribe is programmed in roughly the same way, the common social values of the tribe will feel like objective absolutes to tribal members. People will have little need to question social values, little reason to reflect on the nature of value differences, and no comparative basis from which to criticize the sources of introjection that gave them their values.

I don't mean to imply that tribal life is simplistic or unimportant, but when compared to modern pluralistic cultures, achieving social goals through social-ization would be a relatively simple matter. Imagine how straightforward issues would seem if we had only one set of major social norms to transmit to each tribal member. In many ways the process would be similar to teaching the Boy (Girl) Scout Code (a boy scout is trustworthy, brave, clean, loyal, reverent, courteous, kind, thrifty, helpful, etc.). There is no encouragement to pay attention to the intrinsic differences between the values; value choice is, therefore, kept to a minimum. The way Zimbardo's prisoners were forced to memorize and obey rules provides a good example of this approach. No matter how absurd the rules (like "No laughing!" or "Prisoners must eat at meal times!"), they were all treated as equally important and beyond debate.

Lawrence Kohlberg refers to this style of moral socialization as the BAG OF VIRTUES[1] approach to moral education. The authority figures who impose the values act as though values are all of the same logical type: they are lumped together in an "absolute bag" to be obeyed without question. It also does not matter if they are arbitrary so long as each tribal member adopts them. This method works well in closed tribal societies and with young children (it is even necessary when children are too young to discuss values). It has the advantage of creating group solidarity, stable expectations, and a sense that everyone shares a natural heritage.

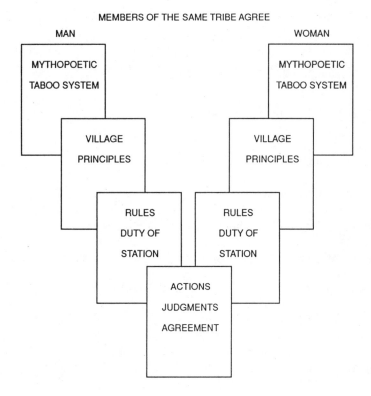

MEMBERS OF THE SAME TRIBE AGREE

■ Tribal Duties of Station

The term DUTY OF STATION refers to 'all those special duties (and rights) that we get when we move into an institution'. In a tribe clear rights and duties of station tell others in an immediate, concrete way what they can expect from us in institutional settings. For example, the word "Father" is tied to concrete social expectations. There would be room for some individual differences, but the important aspects of the role would be prescribed by clear institutional rights and duties that applied to all the "Fathers" in the tribe. The same would be true for all "Mothers." If there is no way to make comparisons with forms of parenthood in other tribes, standard-ized duties of station will dominate tribal parenting and leave little room for individual lifestyle choice.

The Zimbardo prison community provides an artificial but good example of a closed form of tribal existence. Because the inmates were isolated from the outside world, the broader concerns of their larger community of origin receded, until their only reality gradually came to be the local duties of station in their closed institution.

For most of us, however, the simple "good old days" of tribal certainty and security are gone forever. Value comparisons have made individual lifestyle choice a fact of life. Since this kind of choice often leads to value confusion (especially

·when the values involved have arbitrary foundations), it is difficult to maintain the feeling of security that was available when there was no choice.

When the opportunity for comparisons arises, authorities may be forced to justify rules to tribal members. If the values underlying tribal duties of station turn out to be arbitrary, tribes may well experience a legitimation crisis—which means tribal members may begin to challenge the legitimacy of institutional offices. We can understand the inherent inadequacy of arbitrary rules if we consider a statement attributed to prisoner 416 of the Zimbardo Prison experiment. (Remember, 416 was an "outsider" brought in on Wednesday, so he was still in a position to make fresh comparisons).

> I don't understand it, any of it! Nothing makes sense in here and no one is concerned that nothing makes sense. Everybody has gone mad in this place and they don't know it. No one person sees the change in him because the place and all the others are all mad in the same way he is. Whatever craziness he feels or does seems appropriate—it fits. As long as it fits, it doesn't have to be rational, doesn't have to make sense. No one questions all these arbitrary, insane rules. "You have to eat at meal times," even if you are not hungry or don't want to, "No talking allowed during meals," and any of a score of other rules. I can't tell whether the guards are more into this insanity than the prisoners or if it's the other way around. If you don't smile when that blond guard tells a dirty joke, you get punished. When he repeats it and you do smile, you get punished again for overreacting. You can't even predict whether a guard will give you a straight answer or ridicule you when you ask a question.[2]

Prisoner 416 was confused because the rules were arbitrary rather than grounded in reason. "Arbitrary" is not synonymous with evil. It only means there is no particular reason for a value. If there is a reason for a value or rule, and the reason goes beyond the personal whim of some authoritative tradition, then the value is not arbitrary, even if the reason may not be a good one. In a closed tribe arbitrary rules would probably not be a problem, since no one would think to question a rule in any case. Thus, the primary benefits of tribal life (social solidarity and security) could be maintained even with rules that could be seen to be arbitrary from a nontribal point of view.

Of course, the arbitrariness of the Zimbardo prison went beyond arbitrary rules. Because authorities could make changes in the rules on the basis of personal whim, one of the chief benefits of tribal life—security—was also missing. When nothing makes sense because everything arbitrarily changes moment by moment, the faculty of reason becomes useless. In the presence of arbitrary contradictions there is nothing for reason to do. It is impossible to predict outcomes—one cannot make even elementary plans—so we begin to feel childlike in our vulnerability. Arbitrary treatment by authorities is the primary technique used in brainwashing, where the goal is to cause a person to developmentally regress, as a way to prepare the ground for a kind of resocialization that is a clear case of immoral situational control.

Because arbitrary changes confuse and frighten people, we should strive to avoid being arbitrary at each and every level of social consideration. This is especially true in the modern world, now that so many of us live without the stability provided by some ancient, protected tradition. For example, many urban dwellers in pluralistic, rapidly evolving cultures are literally missing a concrete past. Since the urban world is remodeled every decade or so, often childhood landmarks and styles of life have simply disappeared, replaced by parking lots and skyscrapers. This lack of continuity in heritage can make it difficult to understand people who may be only a decade older or younger.

■ *Social Pluralism*

When people from different tribal backgrounds must live in the same area, we have pluralism. SOCIAL PLURALISM is a condition in which 'groups with different life-styles and moral points of view exist in the same society'. Even if we have been socialized in tribe "A," we will be in a position to compare ourselves with those socialized in tribe "B." When comparisons are possible, people may even begin to question their own socialization, and in advanced pluralistic cultures it may be common for people to belong to several different and incompatible institutions at the same time. Value pluralism, then, leads directly to fundamental value choices,

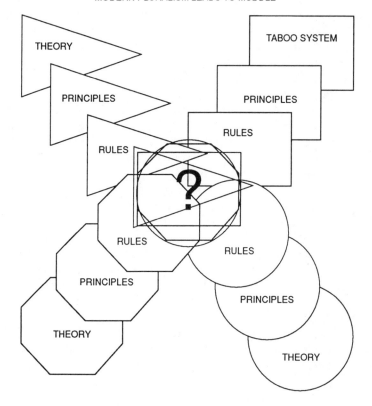

MODERN PLURALISM LEADS TO MUDDLE

and thus to the confusion and conflict that is symbolized by the question mark in the center of the following chart.

In a pluralistic culture, what does it mean to be a man or woman, a solid citizen, a loyal employee, a moral person, a husband or wife, a mother or father? Which version of a role is right from the moral point of view? Which version is better from a personal point of view? These kinds of value comparisons are becoming more common every day, around the world. A tribe would have to remain very isolated or extremely totalitarian to avoid the confusion such questions can cause.

A film presentation by Dr. Morris Massey called *What You Are Is Where You Were When*[3] explains some of the strange consequences of being socialized in a pluralistic culture. Using the language of computers, Massey calls the process of socialization "gut level value programming." He argues that in the modern world different generations are socialized to have different gut level feelings or values in ten-year intervals (because of the acceleration of technical innovations, now it may be even a shorter span of time). The diversity of programming helps us understand why there is so much conflict between different age groups and between people from different locations.

When one person or group says that something is good or right and others say that it is bad or wrong, how should we resolve the dispute in a pluralistic culture? What role should power play in resolving such disputes? For example, was it right for the guards in the Zimbardo experiment to threaten to deprive all prisoners of visiting hours in order to control prisoner 416 (see Chapter One)? Punishing an entire class to make a few deviates fall in line is a common practice in school systems. Since it is an effective means of social control, some people think it is ethically correct to use this technique to resolve disputes. Is it? What about disagreements concerning dress codes, drug use, or sexual norms? In radically pluralistic cultures, people develop different feelings about all of these topics. What should we do about such diversity? Although most of what Massey says about value programming is consistent with what psychologists tell us about introjection, he does make one very controversial claim about the status of conflicting introjected values. He says: "No matter what you believe about music, money, food, the family, about anything, you are 100% correct. The surprising thing is everyone else is 100% correct as well." This statement is a good example of how value diversity can make things seem to be utterly confusing. If every choice about values, no matter how different the alternatives, is 100% correct, there is no reason for people to search for the best value choices. You cannot do any better than 100% correct. We might as well flip a coin to settle all value disputes, since any choice is as good as any other. This approach to values reduces all values to a subjective arbitrary level. This is the opposite of the "bag of virtues" approach to understanding values, and has serious consequences for the possibility of rational ethical debate.

For example, if my neighbor feels it is right to torture babies for the fun of it, and I feel it is wrong, does the fact of introjected value diversity prove that I must assume we are both 100 percent correct? Are we merely disagreeing about arbitrary personal preferences so that it does not matter whose values are adopted? We need to be careful here. If I really believe all values are merely subjective personal preferences (that is, personal feelings resulting from having arbitrary rules introjected into me), then I have no objective basis from which to judge the sadist for having a preference for torturing babies.

While it is commendable in pluralistic cultures to be tolerant of different feelings, tolerance does not have to imply that there is no rational basis for making ethical judgments (is tolerance itself just a subjective preference?). As we shall see later when we contrast relativism with absolutism, there are good reasons to believe that ethics involves much more than a mere assertion of personal preferences. Keep in mind that even if a value was introjected, it also does not necessarily mean it is arbitrary. The process of introjection tells us how a value originated; it tells us nothing about the rationality of the value. There may be good reasons for some introjected values, while others may be arbitrary. It is important to find a method that can help us distinguish between arbitrary and rational introjected values. Before we pursue this issue, however, let's look at some other ways that pluralism can cause value confusion.

■ THE MORALITY OF MUDDLE

As we have seen, pluralism can stimulate a search for greater understanding, but it can also create barriers to it. People need time to adapt to fundamental changes, but the pace of modern life does not give us much time. Too much change—too many choices—can cause confusion or muddle. Sabini and Silver argue in *Moralities of Everyday Life*[4] that, on the whole, people in our pluralistic culture are a morally mixed-up lot. Life has accelerated to the point where there are simply too many choices, so many lifestyles to choose from that the average moral agent feels unsure of himself.

There are two forms of extreme reaction to pluralism that appear to be a little neurotic. First, there is a kind of debilitating mental numbness that sometimes afflicts people who have not experienced much change in their life. Alvin Toffler calls this FUTURE SHOCK,[5] since it results from "too much change too fast." The person who says, "I don't understand what the hell the world is coming to" may be suffering from a bit of future shock. Pluralism is less likely to cause this reaction in young people. They are so accustomed to value changes that they have a contrary tendency to assume that nothing is permanent, that no value can deserve the kind of respect that lasts for generations. To them, ethical values appear to be fads that come and go like tastes.

Second, sometimes the neurotic overreaction appears as DECIDOPHOBIA,[6] which is an irrational fear of making decisions. Because pluralism allows for so many legitimate value differences people may be afraid that either there is no right answer at all, or if there is a right answer they will fail to see it. Decidophobes tend to procrastinate until someone else tells them what to do or until the problem solves itself by going away or becoming unmanageable.

Social scientists have recorded several other inappropriate but more common reactions to the growth of pluralism. For instance, there is conceptual BIGOTRY, which means that 'one simply refuses to acknowledge that competing value alternatives might have some legitimacy'. Having so many choices seems to frighten some people so much that they react by portraying complex moral issues in overly simplistic terms. They commit the "black/white fallacy," which is the logical mistake "of treating one side of a complex debate as though it is completely right and the other side as though it is completely wrong." This move is inappropriate, because it hides the complexity that confuses people who are willing to look at both sides of the issue, and the complexity ought to be discussed.

Usually a MORAL DILEMMA is defined as 'a situation in which mutually exclusive moral actions or choices are equally binding'.* That is, we have a moral dilemma when two or more conflicting duties obligate us at the same time. Since I am emphasizing social conflict, however, I am also using the term to refer to the kind of complex social issue that can divide reasonable members of a community. When reasonable people can be found on both sides in a conflict, it is usually complex enough to be confusing to anyone who is open-minded. Let us define a SOCIAL MORAL DILEMMA as 'a value conflict that is so complex, reasonable people can disagree with each other about the proper solution to the conflict'.

For example, a dispute over whether to torture babies for fun or profit is not a social moral dilemma. We do not find reasonable people on both sides. Only a sadistic psychopath might be confused about the moral status of this issue. But not all issues are this clear. Sometimes issues require reasonable people to engage in agonizing debate about how to resolve them. Disputes over issues like capital punishment, abortion, employee rights, affirmative action, and premarital sex represent "social" moral dilemmas. Reasonable people can be on either side, so we must seriously consider the arguments of reasonable opponents. The fact there is a social dilemma does not necessarily mean both sides are right; it only means that, so far as we can tell at this time, either side could be right.

In these contexts, committing the black/white fallacy helps people avoid the anxiety of having to make a tough choice. For example, when people make simplistic statements like "Abortion is wrong because it is the murder of little babies," or conversely, "Abortion is okay because a woman has a right to remove a parasitic growth from her body," they are ignoring the complexity of this issue. In both statements, a tough moral choice is turned into a simplistic choice by ignoring the considerations that are important to a reasonable member of the opposition.

Bigots resist critical inquiry into values by treating their own values as absolutes that cannot possibly be in error. They are not interested in debate; they are

---

* Peter A. Angeles, *Dictionary of Philosophy* (New York: Barnes & Noble, 1981), p. 64. Many ordinary-sounding terms have special philosophical meanings. When reading in a specific academic discipline it's useful to have a dictionary from that discipline. This text is one of my favorites.

interested only in getting others to be obedient to their values. For the sake of stability, they may favor authoritarian ways of resolving value differences. This seems justifiable to them, since they have already defined their opponents to be either evil or fools. Authoritarian solutions to the kinds of dilemmas created by pluralism are especially unfortunate, since these solutions stifle moral debates that could lead to creative rational ways of resolving the value conflicts.

SUBJECTIVISM and/or MORAL CYNICISM are also common reactions to social pluralism. Some people are so impressed with the diversity of values in the world, they assume it is impossible to establish any reasonable priorities. Subjectivists argue that "all values are the result of private feelings and are thus ultimately arbitrary." As stated above, if all values are reduced to this subjective level, there is no reason to make serious judgments between them (subjectivism will be discussed in more detail below).

One occasionally hears CYNICS argue that in the "real world" morality is just used as a political tool, since in the crunch of real conflict no one really uses principles. Cynics believe that people will always act on selfish interests, so even if there are higher ethical values there is no need to figure out what they are. Some cynics even argue that "right" only means what is in the interest of the person who has the most power. Some of the prisoners I've taught have adopted this point of view. They think only fools like Socrates will restrict themselves by worrying about what is right. As Massey says in his videotape, many people today believe the "now" value is "Don't not do it, just don't get caught if you do do it." Sometimes a person who looks cynical may actually be suffering from NIHILISM. This is a 'psychological and/or philosophical state of mind in which a person has lost the ability to believe in any values at all, whether they are religious, political, moral, or social values'. Nihilists argue that ethical terms are worthless, irrational, meaningless, or absurd.

Cynicism and/or nihilism should not be confused with healthy skepticism. Skepticism is valuable, since it motivates one to question values and investigate alternatives. Cynics (nihilists and subjectivists), however, take a different path. They do not strive for greater sophistication in their ability to analyze values. Why bother if moral knowledge is either impossible or useless?

■ *Moral Drift*

The reactions to pluralism mentioned above are examples of an unfortunate and even dangerous kind of muddled thought. Before discussing the philosophical cure to muddle, I would like to focus more sharply on why muddled thinking is dangerous. All these reactions to pluralism can contribute to a phenomenon known as MORAL DRIFT. Drift occurs 'when people make a series of small decisions, without paying attention to the overall goal toward which the series of small decisions is gradually carrying them'. In their study of the morality of muddle, Sabini and Silver use Stanley Milgram's Yale authority experiment[7] to illustrate moral drift.

Milgram asked a number of subjects to participate in an experiment that was ostensibly designed to study learning. In fact, it was designed to study research subjects' obedience to a malevolent authority figure. The research subjects were assigned the role of "teacher" and were told to deliver electrical shocks to a "learner" every time the learner made a wrong response to a question. The learner was in another room, so he could not be seen by the teacher. As far as the teacher knew, some learner (who was hooked up by wires to a voltage machine in front of the teacher) would suffer a shock every time the teacher moved a lever on the machine. Each time a question was missed, the teacher moved the lever up another notch on a scale of increasing voltage (from minimal volts up to 450 volts, which is lethal). At the end of the scale clear signs warned that the voltage was reaching a point where it could be lethal. In actuality, the learner was really an actor who read a prepared script. He was not hooked to the machine, and he did not receive any shocks. He merely gave rehearsed standardized responses that were correlated with the different levels of shock—he would protest at first, then shout, then moan, and finally, after 300 volts were supposedly delivered to him by the teacher, he would become silent as though unconscious or dead. Remember, the research subject teacher did not know the learner was not actually hooked up to the voltage machine.

Forty psychiatrists agreed ahead of time that the majority of subjects would go beyond 150 volts, but that only the rare sadistic sociopath would go all the way to 450 volts. What surprised everyone was that although a few subjects refused to keep delivering increasingly severe shocks, an amazing 62 percent of the subjects in the experiment continued escalating the severity of the shocks until they reached the lethal level. This means the subjects were willing to risk doing tremendous harm to innocent people on orders from an institutional authority figure—a Yale scientist. Many of the subjects who went all the way up the scale showed a great deal of stress, but they nonetheless continued to escalate the shocks on orders from the psychologist conducting the experiment. One who went to 180 volts said, "He can't stand it! . . . you hear him hollering? . . . what if something happens to him? . . . I mean, who is going to take the responsibility if anything happens to that gentleman?" (Milgram, p. 376). When the researcher said that he would take responsibility, the subject said "all right" and continued to deliver the shocks.

By focusing only on each small step and by refusing to challenge the experimenter's institutional authority, the subjects in the experiment clearly displayed moral drift. They drifted up the scale to the lethal level of shock without ever explicitly making the significant moral choice to deliver a potentially lethal shock. It is important to recognize that when each small decision is considered in isolation, it is not in itself an evil action. After all, the subjects had volunteered to participate in an experiment at a prestigious university; they did not intend to electrocute anyone. If the researcher had told them to go from zero up to a lethal shock in one move, many more would have refused. But they never had to confront the overall pattern of what they were doing. They drifted along, trusting the institutional authority, taking responsibility for their tiny actions, but refusing to take responsibility for the pattern being created by their overall behavior. In a sense, they were simply blindly following their duty of station (doing their job), which is precisely what malevolent authority figures often want us to do.

Milgram's research surprised many people. On the surface, it appears as though ordinary good people are prepared to abandon their commitment to human values in order to obey a malevolent authority figure. If this interpretation were accurate, it would be startling and controversial. We must be careful, however, how we portray what occurred in this research. Milgram's own analysis attributed the results to a variety of factors.[8] He argued that because the subjects had given up their decision-making role to become an instrument for carrying out another person's wishes, they no longer felt responsible for their actions. In addition, their obedience was influenced by other variables such as their belief that the experiment served a useful purpose, the sequential nature of each small step, their interest in the technical side of the experiment, and their general tendency to be polite rather than withdraw from an activity for which they had volunteered.

I think we should also give considerable weight to the factor of institutional prestige. Remember, the sixth feature of socialization refers to our tendency to give institutions (and their officers) the benefit of the doubt. Why should Milgram's subjects think that there is anything amiss? They were focusing their attention where it is natural to focus, on their duty of station as volunteers participating in a benevolent experiment (not malevolent). They assumed the background against which they evaluated their choice was exactly as it was reported to be. A scientist in a respected research institution was doing research to benefit mankind. It is reasonable to trust a research scientist at a respected Ivy League university. It makes sense to assume he will be careful to obey the principles that regulate research on human subjects. These background expectations colored their interpretation of the foreground (what was happening at the moment).

In a recent discussion of the experiment, Moti Nissani made a similar point. He said his research on "conceptual conservatism" shows that once people have committed themselves to seeing their behavior in a certain light, it is very unlikely that they will readily change their mind and rethink what they are doing.

> Even when we deal with ideologically neutral conceptions of reality, when these conceptions have been recently acquired, when they came to us from unfamiliar sources, when they were assimilated for spurious reasons, when their abandonment entails little tangible risks or costs, and when they are sharply contradicted by subsequent events, we are, at least for a time, disinclined to doubt such conceptions on the verbal level and unlikely to let go of them in practice.[9]

Once the subjects decided they were participating in valuable research, it was very hard for them to reconceptualize and entertain the notion that the researcher was either evil or incompetent. As support for his interpretation, Nissani points out that this kind of behavior changes to a degree when the background is altered. In a follow-up of the Milgram experiment, the obedience rate dropped from 62 percent to 48 percent when the subjects were told the experiment was being conducted by a private research firm. And it dropped to 40 percent when the experiment was altered to expose the subjects to an instance of betrayal and clear injustice on the part of the researcher (in order to give them reasons to question his moral integrity).[10] (Of course, 40 percent is still too high given that moral agents are supposed to take responsibility for their participation in institutional activities. On the other hand, when the experiment was run in Germany 80 percent of the subjects went to the lethal level. Perhaps the U.S. tendency to emphasize individual responsibility has a positive effect.)

This kind of research has important implications for applied ethics. Since people obviously have a difficult time reconceptualizing what they are doing, the background context must be designed to ensure that they start their tasks with adequate ideals and practical information about what is really going on. But, in the modern context of background pluralism, adequate ideals and information are often difficult to achieve. These considerations help us understand why so many people seem to be poorly prepared for moral life in pluralistic cultures.

1. People do not feel sure of themselves when they are muddled or confused. Thus, they are ready to turn over responsibility to authority figures, hoping that authorities are not themselves muddled moral agents.
2. There is also a tendency to focus narrowly on duty of station, the level of ethical consideration most closely related to our immediate situation. Dedication to duty of station is an important virtue, but it can also keep people from developing the broad understanding needed to judge the background context of their immediate situation.

■ The Banality of Evil

Remember the reference to levels of justification in Chapter One? If we focus only on local rules or immediate duties of station, we may develop muddled thinking about the ideals at higher levels that justify them. When we focus only on concrete commands we are vulnerable to treating others in unethical ways without explicitly meaning to be immoral. We can get a better understanding of this point if we consider the significance of something called the BANALITY OF EVIL, which refers to 'evil that results from motives that are not in themselves wrong in a proper context, but which seem excessively inappropriate as moral motives in complex contexts that require a careful evaluation of right and wrong'. In her book on Adolf Eichmann's trial for Nazi war crimes against humanity, Hannah Arendt said that when she went to Jerusalem to report on Eichmann's trial, she was fully prepared to find a moral monster. Instead she found a man whose motives seemed excessively banal given the context of the Holocaust.

When I speak of the banality of evil, I do so only on the strictly factual level, pointing to a phenomenon which stared one in the face at the trial. . . . Except for an extraordinary diligence in looking out for his personal advancement, he [Eichmann] had no motives at all. And this diligence in itself was in no way criminal; he certainly would never have murdered his superior in order to inherit his post. He *merely,* to put the matter colloquially, *never realized what he was doing.* It was precisely this lack of imagination which enabled him to sit for months on end facing a German Jew who was conducting the police interrogation, pouring out his heart to the man and explaining again and again how it was that he reached only the rank of lieutenant colonel in the S.S. and that it had not been his fault that he was not promoted. In principle he knew quite well what it was all about, and in his final statement to the court he spoke of the "revaluation of values prescribed by the [Nazi] government." He was not stupid. It was sheer thoughtlessness—something by no means identical with stupidity—that predisposed him to become one of the greatest criminals of that period. [11]

Whether or not you agree with Arendt's assessment of Eichmann, her views about the ethical predicament facing banal people raise some profound questions. Can people participate in massive evil for motives that may not, in themselves, be evil? Eichmann said: "I was doing my duty; that is a virtue, isn't it?" The answer is "yes" and "no." Ethical life is not that simplistic, and it seems banal in the modern world for a person to approach it only on the level of duty of station. Because banal people never carefully judge either their own motives or the duties they are given by institutions, they inadvertently help to maintain and promote evil. Eichmann participated in the Holocaust—the extermination of millions of people—yet he was motivated almost exclusively by a concrete desire to advance in the Nazi SS hierarchy by obeying orders. This exclusive egocentric focus on a personal agenda seemed to blind him to the larger social context of his actions, and that is so banal as to be evil.

Eichmann's case is an extreme example, but there are similarities to the people in Zimbardo's experiment, Jones's experiment, and Milgram's experiment. Many had motives that were not evil, and were surprised when they found themselves contributing to evil. All agreed with hindsight that they should not have cooperated with the institutions that controlled them. But at the time, they remained banally oblivious to the broad ramifications of the many small steps they were required to take. By the time they understood, they felt powerless to stop what they were doing.

The banality of evil appears to be related to a lack of enough courage or understanding to properly confront immoral institutions. Reread the "good" guard's comments from the Zimbardo experiment. Although he eventually came to realize that he didn't like his role, he seemed too confused to do anything about changing the institution. Zimbardo points out that the passivity of these "good" guards helped maintain the prison environment. The fact they did not speak up seems rather banal, given the context. It is not enough to recognize that something is wrong; to be good moral agents we must also know how to confront the wrongful behavior.

When we are banal we are not choosing harm as our ultimate goal, so in a sense we are not intentionally contributing to evil. Yet because we do contribute to evil in the world, we should be blamed. Perhaps we can use moral drift to excuse children, since they cannot delay gratification or accept the personal sacrifice for which morality sometimes calls. But we expect more from adult moral agents. Adults should not be excused when they act in a trite fashion. In this text, the concept of banality is not used as an excuse; it is used to help us understand situations in which agents do not appear to have evil intentions even though they become involved in situations that are obviously immoral.

Because I think the banality of evil is a fairly common phenomenon, and because it is hard to believe that decent people can do evil things for fairly trivial reasons ("trivial" must be judged in context), I'll mention a couple of other famous cases where I see this tendency at work. Although the following examples are extreme, which is why the people who participated in the evil were mostly amazed and chagrined to find themselves doing what they were doing, it is my belief that such instances are far more common than we would like to believe, albeit in much less extreme forms.

Amnesty International published a study of soldiers who became torturers in Greece's political prisons.[12] It documents how evil authorities can brutally socialize good, simple people into roles that call for sadistic behavior. How does a corrupt regime induce ordinary soldiers to torture their fellow countrymen? Do they put out advertisements saying: "Needed at local political prison: burly sadistic men to torture prisoners; good fringe benefits and opportunities for innovative work"? People might like to comfort themselves with the belief that people who abuse others are atypical in this way, but we must remember that the John Wayne guard started out as an avowed pacifist. We must remember that forty psychiatrists predicted only the very rare sadist would go up to 450 volts in Milgram's experiment— yet 62 percent of these normal average subjects went that high. The people in these situations are not different from you and me; they do not start out with evil intent.

The soldiers in Greek political prisons were conscripted; they were not sadistic volunteers. They were socialized to become torturers, and many felt profound guilt when society confronted them after they were "liberated" from army duty. Many came from "respectable, middle- and working-class families throughout the countryside, and there is no doubt that their relatives and friends felt shocked and bitter at what had become of the promising young men they had known" (p. 35). In the end, when some of the soldiers went to trial, even the prosecutor did not know who to blame. He said in his closing address:

> . . . The subordinate ranks were . . . conscripted. They were not, as some people have tried to pretend, volunteers. After they had every trace of individuality and humanity crushed out of them at KESA, after their lowest instincts had been aroused, after they had been threatened, terrorized and misled, they were let out like wild animals from their cages and set on their brothers to tear them to pieces. Most of them, not having the strength to resist, followed their orders. Some adjusted and identified themselves (with the procedures), after which they acted on their own, varying the repetitive monotony by personal initiatives. How can we today, members of the tribunal, go deeply enough into this to find out who are the guilty? (p. 35)

I think that it is interesting that so many of the soldiers who passed through KESA (a special army unit) were from small villages. They had a good tribal heritage but little experience with value choice in the wider community. They entered the army with a naive narrow understanding of political reality, believing that if they followed orders everything would be fine. In short, they lacked crucial experience about how to save themselves from moral corruption. At the time, being young naive soldiers, they did not understand the broad ramifications of the many small steps they were required to take during their brutal training. By the time they understood, they felt powerless to stop what they were doing.

Without the education we get from real practical experience, we will be vulnerable to either choosing inappropriate means for implementing ideals or standing by in confusion while things we disapprove of take place under our noses. The practical wisdom required in applied ethics develops slowly. We all begin life inexperienced and prepared to be morally banal until we learn. Like most other activities, moral expertise requires practice. Thus, we need moral fire drills to prepare us for acting in crisis situations and to help us avoid getting into those situations in the first place. Fire drills give practical insights and also help us develop the confidence and courage to act when the time comes. Moral life is a lifelong activity, so the point is to keep trying and to generate new insights with each attempt.

A different kind of dangerous banality occurs when idealists are so out of touch with immediate reality that they think their noble intentions can justify any means they choose. Sometimes people focus on abstract slogans and ignore the immediate concrete pain they cause in the pursuit of their ideals. This form of banality is documented in Robert Jay Lifton's study of Nazi doctors who participated in the Holocaust.[13] To investigate how professionals in the medical field could have conducted grisly experiments on human subjects, he went to Europe to interview some of the doctors who served in the death camps. He arrived at conclusions similar to those of Arendt about the banality of evil. He reports that many of the doctors felt that the horrible experiments on humans that took place in the concentration camps served a noble end. In the context of the eugenics movement fashionable in the 1930s, these "doctors came to see themselves as vast revolutionary biological therapists."[14] The killing itself came to be projected as a medical operation. In short, the doctors viewed themselves as scientific idealists at the same time that they presided over torturous killings.

Because these doctors seem more consciously evil than the subjects in the other examples of banality, I hesitate in using them as examples of the banality of evil. However, there are aspects of their situation and character that do seem rather banal. Lifton points out that the doctors used standard psychological forms of self-delusion. One technique was "psychic numbing," which results from talking compulsively about QUANTITATIVE data—that is, focusing on taking detailed measurements and recording only technical properties. This helped them avoid confronting the reality of the massive suffering present. Since suffering involves the QUALITATIVE, or value, dimension of experience, it is a variable that can be ignored when one is looking only for quantifiable, "scientific" data. But from a moral point of view, it is banal to even adopt such a narrow perspective on how to collect data. When the "object" being studied is actually a subject—a human being—qualitative features of the research (such as suffering) *are* morally relevant. In their pursuit of moral ideals, the doctors ignored the most relevant moral variables. In this context, exclusive dedication to an abstract ideal seems excessively banal.

Again, we see how crucial it is to focus on the proper level of ethical consideration. When debating hypotheses about ideal possibilities, paying attention to concrete events may not seem too important. But once we change the level of consideration and start implementing a hypothesized ideal on the concrete level, immediate concrete moral consequences deserve most of our attention. If the chosen means to an ideal involves great risk to innocent people, it is evil and excessively banal to refuse to abandon the means (if not the end). Eichmann focused exclusively on narrow concrete motives and ignored ideals, and the doctors focused exclusively on abstract ideals and ignored immediate concrete consequences, so both were excessively banal (and evil) from the moral point of view. When adults drift in this way, we hold them responsible. Good intentions are not enough. We assume these adults are either not being conscientious moral agents (thus can be blamed), or that they have failed to develop reasonable skills for moral agency (thus have been irresponsible).

■ The Virtue of Understanding

We know that the reactions to pluralism mentioned above are unsatisfactory, but are there more effective ways to deal with pluralism? Sometimes it is helpful just to have more understanding. To promote the virtue of intellectual understanding, Zimbardo set up a group encounter at the end of his experiment that was to be ". . . a time for moral reeducation . . . so that hopefully we would all behave more morally in future real-life situations." (See p. 19 of this text.) Jones also emphasized the virtue of "strength through understanding" at the Friday mass assembly. In a similar way, we all need to develop broad background theoretical understanding that can provide some conceptual coherence to our experiential encounters with value diversity. This is what philosophers are striving for when they engage in metaethical discussions to clarify the context for making value judgments.

■ METAETHICS: THE MEANING OF ETHICAL TERMS

There is a rich body of metaethical literature that attempts to clarify a background for ethical statements and actions. There is no need to review all the literature at this time. I will mention two extreme positions, and then go on to discuss one contemporary approach that attempts to reach a compromise.

■ Naturalism versus Emotivism

Until this century, philosophers generally treated value statements as though they were similar to descriptive statements that attribute some property to an object.

It was generally believed that the evaluative statement "the sunset is beautiful" meant that the sun had the property of beauty, just as the descriptive statement "the rock is round" meant the rock had the property of roundness. True value statements accurately described value properties in the world, and false statements inaccurately described them. This makes sense only if one assumes values exist as properties that can be perceived by moral agents. Eighteenth-century Scottish philosophers went so far as to claim that humans have a special "moral sense" (like a sixth sense) that enables them to "see" a natural moral property like benevolence. Others argued that our special human capacity to reason enables us to reflect on events in the world and discover natural moral values or laws. Because these approaches shared the common assumption that 'values are objective properties that in some sense exist naturally in the world', their position in ethics has generally been called NATURALISM.

The most radical modern challenge to naturalism comes from a position known as "logical positivism," which is clearly stated in A. J. Ayer's *Language, Truth and Logic*.[15] This metaethical position is called EMOTIVISM, because it claims that 'value statements are merely expressions of emotion that lack the cognitive content that truth claims are supposed to have'. This means we should not think of value claims as the kind of statement that could be true or false. It is meaningless to even ask about the truth value of value statements. For instance, is "Hooray for our team" a true or a false statement? It is neither, Ayer argued, since it merely expresses an emotion about a team. It is not a truth claim at all, and every other value statement has this same logical structure.

Ayer's position seems reasonable when emotional utterances amount to no more than a cheer for a team. When applied to ethical statements, however, the emotivist's metaethical theory seems less reasonable. Their theory reduces the statement "Hitler was an evil man" to being merely a sophisticated way of saying "Boo for Hitler." This is definitely not compatible with commonsense notions about ethical language. Emotivists are telling those of us who want to say it is true that "Hitler was an evil man" that we are merely confused about the cognitive status of value judgments.

As we saw earlier, Massey says all gut-level judgments are 100 percent correct because they amount to no more than expressions of introjected values. Someone like Ayer would point out that calling them correct does not say much. It only means they are accurate expressions of the speaker's emotions. That is, they are not truth claims about the status of the world; they are only reports about the feelings that have been introjected into the speaker. Because of their emphasis on emotional expression, emotivism has been facetiously called the "Boo–Hooray" theory of ethics.

■ Subjectivism

Emotivism as expressed by Massey is a form of SUBJECTIVISM. Subjectivists often say things like, "Hitler was right from his point of view, and his victim is right from her point of view." "Both the John Wayne guard and prisoner 416 are right."

Ethical arguments can have a role to play in subjectivism, but only as verbal devices used to sway emotions. Again, this position seems very confusing to common sense. It implies that there are no grounds on the basis of which we can say it is true that torturing babies is wrong, and yet, most of us believe such acts are objectively evil.

Massey is not really a thorough subjectivist, however, because he is not talking about *all* value claims. His videotaped presentation is about the etiology (causal history) of a certain class of values, namely those that are introjected and turn out to be merely tastes. Tastes are a special kind of value. There may be no objective reason for a taste, for example, either you like the taste of chocolate or you don't. Because there seems to be no objective justification for personal preferences of this kind, we say they are subjective. They are also private in the sense that they only need to affect the person who has them. For our purpose, then, we will define MATTERS OF TASTE as 'subjective values that are so private they can only be judged from the point of view of the person who has them'. Where taste is concerned, we can simply agree to disagree. In this narrow context, it makes perfectly good sense to say that all judgments are 100 percent correct. Of course "correct" means no more than the assertion that I have the preference. So long as we focus only on tastes, then, subjectivism is not confusing, but it does seem trivial.

Subjectivism tries to reduce all values to one logical type, which is often set at the lowest common denominator of arbitrary introjected tastes. But the fact that *some* values may only be judged relative to the subjective context of an individual does not prove that *all* values are subjective in this sense. As mentioned earlier, a value's causal history only explains how it came about; it does not tell us anything about the rational or cognitive status of the value. The truth value of a judgment does not depend on causal origins; it depends on whether or not there are independent reasons that would justify the judgment.

■ Ethical Values Are Not Matters of Taste

In this light, it becomes clear why some introjected or gut-level values should not be treated as though they are a matter of taste. Some of these values have serious public consequences. If I was "value programmed" to be a sadist, then even though the taste was caused by introjection, the value does not belong in the category of taste. There is nothing private about such a preference. By definition, torture requires the unwilling participation of another, so the sadist's practices are a matter of public concern. We cannot agree to disagree about sadistic practices.

Ethical categories were developed to judge interpersonal conduct, not matters of taste. Ethics tell us how we ought to treat one another, thus it is a conceptual mistake to treat ethical values as though they could be a matter of private concern. Tastes and ethical values belong in different bags. Even if they both share a causal history—for example, they both resulted from introjection—they are still logically different kinds of values with regard to their purpose, consequences, and justification. I may not be able to give good public reasons to justify my dislike of chocolate, but I can give good public reasons to support my judgment that sadistic behavior is wrong. I am not willing to agree that the sadist and I are both 100 percent correct about the value of sadism.

One of the biggest problems with subjectivism is the way this metaethical position makes it difficult to talk in a practical public way about these ethical concerns. For example, bigotry is a value that is not generally considered to be a matter of taste. However, because Massey does not distinguish between types of introjected values, he is forced to discuss bigotry as though it were just another taste. In his videotape he says: "I'm a bigot. I was value programmed in Waco, Texas, and if you had been programmed in Waco, you would be a bigot, too. But now I am in Boulder, Colorado; I cannot afford to be nor do I want to be a bigot." This statement implies that the reason Massey rejects bigotry is because it is inconvenient now that he has changed geographical location. It is not that bigotry was wrong in Waco, it is just that it is not the style in Boulder. Are we to assume that if he returns to Waco it will be all right to return to being a bigot? Is bigotry a matter of taste? Not really, which is why he does not "want to be a bigot." Maybe he has learned something in Boulder about the objective harm caused by bigotry.

Actually, by bringing in the issue of different cultural locations, Massey has shifted ground. When he contrasts Waco with Boulder, he is sounding more like a "cultural relativist." This position takes the subjectivist's major insight and makes it more general by applying it to a cultural context. Since relativism is the major antagonist of those who are searching for transcendent absolutes, we need to turn to this metaethical position in the next chapter.

■ STUDY QUESTIONS

1. In what way does pluralism lead to ethical choice and tribalism discourage it?
2. Why might arbitrary duties of station lead to confusion in pluralistic environments?
3. Why does the morality of muddle indicate that we need to engage in metaethical reflection?
4. Why are moral drift and the banality of evil inconsistent with the kind of moral responsibility we expect in moral agents?
5. Why do commonsense notions of morality lead us to think that people generally ascribe a different meaning to ethical statements than they do to matters of taste?
6. In what way does subjectivism make it difficult to talk about the immorality of bigotry? Does naturalism have the same difficulty?
7. Give one example of how subjectivism or the other reactions to pluralism can stop us from seeking greater ethical understanding.

■ NOTES

1. Lawrence Kohlberg and Elliot Turiel, "Moral Development and Moral Education," in G. Lesser, ed., *Psychology and Educational Practice* (New York: Scott, Foresman, 1971), p. 412.

2. Craig Haney and Philip G. Zimbardo, "The Socialization into Criminality: On Becoming a Prisoner and a Guard," in Jane Louin Tapp and Felice J. Levine, eds., *Law, Justice, and the Individual in Society* (New York: Holt, Rinehart and Winston, 1977) pp. 209–210.

3. All of the following quotations attributed to Dr. Morris Massey were taken from his popular video presentation, *What You Are Is Where You Were When*, produced by Magnetic Video Library, 23705 Industrial Park Drive, Farmington Hills, MI 48024, phone (313)476-1920.

4. John Sabini and Maury Silver, *Moralities of Everyday Life* (Oxford: Oxford University Press, 1982).

5. Alvin Toffler, *Future Shock* (New York: Bantam Books, 1971).

6. Walter A. Kaufman, *Without Guilt and Justice: From Decidophobia to Autonomy* (New York: P. H. Wyden, 1973).

7. Stanley Milgram, "Behavior Study of Obedience," *Journal of Abnormal and Social Psychology*, 67, 1963, p. 376.

8. Stanley Milgram, *Obedience to Authority* (New York: Harper & Row, 1974), pp. xiif, as cited in Moti Nissani, "A Cognitive Reinterpretation of Stanley Milgram's Observation on Obedience to Authority," *American Psychologist*, December 1990, pp. 1384–1385.

9. Moti Nissani, "An Experimental Paradigm for the Study of Conceptual Conservatism and Change," *Psychological Reports*, 65, pp. 19–24, as cited in Nissani, endnote number 8, p. 1384.

10. Milgram, *Obedience to Authority*, pp. 66–69, as cited in Nissani, endnote number 8, p. 1385.

11. Hannah Arendt, *Eichmann in Jerusalem, A Report on the Banality of Evil* (New York: Penguin Books, 1963), p. 287.

12. "Chapter III. The Soldiers," *Torture in Greece: The First Torturer's Trial 1975* (An Amnesty International Publication, 1977), p. 36.

13. Robert Lifton, *The Nazi Doctors* (Basic Books, 1986).

14. These quotations are taken from an article discussing Lifton's research in *Time*, June 25, 1979.

15. A. J. Ayer, *Language, Truth and Logic* (New York: Dover Publications, 1952).

■ CHAPTER FOUR

Metaethics and Rational Understanding

■ CULTURAL RELATIVISM

CULTURAL RELATIVISM is a metaethical position that claims 'ethical values can only be judged relative to the particular culture within which they arose'. Relativists argue that since social values evolve within ways of life, such values only make sense in the context of the way of life that created them. Since they assert ethical norms are cultural preferences, they argue that ethical judgments can only be right or wrong relative to the dominant preferences of the relevant culture.

Cultural relativism is more optimistic about ethical judgments than simple subjectivism, since it explains how ethical rules can function to resolve certain value conflicts. Ethical values transcend individual preferences within a culture, so we can resolve disputes between individuals and subgroups by appealing to the authority of the values that are universal to the culture.

But what if someone asks how we should resolve ethical disputes between different cultures? At this point, some cultural relativists argue, we can only remain silent. Others elaborate by becoming prescriptive and asserting that we *ought* to remain silent; that is, since cross-cultural judgments are bound to be ethnocentric, they claim it is wrong to make such judgments. This means we shouldn't condemn what looks evil in another country, since we would only be judging from our culture's perspective. (Does this mean that although we do not have to be individual subjectivists, we do have to be cultural subjectivists?)

Notice the subtle shift from descriptive statements to prescriptive statements that took place in the preceding paragraph. This is a common mistake. Cultural relativists start out with a strong descriptive position. They observe the fact that "different cultures have different value systems." As a descriptive piece of data their point is well established, but many people respond to this data by saying, "So what." It is one thing to notice that values vary from culture to culture; it is another thing to prove there are no universally transcendent values that ought to be used to judge between cultures.

When a cultural relativist says we "ought to" refrain from cross-cultural judgments, she has moved from descriptive relativism to a normative position, and the shift is logically inappropriate. The statement "It is wrong for one culture to judge another" is a moral claim. Is this value judgment relative as well, or is it logically different from the other cross-cultural value judgments it is condemning? If the judgment is relative to its own culture, it has no special transcendent status as a judgment and contradicts its own claim that cultures shouldn't make cross-cultural judgments. It is very difficult to make sense of a cross-cultural judgment about not making cross-cultural judgments.

Normative relativism shares some of the same problems as subjectivism. The mere fact that there are different value positions in the world does not tell us anything at all about the validity of any particular value position. Culture A may be different from culture B, but why do we have to suppose that they are both "right" in some sense? Why not assume one may be better than another, or that both could be wrong? It is true that some cross-cultural judgments are ethnocentric, but why assume all of them are? There are other alternatives. Some judgments *are* more ethnocentric than others. How can we know this if we can't make cross-cultural comparisons? Can we maybe attain greater insight into better ways to live by making and evaluating cross-cultural comparisons? Perhaps some cultures have values that are closer to being absolute than the values found in other cultures. If so, then cross-cultural judgments would make sense.

Relativism's strength as a metaethical theory comes from its emphasis on paying attention to context. We cannot adequately judge an action or value unless we understand its historical cultural context. Relativism's weakness lies in its

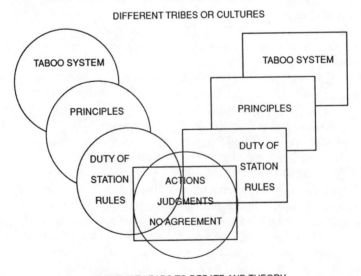

DIFFERENT TRIBES OR CULTURES

TABOO SYSTEM

TABOO SYSTEM

PRINCIPLES

PRINCIPLES

DUTY OF

DUTY OF

STATION

STATION

ACTIONS

RULES

RULES

JUDGMENTS

RULES

NO AGREEMENT

CONFLICT LEADS TO DEBATE AND THEORY

assumption that the importance of context proves it is not possible for one context to be superior to another in some transcendent sense.

What should we do when two cultures clash? One culture could simply impose its will, that is, conquer a weaker culture, then exterminate or assimilate their values. Or cultures could reach diplomatic accommodations by setting aside geographical areas that would allow each group to maintain a separate existence. Or perhaps the ideal would be for both to merge and evolve into something different, with the hope that the new way of life would combine virtues from each to create some transcendent vision that would be better than the ideals advocated by either of the previous ways of living.

Is transcendence a viable notion? On the surface, the facts of socialization and modern pluralism make it seem unlikely, and yet the potential rewards of finding a transcendent perspective have motivated philosophers for centuries. They continue to search for universal prescriptive values that can help establish meaningful priorities. To these philosophers the facts of cultural relativism are simply irrelevant. They treat introjected value differences as mere starting points to be transcended. This allows them to say that "While it may be normal to be a bigot if programmed in Waco, and while normal values may feel right relative to their place of origin, it is nonetheless possible for norms to be wrong from a broader perspective." The viability of this approach, of course, rests on the assumption that it is possible in some meaningful sense to transcend and judge different cultures.

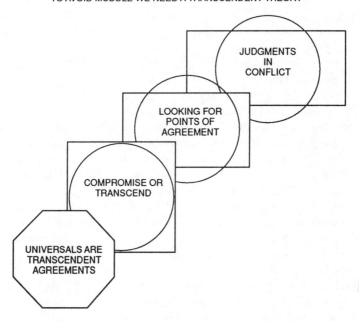

TO AVOID MUDDLE WE NEED A TRANSCENDENT THEORY

JUDGMENTS IN CONFLICT

LOOKING FOR POINTS OF AGREEMENT

COMPROMISE OR TRANSCEND

UNIVERSALS ARE TRANSCENDENT AGREEMENTS

■ ABSOLUTISM

The metaethical opposite of relativism assumes that "there are some universal transcendent truths in ethics." An ABSOLUTIST argues that no matter what culture we are from, we "ought" to give priority to absolute universal norms when they conflict with local customs. All we need to do is discover the content of the absolutes and then learn how to balance them with local customs. Absolutists are well aware of the descriptive facts that so impress relativists. Some absolutists expect and even welcome cultural diversity on the concrete level, where individuals make specific choices about how to apply absolutes. To be an absolutist does not require one to be inflexible and/or totalitarian in thought. It would be foolish not to expect local customs and environmental circumstances to influence the intelligent application of absolute principles. But, as we move up to increasingly abstract levels of ethical consideration, absolutists generally expect to find rational people moving toward a consensus about which principles are truly universal in application.

In the eighteenth-century Age of Enlightenment, the search for absolute universal standards stimulated intense philosophical investigation. Whether philosophers of the period relied on a divine light of reason, an appeal to natural laws, or a moral sense theory, the goal was the same: to transcend social and cultural idiosyncrasies by grounding moral judgments in universal principles. For example, Scottish moralists believed that because all men of good character shared a common moral sense, they would perceive the same moral truths if given the chance. The farmer was as capable as the scholar of apprehending moral truth.[1] These early absolutists did not believe, however, that the capacity to apprehend universal moral truths was a simple genetic gift. Environment also had a role to play. Since faulty nurturing could corrupt a man's natural capacity it was important for everyone to experience a healthy moral heritage so that their moral understanding would naturally unfold.

We can create a useful analogy by comparing the Enlightenment's faith in natural development with modern ethological ideas about the development of genetic predispositions. In response to a debate about the possibility of *in utero* (in the egg) learning, Konrad Lorenz agreed that a chicken might have to learn elements of pecking behavior prior to hatching by having its embryonic head passively bounced up and down by the beating of its heart.[2] But this learning may in turn require that the embryo position itself properly, a behavioral predisposition which may itself be a genetically determined adaptation to a fairly stable nest. Evolutionary theory assumes that the development of complex skills always depends on a sequence of mutually supportive genetic and environmental factors.

Now suppose we intervene in the chick's nest (its normal species environment) by rolling the developing egg in such a way as to prevent the heart from properly stimulating the nodding movement in the chick's head. Because the chick would miss the developmental stage in which it should learn elemental behaviors required for pecking, when the natural time for hatching arrived the chick would not be able to peck its way out of the egg. Clearly, the existence of normal adult chickens testifies to the fact that their eggs were not inappropriately rolled.

In an analogous manner, Enlightenment philosophers believed men would naturally develop a rational capacity (or alternatively, a moral sense) for apprehending universal moral truths so long as no one figuratively rolled their eggs at some time when they were especially vulnerable to maladaptive learning. By appealing to such developmental misadventures, Enlightenment thinkers could explain away some of the more obvious moral differences, such as when deviants with sociopathic personalities disagree with good men. Sociopaths are exceptions to the norm. Like blind men, they did not develop the equipment for "seeing" the ethical truths that are self-evident to men who experienced the normal tribal heritage that prepares us for moral life. If we can account for many of the concrete value differences in this way, then moral relativism can be shown to be a product of diverse social interventions that may ultimately be irrelevant in the natural order of things.

But what about theoretical differences between people who apparently experienced stable "nests"? Alasdair MacIntyre argues that the plurality of philosophical traditions proves that Enlightenment philosophers were overly optimistic.

> . . . Both the thinkers of the Enlightenment and their successors proved unable to agree as to what precisely those principles were which would be found undeniable by all rational persons. . . . Nor has subsequent history diminished the extent of such disagreement. It has rather enlarged it. Consequently, the legacy of the Enlightenment has been the provision of an ideal of rational justification which it has proved impossible to attain. And hence in key part derives the inability within our culture to unite conviction and rational justification.[3]

Because of the considerable formal agreement between Western traditions, I am not yet ready to abandon the Enlightenment's optimism. It may be useful, however, to modify the Enlightenment search for an absolute so as to emphasize the search rather than the result. The goal would be increasingly better transcendent "truths," which in their own turn would need to be historically transcended. But perhaps even the idea of transcendence is overly optimistic.

■ PLURALISM AND ABSOLUTES

MacIntyre's challenge to the philosophical enterprise is profound and disturbing to absolutist philosophers. MacIntyre's position, however, is not the same as relativism. He is still willing to assert that some positions are better than others. His metaethical position is closer to being a form of pluralism. PLURALISM asserts that 'there are a number of higher but irreducible ways of living, none of which can have absolute priority over the others.' Pluralists believe people can transcend ego and ethnocentric concerns in some contexts (which is why people continue to do research and seek therapy), but we may never be able to establish any ultimate priorities between the major belief systems themselves. The background conceptions that support belief systems are simply INCOMMENSURABLES, which means that 'there is no common standard or measure against which different values can be judged'. For example, MacIntyre argues that each of the protagonists in an ethical argument

> . . . reaches his conclusions by a valid form of inference from his premises. But there is no agreement as to which premises from which to start; and there exists in our culture no recognized procedure for weighing the merits of rival premises. Indeed it is difficult to see how there could be such a procedure since the rival premises are—to borrow a term from contemporary philosophy of science—incommensurable. That is to say, they employ and involve concepts of such radically different kinds that we have no way to weigh the claims of one alternative set of premises over against another. . . .
> Perhaps not all moral disagreement in our society is of this kind, but much is and the more important the disagreement the more likely it is to have this character.[4]

As we saw in the previous chapter, value pluralism on a concrete, gut level is very confusing. It is even more difficult to deal with pluralism on a theoretical level. How, then, should we proceed? Let's return to the more concrete, gut level first, to find a strategy that can help us deal with it. Perhaps the same strategy can then be used at the theoretical level.

In the second half of Massey's videotaped presentation about value diversity, he recommends that we "Stop! Pull back! And rationally, objectively, critically consider—where were they [people] when they were value programmed? If we will do this, then our judgments will be better." Massey claims that objectively reviewing a situation may create a significant emotional event that will cause a moment of MENTAL ARREST, which means 'an opportunity to pause and reflect on our own ongoing evaluative process'. He recommends that we make use of these moments of mental arrest to ask self-reflective questions about our own value programming; for example, "Wait a minute! What do I believe? What is right, correct, normal, and good (or bad)?"

By pointing out that it is possible to become critically self-reflective, Massey appears to be recommending that we strive for a higher level of understanding, one that can transcend our previous orientation. But why bother to change? Previously, he asserted that all our value judgments are already 100 percent correct. He cannot have it both ways. If objectively reviewing a situation can lead to "better" judgments, then obviously not all judgments are 100 percent right or correct. By the end of his videotape, Massey is beginning to sound like an absolutist. He is implying that even though some values may be "normal" given a certain programming context, it is still not necessarily the best programming a person could have received. This implies there must be some higher transcendent perspective we can use to make comparisons at lower levels. In the end, Massey is neither a simple subjectivist nor a pure cultural relativist; he is advocating a form of rational objectivity.

■ THE NEED FOR RATIONAL STANDARDS

It may be that the best we can do at any level of ethical justification (when confronted by pluralism) is to follow Massey's advice, and stop to pull back and reflect. For a *causal* explanation of differences we will have to turn to science. For a *justification* of differences we will have to evaluate styles of evaluating. This is precisely what we are supposed to do when we study philosophy. Philosophers keep asking "Why?" until they have pulled back as far as they can go, all the way back to the fundamental foundations for all beliefs and actions with which they are familiar. Philosophy makes use of the unique human capacity to disengage from the world and look back on it. This capacity is the psychological foundation for rational inquiry. It is the key to understanding the optimism behind mainstream philosophical theories, since the search continues to lead us to rich new insights.

■ *Kant and the Recursive Nature of Reason*

To get a clear idea of what it means to "Stop. Pull back, and critically, objectively reflect," let's return to the eighteenth century's Age of Enlightenment, the age during which many of the details of modern conceptions of rationality were developed. Many scholars agree that the Enlightenment reached its peak in the philosophical works of Immanuel Kant. In her new, seminal book, *Constructions of Reason*, Onora O'Neill clarifies Kant's rational approach to pluralism and to the critique of reason itself.[5] In the first place, an adequate criticism of reason must be recursive, that is, a self-criticism that results from self-reflective moments of mental arrest. Any attempt to establish a grounding for the criticism of reason in some outside authority would simply transfer all the skeptical questions that need to be answered to that "new" foundation. As Kant says:

> . . . [I]t would be absurd to look to reason for enlightenment, and yet to prescribe beforehand which side she must necessarily favor. Besides, reason is already of itself so confined and held within limits by reason, that we have no need to call out the guard, with a view to bringing the civil power to bear upon that party whose alarming superiority may seem to us to be dangerous. In this dialectic no victory is gained that need give us cause for anxiety. . . .
>
> Allow . . . your opponent to speak in the name of reason, and combat him only with the weapons of reason.[6]

O'Neill summarizes the consequences of Kant's theory about how practical reason functions as follows:

> The problem of seeing which modes of thinking—if any—are authoritative presupposes not only the lack of a "dictator," but the presence of a plurality of noncoordinated (potential) actors or thinkers. Kant uses the imagery of "citizens" or "fellow workers" to contrast the situation with that facing the subjects of a dictator who imposes

common standards. He does not suggest that reason's authority is based on a constitutional convention, but reminds us that there is a plurality of potential reasoners.[7]

What this means is that reason is ideally suited for the task of dealing with value diversity. It requires respectful tolerance for opposing traditions, it respects open debate, and it acknowledges the social dimension of reason by including a plurality of participants. But does this lead to an empty acceptance of every lifestyle choice no matter how immoral? No. Reason's tolerance has a cutting edge. It cannot tolerate the destruction of those conditions necessary for us to lead rational, social lives. As O'Neill points out, according to Kant, people who are in disagreement

> cannot even begin to share a world if there is no cognitive order. The most then that they can do is to reject basic principles of thought and action that are barriers to cognitive order. A minimal, negative step toward any solution must be to refrain from adopting plans that others cannot adopt. Those who are to be fellow workers [in the search for truth] must at least refrain from basing their action on basic principles that others cannot share. Those who act on such maxims are not guaranteed agreement at all points; but if they wholly reject it, communication and interaction (even hostile interaction, let alone coordination) will be impossible. To act on this maxim is simply to make what Kant elsewhere calls the Categorical Imperative the fundamental principle of all reasoning and acting.[8]

We will explore the Categorical Imperative in Chapter Ten; at this point we need only to emphasize that this way of characterizing reason leads logically to three practical principles that ought to be adopted by any rational moral agent from any culture who is trying to find the truth. These principles emphasize an obligation to keep open the possibility for "continued action, interaction, and communication." Kant is above all a philosopher with a keen sense that progress takes place in and through social interaction. As summarized by O'Neill, the three principles are:

> [1] . . . to think for oneself. Only those who think for themselves have any contribution to make to a debate or plan. . . . parroted words cannot be taken as expressions of judgment or as acts of communication. . . .
> [2] . . . to think from the standpoint of everyone else. Only those who . . . strive to listen to and interpret others and to see the point of their contributions are genuinely aiming to be "fellow workers" and to avoid maxims to which others cannot agree. . . .
> [3] . . . always to think consistently. This is . . . a never-ending task. The set of judgments that we independently form, then revise as we shift our standpoint to take account of others' standpoints, will constantly change, and so may repeatedly fall into inconsistency.[9]

O'Neill's work on Kant carefully constructs an interpretation of his philosophy that highlights the social (public), practical character of reason as well as its self-reflective and self-critical aspects. To see how these features would show up in an institutional setting designed to help us reach rational solutions to conflicts, we can review how similar ideals have been built into our judicial process. To focus attention, I will discuss only that part of the system that requires a jury trial.

■ *The Jury Box as a Model of Rational Reflection*

If you were accused of a crime but were innocent, what decision-making model would you want your accusers to use? Would you rather be tried by a tribal opinion poll, an arbitrary flip of a coin, trial by combat, an angry mob of the alleged victim's relatives, a single authority figure, or a body of concerned citizens who were judging you according to guidelines designed to get them to stop, pull back, and critically, objectively reflect on the merits of the case? There is no procedure that can guarantee mistakes won't be made. Innocent people may be convicted and the guilty may go free. But some ways of making decisions in this context are more responsible than others. People who are MORALLY RESPONSIBLE are guided by two dominant virtues: rationality and caring (the latter term is similar to what Good-paster[10] calls "respect for persons"). Morally responsible people will use whatever decision-making procedure is most likely to get at the truth. In a jury trial, justice demands that we take a morally responsible approach, so let's examine how the jury system has been explicitly designed to encourage responsible decision making.

1. There is a judge who is supposed to be an EXPERT ON RULES AND EVIDENCE. In complex cases she uses her expertise to help the jury understand what is relevant to the case. We do not want irrationality or arbitrary preferences to rule in matters of justice.
2. The members of the jury are supposed to be IMPARTIAL, in the sense that they avoid personal agendas when deciding the case. However, while they are not supposed to have a personal interest in the outcome, they are still supposed to care about the truth of the outcome.
3. We want people who serve on juries to be our PEERS, so they will be more likely to care about us and understand any unique circumstances that are relevant to our case. We all know introjected values affect decision making. Do we want to be judged by people who might have introjected values that are radically different from ours? Peers are more likely to understand us.
4. Furthermore, we want to be judged by rational people who EXPLORE ALL THE FACTS from the relevant alternative points of view. We want them to listen to evidence from all sides—pro and con—and then debate the issue, so that the judgment will reflect the merits of the case rather than being a lopsided interpretation due to irrelevant things like personal desire, political expedience, or delusions.
5. Jurors need a period of REFLECTIVE EQUILIBRIUM.[11] They should retire to a jury room, so that irrelevant stress or emotion will not cloud their judgment during their deliberations on the case.
6. And finally, decisions should be constrained by the demands of PUBLIC DEBATE. This means that trials should be conducted in a public arena, so that the entire judicial process can be publicly critiqued. Furthermore, when jurors try to persuade other jurors to vote their way, the evaluation of the evidence is again subject to critical public debate in the jury room. Fallacious rationalizations are more likely to be exposed when views are exchanged in a public debate.

If we can trust this kind of decision procedure to help us be more responsible when making value choices, then we have good reasons to believe that it is possible to strive for objective public considerations. The decision procedure presented in Chapter Two was designed to keep us focused on some of these same concerns. To use it effectively, it too should be used in a public setting that encourages debate. Standards of rationality developed over time as historical circumstances taught us that just decision making in pluralistic environments could not be based exclusively on either authority, personal preferences, or ethnocentric codes. Peters argues that because of this, a rational approach to morality amounts to a way of life.

> . . . An attempt is made to base conduct and assessment of people on reasons which fall under principles which make them relevant. In the history of man this is a rare phenomenon. The more usual practice has been to rely on tradition or on some authoritative source, as in most religions. This way of conducting life developed precisely because there was a clash between codes which had a traditional or authoritative basis. When faced with discrepant demands, men had to reflect, to go behind "convention" to "nature" or some other standard codes. And in coming together in this way men presupposed certain principles such as impartiality, freedom, truth-telling, the consideration of interests and respect for persons which provided general criteria by reference to which they could weigh up different codes of conduct. A form of experience gradually emerged under which contents deriving from different traditions were fitted. This form of experience is what I call "rational morality."[12]

Peters calls rational morality "a way of life," and within that way of life, as MacIntyre pointed out, we still have disagreements over background theoretical fundamentals. Obviously, the search for the best moral point of view is not over. The debate has simply been transferred to questions about the nature of rationality itself. There may be a number of different views about what a rational way of life looks like. To avoid ideological uses of reason, we need to encourage those pursuing the Enlightenment goal to emphasize the process of the search for truth rather than a closed commitment to a favored final solution.

I believe Kant's analysis of rationality, with its emphasis on reason's public and self-critical nature, is not just another simple ideological position. By its nature it is open to critical review from within and without and is able to be modified by considerations of practical necessity. Of course, some modern critics assert that advocating openness and a search for transcendence is itself ideological, since it undercuts deep emotional commitment to a favored way of life. I am skeptical of this psychological claim, but even if it were true, it is not clear that we have any other alternative to rational debate, given that there is a need in pluralism to keep the door open for communication between traditions. As O'Neill says:

> Those who flout reasoned maxims of communication risk damage to shared standards of reasoning, which are essential for addressing the world at large and to some extent

required even by those who seek to address only their own sect or friends or the politically or religiously or otherwise like minded.[13]

■ *Hermeneutics and Rationality*

The debate over conditions for reason and forms of reason continues. Some modern critics have even challenged the usefulness of the absolutist/relativist distinction itself. For instance, Hans-Georg Gadamer argues that human conceptions are always historically situated, thus there is no possibility of ever discovering some kind of absolute outside of history that can be used to ground cultural norms. He says:

> In fact history does not belong to us, but we belong to it. Long before we understand ourselves through the process of self-examination, we understand ourselves in a self-evident way in the family, society and state in which we live. The focus of subjectivity is a distorting mirror. The self-awareness of the individual is only a flickering in the closed circuits of historical life. That is why the prejudices of the individual, far more than his judgments constitute the historical reality of his being.[14]

Gadamer's use of the term "prejudices" is similar to what I have been calling the "background" assumptions that underlie any ethical position. But Gadamer argues that at any given time, because we are bound by the assumptions of history itself, individuals can never transcend their own historical situation. On the surface, his emphasis seems to be more sympathetic to the cultural relativists than to those who are striving for an absolute that can transcend cultural heritage. However, although Gadamer's position gives primacy to history, it also allows for a conception of rational progress if it results from developing historical or cultural forces. He is not a relativist, he is working within the hermeneutic tradition. As G. B. Madison says, HERMENEUTICS

> . . . is not a form of irrationalism and does not entail a rejection of reason. . . . Hermeneutics entails a critique of scientific reason (what Gadamer would term "method"). . . . [But] it does not entail relativism. . . . Reason's claim to universality is something that thinkers like Gadamer and Ricoeur are not in the least prepared to relinquish. . . . When hermeneuticists say that all understanding occurs within (and is, in this precise sense, dependent on) a context, they are not saying as relativists do that we are imprisoned in closed, incommensurate universes of discourse; they are simply saying that in our ongoing search for ever greater understanding we are not supported in this endeavor by nothing. . . . [They defend] . . . what might be called the pursuit of truth, i.e., an understanding of things that is animated by a drive for universality . . . which must nevertheless remain always only presumptive. . . . Some statements or interpretations of the world are, at any given time, better, more rational (more arguable) and thus "truer" than others. . . . People with different backgrounds . . . will, if motivated by good will and the desire to reach an agreement, attempt to discover the grounds they do share and on whose basis a consensus can be built.[15]

According to the hermeneutic approach to reason, then, the fact that I believe that one solution is better than the other does not mean that I claim to already possess an absolute truth. It only means I have made progress. I can respect and take seriously the position of those who come from a different heritage, so long as they are being serious about being responsible, and so long as they are not being banal or making obvious mistakes of a kind that my tradition has already transcended (if I have no acquaintance with a tradition, I cannot say that I have transcended it).

Notice the way in which we have been shifting back and forth between individual consciousness and the influence of historical and cultural forces. Gadamer places emphasis on historical traditions and deemphasizes individual contributions (individual "self-awareness . . . is only a flickering in the closed circuits of historical life"). One of his major critics tries to account for these relationships in a way that leaves more room for individual transcendence. Jürgen Habermas[16] argues that individuals can develop emancipatory, self-reflective virtues that enable them to transcend their initial ethical context, or at least consciously choose to build upon it and move forward. (This issue will be discussed in more detail in Chapter Eight.)

Hermeneutic philosophers (working in a modified Kantian tradition) agree that there is room in a complex world for alternative visions, but they do not see why a plurality of visions has to lead to relativism. When visions conflict, they believe rational debate can help us figure out caring, respectful ways to deal with the value differences. These interesting philosophical issues take us well beyond the purpose of this chapter. For the reader who would like to pursue these issues in more detail, endnote 16 suggests additional readings.

One may still wonder why individual moral agents within any particular tradition should have to worry about justifying social values on such an abstract level. Can it be that we are asking too much of the ordinary busy citizen? Why isn't it enough to just be loyal to the duties of station in our own heritage? The problem is, in a pluralistic world ordinary people like you and me are called upon to make the most amazing judgments. The responsibilities that come with "moral agency" and "government of the people" mandate that we be informed, and that we take our mission seriously. We will be held responsible whether we accept the challenge or not. At the very least, then, we should occasionally challenge ourselves to transcend our previous orientations. Unfortunately, we do not always stop and pull back and ask "Why?" when we ought to. Too often, we are so busy with daily life that we fail to engage in serious critical reflection about overall patterns, so we drift along hoping others will take care of the moral world for us.

Although Zimbardo and Jones were both highly impressed with the power of institutions to control their subjects, they also believed their subjects could do something to improve. Their solution was to encourage the development of the broader understanding that comes with reflection during moments of mental arrest. Zimbardo's discussion group and Jones's Friday assembly gave everyone an opportunity to pause and ask "Why?" and then publicly debate possible explanations for what they experienced. In a similar manner, the best time to reflect on our own moral heritage is during moments of mental arrest. At those moments we may have the opportunity to modify the background assumptions we have been using to organize our experiences (assuming we discover a reason to modify them).

The goal, of course, is to develop a well-thought-out critical theory that can help us rationally choose our future actions rather than habitually react to forces without reflecting. The best theory will be a moral point of view that will appeal to all those moral agents who care about ethics and are searching for the highest standards currently available. We need to focus now on developmental research that investigates "how" people develop the prerequisite virtues that enable them to care and understand in this moral sense. As we shall see, a major developmental shift in the way we orient to the world must occur before we can make the transition from childhood egocentrism to full moral agency. To clarify this shift, the next two chapters review empirical research on individual cognitive and moral development. As we will see when we get to Chapter Eleven's discussion of how to implement theories, this developmental information serves a very important background purpose in applied ethics.

■ STUDY QUESTIONS

1. Why is it a logical mistake for a descriptive cultural relativist to make prescriptive statements about how we should judge other cultures?
2. How do absolutists explain the fact that there are different value systems in different cultures?
3. How did Scottish philosophers account for the fact that deviant people do not seem to share the same moral intuitions as the average moral agent?
4. What do metaethical pluralists mean when they say that different fundamental value systems may be incommensurable?
5. In what way can a moment of mental arrest provide an opportunity to reevaluate a belief system?
6. Why does Kant think that reason is inherently social, self-critical, and practical? Does this support the idea that reason is not necessarily ideological?
7. Explain how the jury box model of rationality can be construed to be an illustration of the ideals behind responsible decision making?
8. In what way does the hermeneutic approach to metaethics offer a compromise between the aspirations of the absolutist and the relativist?

■ NOTES

1. For a good discussion of this commonsense point of view, see Garry Wills, *Inventing America* (New York: Vintage Books, 1978), pp. 184ff.

2. Konrad Lorenz, *Evolution and Modification of Behavior* (Chicago: The University of Chicago Press, 1965), pp. 23–27, 79–83.

3. Alasdair MacIntyre, *Whose Justice? Which Rationality?* (Notre Dame, IN: University of Notre Dame Press, 1988), p. 6.

4. Alasdair MacIntyre, "Moral Disagreements," in Tom L. Beauchamp, ed., *Philosophical Ethics* (New York: McGraw-Hill, 1991), p. 56f.

5. Onora O'Neill, *Constructions of Reason: Explorations of Kant's Practical Philosophy* (Cambridge: Cambridge University Press, 1989).

6. Immanuel Kant, *Critique of Pure Reason*, transl. by Norman Kemp Smith (London: MacMillan, 1938), pp. A747/B775, as cited in O'Neill, p. 16f.

7. O'Neill, p. 16.

8. Ibid., p. 23.

9. Ibid., pp. 25–26.

10. Kenneth E. Goodpaster, "The Concept of Corporate Responsibility," in Tom Regan, ed., *Just Business* (New York: Random House, 1984), p. 301.

11. John Rawls, *A Theory of Justice* (Cambridge, MA: Harvard University Press, 1971), pp. 20ff, 46–48.

12. R. S. Peters, *Reason and Compassion* (London: Routledge & Kegan Paul, 1973), p. 15.

13. O'Neill, p. 47.

14. Hans-Georg Gadamer, *Truth and Method*, transl. by J. Weinsheimer and D. Marshall (New York: The Crossroad Publishing Corporation, 1989), p. 245, cited in Gerald Wallulis, *The Hermeneutics of Life History* (Evanston, IL: Northwestern University Press, 1990), p. 4.

15. G. B. Madison, "Hermeneutical Integrity: A Guide for the Perplexed," *Market Process*, Fall 1988, pp. 2–8.

16. Jürgen Habermas, *Knowledge and Human Interest* (New York: Beaver Press, 1971); see pp. 208–213 and Chapter 10. Also see *Communication and the Evolution of Society*, transl. by Thomas McCarthy (Boston: Beacon Press, 1979). For more information on the hermeneutic approach to philosophy, see Richard E. Palmer, *Hermeneutics* (Evanston, IL: Northwestern University Press, 1969), and B. R. Wachterhauser, ed., *Hermeneutics and Modern Philosophy* (Albany, NY: State University of New York Press, 1986). Also see Richard J. Bernstein, *Beyond Objectivism and Relativism: Science, Hermeneutics, and Praxis* (Philadelphia: University of Pennsylvania Press, 1983).

CHAPTER FIVE

Cognitive and Moral Development

■ COGNITIVE DEVELOPMENT

In the past sixty years developmental psychologists have provided us with a wealth of information on the capacities, both emotional and cognitive, that people need in order to participate fully in the adult world. While this kind of developmental research cannot settle philosophical puzzles, it can help us understand the nature and origin of some disputes and give us insight into what moral agents can do under different conditions. To see this we need to briefly review some leading theories of human development. As we will see in the final chapter, a practical understanding of developmental material will be very useful when we reach the point of establishing concrete policies.

According to the French psychologist Jean Piaget,[1] human intelligence develops through four sequential stages. Before we can develop to a more sophisticated stage we must first master the developmental prerequisites for the earlier stages. The following chart[2] illustrates the sequence of stages and the age range within which the skills are normally mastered.

Some of Piaget's critics claim that he underestimates how soon children can begin to use formal operational thinking. They worry that he does not give enough credit to the effect that an educationally enriched environment can have on development. For instance, L. S. Vygotsky argues that Piaget studies "child thought apart from the influence of instruction," and that this "excludes a very important source of change and bars the researcher from posing the question of the interaction of development and instruction peculiar to each age level."[3] He argues that the development of thinking skills depends on environmental stimulation, so we should expect some variability in the time needed for their development. Enriched environments will speed up the developmental process, while deprived environments can slow it down and even destroy it. However, these differences do not affect the main point, which is that prior to the development of formal operational abilities we find very little self-reflective thought.

SENSORIMOTOR INTELLIGENCE

The child learns to sense the world, move about, and physically manipulate objects in his environment. This stage is amoral; not an agent, a reactor.

SYMBOLIC, INTUITIVE, PRELOGICAL THOUGHT

Language develops. Uses verbal symbols to describe experience, but does not grasp logical or causal relations, Magical thinking, confuses appearance with reality. Uses one variable to solve problems.

CONCRETE OPERATIONAL THOUGHT

Uses a system of classes, relations, and logically invariant properties to manipulate concrete objects. Understands causal relations, conservation of matter, and uses many variables to solve problems.

FORMAL OPERATIONAL THOUGHT

Applies logical operations to logical operations. Thinking about thinking. Evaluating styles of evaluation. Applies operations to thought patterns and systems rather than external objects. Hypothetical-deductive isolation of variables and testing of hypothesis. Systematic isolation of variables and testing of hypothesis before turning to reality. True formal or abstract thought.

Since we are interested in capacities that lead to moral agency and philosophical reflection, at this point I will only discuss the two stages that are especially important for understanding the intellectual side of moral development. The stage of CONCRETE OPERATIONAL THOUGHT develops as we learn increasingly sophisticated strategies for adapting to the demands of the external world. The major intellectual advance at this stage is the ability to think logically and in causal terms about standardized solutions to common concrete problems. Because mental operations are being used to solve external problems, people are not in a position to develop much critical self-awareness about their own habitual use of these strategies.

A major shift begins to appear at about eleven years of age. During this time the FORMAL OPERATIONAL capacities that make it possible to think on a theoretical level begin to appear. That is, while concrete operational thought is used to manipulate the external world, formal operational thought can be used to manipulate mental operations themselves. This capacity is the root of creativity. As R. G. Richmond says:

. . . A formal operation is a mental action in which the statements themselves are combined to produce new statements. The result of this is a further release from the world, for the adolescent is now performing operations on the results of other operations. . . . With formal operations, the given environment can be treated as one of a number of possible conditions. . . . He begins with the possible and proceeds towards the real. Thus, formal operations reverse the relationship between the real and the possible.[4]

Formal operational thinking should be characterized as "thinking about thinking," "using logic on logic," or "evaluating evaluations." The crucial advance is in the capacity to reverse directions and reflect on the process of reflection itself. We could not follow Massey's advice to "Stop! Pull back! and ask: What do I believe?" if we did not have this capacity. The ability to reverse directions and think about that which does not yet exist on the concrete level is the foundation on which all theoretical disciplines must rest (including science and ethics). Although concrete experience precedes formal thought in individual development, the latter logically precedes the former in theoretical disciplines. Formal thought gives us the capacity to think about hypothetical ideals before we know how to deal with them on a concrete level. Neither the scientific theory of relativity nor the ethical theory about inalienable rights could have been conceived of by a concrete operational thinker.

■ MORAL DEVELOPMENT

Piaget's initial research on the development of moral thought[5] has been elaborated on and extended by other developmentalists, most notably the educational psychologist Lawrence Kohlberg. In a series of longitudinal cross-cultural studies,[6] Kohlberg identified three levels of moral development, which he divided into six sequential stages. His method was to interview the same research subjects for over 30 years, and at three-year intervals have them write out solutions to moral dilemmas. Then, according to the type of reasons they offered, he categorized the subjects' reasoning into stages. The following is a typical dilemma used in Kohlberg's research.

> In Europe, a woman was near death from a very bad disease, a special kind of cancer. There was one drug that the doctors thought might save her. It was a form of radium for which a druggist was charging ten times what the drug cost him to make. The sick woman's husband, Heinz, went to everyone he knew to borrow the money, but he could get together only about half of what it cost. He told the druggist that his wife was dying, and asked him to sell it cheaper or let him pay later. But the druggist said, "No, I discovered the drug and I'm going to make money from it." So Heinz got desperate and broke into the man's store to steal the drug for his wife. Should the husband have done that? Why or why not?[7]

People can agree that Heinz should or should not steal (same content) and yet give different types of reasons for their conclusion (different form). For instance, one might say, "Don't steal or else you might go to prison." The form is action guided by avoidance of personal pain. Another might say, "Don't steal because theft hurts people." The form is action guided by concern for others. While the content in these answers is the same, the form of the reasons given to justify their recommendation is so different that Kohlberg thinks the logic of the answer has shifted. What is important to Kohlberg is whether or not the form of reasoning is egocentric (focused on self), ethnocentric (focused on the group), or is governed by universal principles (focused on norms that transcend the contingencies of local circumstances). Kohlberg believes the forms develop naturally during direct confrontations with real day-to-day ethical conflicts. People develop new ways to think when their old strategies don't work. Shifts in the form of thought cannot, however, be taught as specific content by methods* that emphasize habit formation (the bag of virtues approach mentioned in Chapter Three).

It is important to remember that the subjects in Kohlberg's study are solving hypothetical dilemmas. Their answers reflect the highest ideals that come into play when they are sitting at a desk deliberating calmly about how they think they ought to behave. Actual behavior in stressful situations might well be different. Factors such as fear, depression, and desire, which do not have their full impact on us when we are only "thinking" about dilemmas, are likely to affect our behavior in real-life situations. His research showed that the way we think about what we ought to do can change over time. Some people did not change much, and others changed considerably, but changes in form always followed the same sequence. We should keep in mind that no one was ever wholly in one stage. Most subjects gave answers that had the characteristics of at least three different stages (which is to be expected since subjects are in developmental transition). Kohlberg placed a subject into a certain category only if at least 50 percent of his answers had the form characteristic of that stage.[8]

Why should we assume that the stages represent developmental growth rather than arbitrary age-related shifts in style of reasoning? Like Piaget, Kohlberg says a change shows developmental progress when it strengthens a person's ability to remain in a state of equilibrium with his environment, that is, he can solve more moral problems. Each stage is a structure that gives us a more stable and extensive equilibrium by building on earlier structures.[9] Reasoning in the earlier stages, then, is not irrational. It is only an overly simplistic way of seeing the world, because it ignores moral complexity, and so interferes with our ability to solve dilemmas.

---

* There is a debate in the literature between learning theorists (like B. F. Skinner) and cognitive developmentalists over the form/content issue. We do not have time to pursue this debate here. In brief, Skinnerians advocate a learning theory model that places emphasis on the content of rules programmed into us. We do need content to work with, but developmentalists emphasize that the level of conception (the form of mental life) determines the type of content that can be learned as well as how it will be understood and used.

Carol Gilligan's book, *In a Different Voice*,[10] argues that Piaget's (1932) and Kohlberg's (1973) research carries on a tradition in psychological research of focusing almost exclusively on studies of males. She claims the typical modern description of moral development emphasized the "content" areas that are of primary interest to men, that is, justice and individual rights. It is only in the last couple of decades that fascinating research studies[11] on how women come to know about the world have received serious attention in academic circles. In order to add gender balance, I will integrate material from Gilligan's research into Kohlberg's research during the following review of Kohlberg's conclusions (all references to Gilligan are from *In a Different Voice* unless otherwise indicated).

■ The Preconventional Level

Gilligan's research reveals that while women and men focus on different content, they nonetheless share the same common forms of intellectual development. After an initial amoral stage of infancy, male and female children both must move through an egocentric level of development, the *Preconventional Level:* Level I. The child's egocentrism contributes to MORAL REALISM,[12] which is the "child's tendency to treat moral events as though they are independent of the intentions of

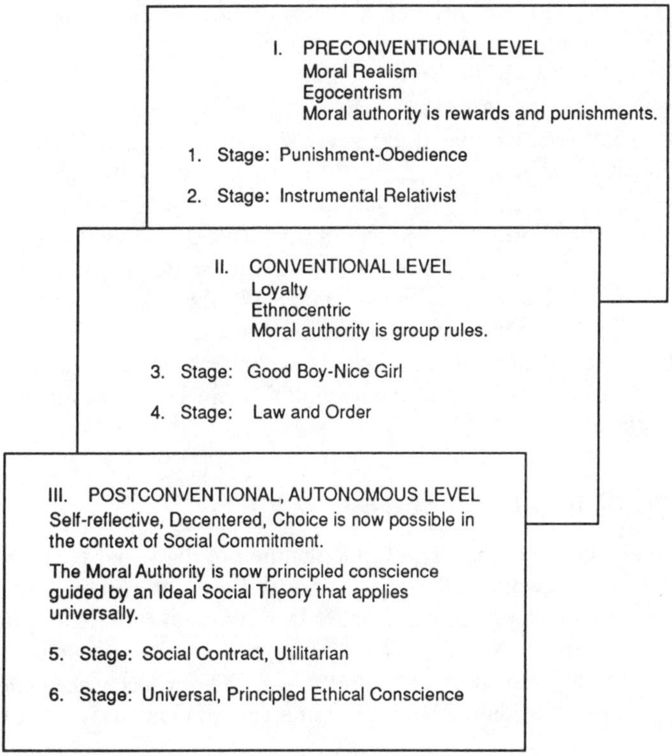

I.   PRECONVENTIONAL LEVEL
     Moral Realism
     Egocentrism
     Moral authority is rewards and punishments.

  1. Stage: Punishment-Obedience

  2. Stage: Instrumental Relativist

     II.   CONVENTIONAL LEVEL
           Loyalty
           Ethnocentric
           Moral authority is group rules.

       3. Stage: Good Boy-Nice Girl

       4. Stage: Law and Order

   III.   POSTCONVENTIONAL, AUTONOMOUS LEVEL
   Self-reflective, Decentered, Choice is now possible in
   the context of Social Commitment.

   The Moral Authority is now principled conscience
   guided by an Ideal Social Theory that applies
   universally.

   5. Stage: Social Contract, Utilitarian

   6. Stage: Universal, Principled Ethical Conscience

people." Children assess blame by focusing attention on the amount of real physical damage done to themselves; they ignore what was intended. "Ought" statements and words like "good" and "right" are defined by references to personal desires for rewards and to the powerful authority figures who make the rules that determine who gets the rewards and punishments. Gilligan found that females who had this egocentric orientation focused primarily on pragmatic concerns and personal survival.

> From this perspective, *should* is undifferentiated from *would*, and other people influence the decision only through their power to affect its consequences. . . . The self, which is the sole object of concern, is constrained by a lack of power that stems from feeling disconnected and thus, in effect, all alone (p. 75).

At this level, the subjects do not have a fully developed "social" nature. Peters[13] argues that "before one can choose a rule, one must first learn what it means to follow a rule." We cannot develop into truly social beings until we first experience social rules that have been imposed on us. At this level, then, what plays the role of MORAL AUTHORITY in one's life is not moral conscience or commitment to social norms but 'deference to whoever happens to control rewards and punishments'. Since egocentric people can only understand rules as external constraints placed on their impulses, a society of them would resemble a gang of pirates rather than a community of moral agents.

In the *Punishment-Obedience orientation* (stage one of Level I), research subjects say you should steal the drug to save Heinz's wife only if she has power (deference to authoritative rules and power for its own sake). In the *Instrumental Relativist orientation* (stage two of Level I), they say Heinz should save his wife only if she has instrumental value from his point of view. One thirteen year old said: "But the husband wouldn't want it [for his wife to die]; it's not like an animal. If a pet dies, you can get along without it—it isn't something you really need. Well, you can get a new wife, but it's not really the same" (Kohlberg, 1971, p. 168). They recognize that others have competing interests, and begin to negotiate deals to get what they want. This helps them understand that rules not only are concrete commands of authority figures but also can be useful instruments for protecting self-interest.

■ The Conventional Level

To develop an adequate qualitative understanding of the social purposes behind rules, we must transcend the Preconventional Level. If caring is one of the prerequisite capacities for full moral understanding, then the tribal heritage that imposes rules on us must also, in some sense, provide each of us with a sense of social identity that can help us transcend our initial egocentric mode. Thus, the family group that initially imposes rules on young members must at the same time affirm their unconditional worth so that they can in return learn to care about social life. To move up to a *Conventional Level* (Level II) and become a loyal member of a group requires a major shift in the form of thought. Obedience to social norms is no longer based only on awe of power (stage one fear) and/or self-interest (stage two manipulations) as it was at the previous level. People are becoming social beings with identities tied to the values of the group. Satisfying the expectations of peer groups and/or the community is perceived as valuable for its own sake, regardless of the immediate consequences to self. What plays the role of MORAL AUTHORITY in one's life has shifted to 'a general respect for group rules'. Because people are less egocentric, they can empathize with the point of view of the group, and for the first time, true self-sacrifice becomes something one can choose. People begin to ask questions like: Was he loyal? Is he one of us? Regardless of what she did, what did she intend to do? Gilligan's research shows that this orientation becomes the dominant theme in the socialization of many young women.

> Where as from the first perspective, morality is a matter of sanctions imposed by a society of which one is more subject than citizen, from the second perspective, moral judgment relies on shared norms and expectations. The woman at this point validates her claim to social membership through the adoption of social values. Consensual judgment about goodness becomes the overriding concern as survival is now seen to depend on acceptance by others. Here the conventional feminine voice emerges with great clarity, defining the self and proclaiming its worth on the basis of the ability to care for and protect others (p. 79).

At the *Good Boy-Nice Girl orientation* (stage three, Level II), subjects may say that Heinz should steal the drug even if he might go to jail, because it is natural and right for a husband to be loyal to his family. Heinz shouldn't be blamed, because any "nice" person (a social being) would do the same. Or conversely, he should not steal the drug because "nice" people do not steal. There is, in short, heavy emphasis placed on "conformity to stereotypical images of majority behavior"[14] (everyone is doing it). The person can clearly differentiate between instrumental values based on needs of the self and social values that serve the needs of the group. At previous levels these two types of values are not clearly differentiated. At the *Law and Order orientation* (stage four, Level II), subjects may say that Heinz should not steal because stealing violates the law. If they say that he should steal the drug they will refer to a legal obligation for which he is responsible—to protect his wife. At this stage people are beginning to give their legal community the highest moral priority. Other groups to which they may belong become morally subservient to the larger society as it is expressed in the law. People have learned to differentiate between acts based on legal duty and acts based on having nice social motives.

■ *The Postconventional Level*

Finally, under conditions of pluralism and after one has mastered these conventional skills, it is possible for a third orientation to develop. People begin to display a postconventional capacity to critically reflect on and improve the social norms that had previously shaped their identity. This is the level where people achieve full moral agency. They finally have the capacity to critically judge (and thus to affirm or reject from a moral point of view) the rules that have been governing them. At the *Postconventional, Autonomous (Principled) Level* (Level III), people are choosing their own principles rather than simply mirroring the introjected and/or legally enforced norms of the current status quo. With the movement away from the unreflective concern with maintaining the status quo for its own sake, theory begins to play a dominant role. Choices emphasize abstract principles that have validity and application apart from the contingent authority of established groups.

This level, where true social criticism becomes possible, should not be confused with the preconventional person's tendency to complain about the norms he sees as external constraints on his personal desires. Since the preconventional person has not experienced the conventional orientation, he lacks qualitative understanding of social relations. His egocentric emotional ignorance amounts to a psychological incapacity that deprives him of the freedom to truly choose moral rules. In contrast, the third level combines a new rational theoretical understanding of values with the previous level's conventional capacity to care about social norms. Together these two developments give people a new capacity to simultaneously evaluate both the rational and the social quality of values. Gilligan says that in women, this third perspective is characterized by

> a new kind of judgment, whose first demand is for honesty. . . . The criterion for judgment thus shifts from goodness to truth when the morality of action is assessed not on the basis of its appearance in the eyes of others, but in terms of the realities of its intention and consequence (p. 83).

Because self-reflective social criticism now plays a role in judgment, this is the orientation of greatest interest to philosophers. Piaget's formal operational thinking reversal has taken place, so now the question "What is it that I ought to do?" is seen as referring to an ideal state of affairs, rather than as being a simple request for information about the content of one's previously established obligations to the group. The MORAL AUTHORITY in one's life has become 'the ideal principles that enunciate an abstract theory about how we ought to live', rather than internalized, concrete social norms that have not been critically judged.

I think this ability to care about abstract principles results from the developmental process called DECENTERING. Normal developmental decentering 'moves from the egocentric child's capacity to care about those who provide for him, through ethnocentric caring about the family or tribe, to a universal perspective where we care about humanity and abstract ideals just like we cared about the norms of the tribe'. Moral development is about transcending human limitations (imposed first by self-interest and then by tribal needs) by universalizing that which is found in self-interest and in family or tribal life—mainly, the ability to care for self, for others, and also for the social norms that make a community possible. It is the transcendence of narrow ego and ethnic concerns that makes philosophical ethics inspiring. Thus, the goal of a moral society should be to encourage people to develop the ability to care (which should be learned on the family level) and then to universalize it. But we must remember that ethical sensitivity goes both ways. While moral saints do not reject their family heritage (they universalize it to include all of humanity), they also do not lose sight of concrete commitments to individuals. One ought to care deeply about background ideal principles but should not lose sight of what they mean for concrete human relations.

At the *Social Contract, Legalistic orientation with utilitarian overtones* (stage five, Level III), one begins to see an emphasis on changing laws to promote theoretical notions of social utility or constitutional rights. Heinz should steal the drug if that will promote the greatest amount of happiness for all concerned, or alternatively, Heinz should not steal the drug because the social contract, which benefits everyone, cannot allow individuals to set aside laws for their own purposes.

Kohlberg says people at this stage realize that personal opinion and local laws may be arbitrary, so they emphasize procedural rules of justice for reaching consensus. Interests are characterized as naturally conflicting, so the conflicts need to be resolved in accordance with some notion of a just contract designed to promote the common good. This implies that obligations have a contractual nature based on social consensus, thus one's specific duty is negative, that is, to avoid violating the social contract or perhaps another person's natural rights.

With this conception, so long as a person does not directly violate contractual or natural rights, he has no other specific duties to others (i.e., to take positive steps to help them). There is, of course, a general obligation of charity, but this positive contribution to the general welfare is classified as an exceptional virtue, that is, a **SUPEREROGATORY** act (which means 'to go above and beyond the call of duty'). A stage five thinker believes it makes sense to say that a person has a right to life (so we have a negative duty to refrain from harming them) but that no one has a positive duty to do something to help promote that right.[15] If you do help someone stay alive, you are acting in a supererogatory fashion. For these reasons Kohlberg says that stage five does not have a complete integration of rights and duties. To help is charity, not duty (I am not my brother's keeper).

In the *Universal, Principled, Ethical orientation* (stage six, Level III), decisions are based on principled conscience in accordance with self-chosen ethical principles that are meant to be universal and consistent at all levels. Rights and duties are completely integrated because, if it makes sense to say that someone has a right (a legitimate moral claim), then everyone in a position to help has a duty to render assistance. Such a general duty of conscience to take positive steps to promote all rights (not simply negatively refrain from violating them) gives fewer opportunities for supererogatory acts. To be charitable, a stage six thinker would have to do something that would be equivalent to giving up his own right to something to help someone else who does not have a greater right. For example, if I choose to give you my turn on the kidney dialysis machine, or I jump on top of a live grenade to save others, only then am I being benevolent in the supererogatory sense.

Some philosophers and some psychologists have criticized Kohlberg's work for being conceptually vague and methodologically flawed.[16] Many of these criticisms raise interesting methodological problems that need to be addressed, but they do not undercut the fundamental point of his and Gilligan's empirical findings, which is: People display different forms of reasoning that are due to developmental changes. Furthermore, their research is part of a rich cognitive developmental tradition in which others have also observed subjects go through similar developmental changes.[17] Researchers may quibble about the details of the stages, but they are very much in agreement on the nature of the formal levels of development.

■ USING THE DEVELOPMENTAL MODEL TO INTERPRET EVENTS

Because the shifts in style of thought show up continually in studies of the general population, it should be a useful model for making sense of some of the value diversity in the world. For instance, the model can be used to explain legal socialization. Felice Levine and Jane Tapp[18] asked the following questions of hundreds of teachers, law students, criminals, and students in primary grades, middle school, and college: "What would happen if there were no rules?" "Are there times when it might be right to break a rule?" "Why should people follow rules?" "Why do you follow rules?"

If developmental studies accurately describe the cognitive transitions in real life, we should see these transitions mirrored in the answers people give to these questions. We would expect more Preconventional responses from the primary school children. We would expect middle school students to begin to see laws in a Conventional manner—that is, as a necessary means for creating social expectations and a sense of identity. And among college and law school students, we would hope to see the emergence of a Postconventional understanding of law. Obedience to the overall system of law would be based on its contribution to the good of humanity (human welfare and justice rather than a need to conform for its own sake). What Levine and Tapp found in their studies fits these expectations:

> The adult data were strikingly consistent with developmental patterns. [Mainly, that most people do not develop beyond a conventional attitude toward social rules.] Most youth by preadolescence emphasized a conventional, system-maintenance view of

rule guidelines that matched adult modes of thought. Across these samples, no one, regardless of age or situation, inferred that rules are needed to protect rights, establish legitimate claims, or guarantee freedoms—reasoning that would have demonstrated aspects of an ethical legality.[19]

To the question "What would happen if there were no rules?" none of the primary and middle school students showed postconventional answers, and most of the subjects gave conventional, system-maintenance answers. While 88 percent of the graduating law students, 90 percent of the teachers, and 56 percent of the prisoners could not even imagine social order without external rules and/or assumed anarchy would result, nonetheless 8 percent of the college students and 16 percent of the criminals did begin to show signs of postconventional thought. (No explanation was given as to why prisoners were more sophisticated than college students. It may be due to the fact that prison populations are older and perhaps have had more conflicts to resolve.)

To the question "Why do you follow rules?" 60 percent of primary school students gave answers that indicated they wanted to avoid negative consequences, and none of them mentioned social conformity or postconventional consider-ations. On the other hand, while 25 percent of college students still said they obeyed to avoid negative consequences, 33 percent now indicated that they obeyed laws for some postconventional principled reasons, and 46 percent of teachers mentioned postconventional concerns. The data suggests that there is, indeed, a movement away from preconventional considerations and toward postconven-tional understanding of rules. While most adults remain in the conventional, system-maintenance mode, a sizable number of adults begin to express postcon-ventional concerns about ideals as their reason for following rules.

The developmental model should also be able to shed light on some aspects of real moral tragedies. Kohlberg's major theoretical contention is that a person's cognitive structure will influence his moral behavior in real-life situations. We should expect, then, to see some correlations between observable behavior and styles of thought when groups of people confront moral dilemmas.

Kohlberg and Scharf[20] analyzed instances of mass violence and reached con-clusions strikingly similar to Hannah Arendt's theory about the banality of evil. They focused most attention on the My Lai tragedy, where American soldiers rounded up the inhabitants of a Vietnamese village and then massacred the captives—primarily old men, women, and babies. In their analysis of the mas-sacre, Kohlberg and Scharf focused on the reasoning styles of three principal characters who were at the scene of the massacre: Paul Meadlow, a private who admitted he was involved in the massacre of civilians; Lieutenant William Calley, the officer who was subsequently court-martialed by the army for ordering Mead-low and others to fire on the civilians; and private Michael Bernhardt, who refused to obey the orders to shoot at Vietnamese civilians. According to Kohlberg and Scharf, Meadlow appeared to function primarily at the preconventional level: You obey orders not because you respect them, but to avoid getting into trouble.

During basic training if you disobeyed an order, if you were slow in obeying orders, they'd slap you on the head, drop-kick you in the chest and rinky-dink stuff like that. If an officer tells you to stand on your head in the middle of the highway, you do it. Why did I do it. . . . We was supposed to get satisfaction from this village for the men we lost. They was all VC and VC sympathizers. I felt, at the time, I was doing the right thing because, like I said, I lost buddies. I lost a damn good buddy, Bobby Wilson.

Nowhere in Meadlow's interview does he refer to principles or human welfare. We do consistently see references to his own egocentric concerns, his desire for satisfaction, and his interest in not getting in trouble. The fact that he grieves for lost buddies shows he is not a psychopath (see the next chapter), but only an egocentric person would think that his personal grief justifies killing babies to get "satisfaction." Meadlow seems excessively banal, which is one of the marks of the simplistic preconventional level of thinking.

Lieutenant Calley, on the other hand, is much more conventional in his orientation. He is concerned about being a good officer, a regular fellow who will be accepted into the system. He also had a tendency to defer responsibility to those higher up in the system.

I was a run-of-the-mill average guy. I still am. I always said the people in Washington are smarter than me. If intelligent people say Communism is bad, it's going to engulf us [*sic*]. I was only a Second Lieutenant. I had to obey and hope that the people in Washington were smarter than me.

Calley shows little comprehension that an order needs to be evaluated by higher criteria or that the military code does allow for this option (it forbids soldiers to obey illegitimate orders). Like most conventional thinkers, he does not look beyond the norms of his immediate social position. If legitimate authorities give an order, a good soldier carries it out, even if it might lead to the death of innocent people. What seems relevant in Calley's conceptual framework is the order or the concrete rule, not the consequences for people who are not part of the social group, and not the order's compliance with abstract principles.

Q. What was your intention in terms of the operation?
A. To go in the area and destroy the enemy that were designated there and this is it. I went into the area to destroy the enemy.
Q. Were you motivated by any other fact besides that they were the enemy?
A. Well, I was ordered to go in there and destroy the enemy. That was my job on that day. That was my mission I was given. I did not sit down and think in terms of men, women and children. They were all classified the same and that was the classification we dealt with them, enemy soldiers. . . . I felt, and still do, that I acted as I was directed . . . and I do not feel wrong in doing so.

In contrast to Meadlow and Calley, Bernhardt's thinking displays clear post-conventional elements. He is willing to accept responsibility for his own actions as a moral agent, and recognizes that a concrete social rule or command from an authority does not alleviate him of the responsibility of choosing whether or not to obey. He is trying to maintain a sense of personal moral integrity at the same time that he is trying to figure out how to create a place for himself in a terrible time of war.

> If I recognize something is right or wrong . . . this is the first step to actually doing right. And this is the thing. I can hardly do anything if I know it is wrong. If I think about it long enough I am really in trouble, and I won't be able to do it. . . . I am just positively compelled. No matter whose law it is, no matter whose leadership I am following, it has never been as good as what I would have done myself. . . . Since My Lai, I have had to follow my own decisions, I have had to follow my own way because nobody else's has been right . . . Now this is what I try to do: I try and apply logic to it rather than anything else; logic to say, "Is this right, or should I do this."

For Bernhardt there are universal standards and principles that have priority over any particular command or law. For him, what is most relevant in a situation is abstract principles as they apply to the local situation.

> The law is only the law, and many times it's wrong. It's not necessarily just, just because it's the law. . . . My kind of citizen would be guided by his own laws. These would be more strict than in a lot of cases, the actual laws. People must be guided by their own standards, by their self-discipline. I was telling Captain Franklyn about an old woman that was shot. I couldn't understand why she was shot because she didn't halt. First of all, she is in her own country. We never found anything to indicate that she was anything but what she appeared to be—a non-combatant. It wasn't a case like we had been wiped out by an old woman with a fish-bag full of grenades. I told him that she was shot at a distance. They said to shoot her was brigade policy. They couldn't think of a better way of stopping her. I would have said, "No." I just wouldn't have stopped her at all. Nothing needs an excuse to live. The same thing goes for bombing a village. If there are people in the village, don't bomb it. . . . When I saw them shooting people I figured, "Well, I am going to be doing my own war and let them do their own war," because we just didn't agree on anything.

The fact that the world is populated with men like these three, men who appear to have strikingly different moral capacities, raises some serious ethical problems that will have to be dealt with in a theory of implementation (see the last chapter). Should our rules and codes of ethics be designed for the Meadlows among us, the Calleys, or the Bernhardts? Can any code of ethics ever be adequate when members of a profession can show such marked contrasts in their moral perceptions? Who is right, after all, Calley or Bernhardt? (I am assuming that Meadlow is wrong.) There are many who would argue that people like Bernhardt are wrong. The Bernhardts amongst us disrupt the functioning of just systems that require obedience—"Ours is not to reason why, ours is but to do or die." Perhaps we should not hold the individuals in a system responsible when the system so obviously tries to socialize them to be obedient by discouraging them from acting on individual conscience.

I think we need to hold both our leaders and the subordinates responsible for their decisions. If we do not hold moral agents responsible, then even very intelligent people may fail to live up to our trust, requiring us to have very tightly organized institutions to rein them in. The practical importance of this issue is well illustrated in President Nixon's apology for the Watergate fiasco.

> The Watergate break-in and cover-up greatly damaged the American political process. While not unusual in political campaigns, these actions were clearly illegal. Over the years, I had been the victim of dirty tricks and other kinds of vicious tactics in the cut and thrust of political warfare. What happened in Watergate—the facts, not the myths—was wrong. In retrospect, while I was not involved in the decision to conduct the break-in, I should have set a higher standard for the conduct of the people who participated in my campaign and Administration. I should have established a moral tone that would have made such actions unthinkable. I did not. I played by the rules of politics as I found them. Not taking a higher road than my predecessors and my adversaries was my central mistake. For that reason, I long ago accepted overall responsibility for the Watergate affair. What's more, I have paid, and am still paying, the price for it.[21]

A study of history shows us over and over again that while many people get away with engaging in evil behavior that is encouraged by institutional authorities, many others don't. We may eventually be held accountable by our victims if not our peers. Greek soldiers who became torturers were put on trial, Calley was tried by his peers, Eichmann was tried by his victims, and many other people of lesser renown have been found to be morally responsible even though they tried to argue that they were under heavy institutional pressure to act as they did. It is clear, according to the historical record at least, that we want to treat adults as autonomous moral agents who can be held individually responsible, even when they have been commanded by apparently legitimate institutions. We want adults to accept this responsibility because we do not want a society where we will need a police officer on every corner.

We need to have a closer look at the idea that individuals have autonomy and can be held responsible. In Chapter Seven we will begin our journey into normative philosophy by considering an ideal interpretation of moral autonomy that can be used to help judge institutions and individuals. Before we turn to that analysis, however, it will be instructive to analyze the way gender differences in ethics can affect ethical perspectives.

■ STUDY QUESTIONS

1. Why is formal operational thinking an essential ability for philosophical ethics?
2. What plays the role of moral authority in the three levels of moral development?
3. What does it mean to decenter in moral development?
4. Why is a complaint about rules logically different when it comes from a stage two agent than when it comes from a Level III person?
5. What does it mean to say that there are more opportunities to engage in supereroga-tory acts at stage five than at stage six?
6. What practical questions about the design of institutions follow from Levine and Tapp's study and Kohlberg's interpretation of the My Lai massacre?

■ NOTES

1. My understanding of Piaget is based on the following sources: Jean Piaget, *Six Psychological Studies* (New York: Random House, Inc., 1967); *The Moral Judgment of the Child* (London: Kegan Paul, Trench, Trubner & Co., 1932); and *The Child & Reality* (New York: Viking Press, 1973).

2. This chart is a modification of one presented in Lawrence Kohlberg, "The Concepts of Developmental Psychology as the Central Guide to Education: Examples from Cognitive, Moral, and Psychological Education," p. 7, in Maynard C. Reynolds, ed., *Proceedings of the Conference on Psychology and the Process of Schooling in the Next Decade: Alternative Conceptions*. A publication of the Leadership Training Institute/Special Education, sponsored by the Bureau for Educational Personnel Development, U.S. Office of Education.

3. L. S. Vygotsky, *Thought and Language* (Cambridge, MA: M.I.T. Press, 1962), pp. 116–117. For a very good discussion of these issues, see Michael S. Pritchard's recent text: *On Becoming Responsible* (Lawrence, KS: University Press of Kansas, 1991).

4. P. G. Richmond, *An Introduction to Piaget* (New York: Basic Books, 1970), p. 58.

5. Piaget, *The Moral Judgment of the Child*, p. 86.

6. Most of the references to Kohlberg's theory on the next few pages are taken from Kohlberg, "The Claim to Moral Adequacy of a Highest Stage of Moral Judgment," *The Journal of Philosophy*, 70, No. 18, October 25, 1973, pp. 630–646. However, the following sources are also very useful: "From Is to Ought: How to Commit the Naturalistic Fallacy and Get Away with It in the Study of Moral Development," in T. Mischel, ed., *Cognitive Development and Epistemology* (New York: Academic Press, 1971); and Jane Louin Tapp and Lawrence Kohlberg, "Developing Senses of Law and Legal Justice," in Jane Louin Tapp and Felice J. Levine, eds., *Law, Justice, and the Individual in Society* (New York: Holt, Rinehart and Winston, 1977).

7. Kohlberg, "From Is to Ought," p. 156.

8. Kohlberg, "Concepts of Developmental Psychology," pp. 8–15.

9. Kohlberg, "Moral Adequacy," p. 641.

10. Carol Gilligan, *In a Different Voice* (Cambridge, MA: Harvard University Press, 1982).

11. M. F. Belenky, B. M. Clinchy, N. R. Goldberger, and J. M. Tarule, *Women's Ways of Knowing* (New York: Basic Books, Inc., 1986).

12. Piaget, *The Moral Judgment of the Child*, pp. 35–37, 111.

13. R. S. Peters, *Reason and Compassion* (London: Rutledge & Kegan Paul, 1973), p. 46.

14. Tapp and Kohlberg, "Senses of Law," p. 91.

15. Kohlberg, "Moral Adequacy," p. 638.

16. For a sample of criticisms and Kohlberg's response, see *Ethics, Special Issue on Moral Development*, **92**, No. 3, April 1982.

17. I found the following sources to be especially informative: Gilligan, *In a Different Voice*; Jurgen Habermas, "Moral Development and Ego Identity," in *Communication and the Evolution of Society*, transl. by Thomas McCarthy (Boston: Beacon Press, 1979), pp. 69–94; and J. Loevinger, *Measuring Ego Development* (San Francisco: Jossey-Bass, 1970).

18. Felice J. Levine & Jane Louin Tapp, "The Dialectic of Legal Socialization in Community and School," in Tapp and Levine, eds., *Law, Justice, and the Individual in Society*, pp. 163–182.

19. Ibid., p. 169.

20. All of the quotations that follow are taken from Lawrence Kohlberg and Peter Scharf, "Bureaucratic Violence and Conventional Moral Thinking," a paper given at the 49th Annual Meeting of the American Orthopsychiatry Association, Detroit, Michigan, April 5–8, 1972.

21. Richard Nixon, "I Could See No Reason to Live," *Time*, **135**, No. 14, April 2, 1990, p. 38.

CHAPTER SIX

Gender Differences in Ethics

■ THE FOCUS ON DIFFERENT CONTENT

As we saw in the previous chapter, Carol Gilligan[1] argues that during develop-mental transitions males and females both first encounter rules as external constraints, then they embrace them as a source of identity, and finally they develop a capacity to criticize and reform them so that they will evolve with the individual's developing "principled" conscience. However, while women and men appear to share these same forms or perspectives during intellectual transi-tions, the content that receives emphasis in their respective ethical orientations is quite different.

Typically, women treat virtues such as caring and social responsibility as ultimate moral values, in contrast to the typical male emphasis on impartial justice and individual rights. Of course, some women approach morality in ways that do not appear to be different from men. But in Gilligan's recent studies of men and women who do take up one orientation or the other, it was found that while fifty percent of the women focus on justice and fifty percent focus on care, nearly all the men (who focus) are focused on issues of justice. The interesting consequence of these differences is that "if women were eliminated from the research sample, care focus in moral reasoning would virtually disappear."[2] This is a serious matter. If males experience a different ethical world than females, and males are a dominant voice in the construction of ethical theory, ethical theories will reflect the male experience but not the female point of view. But is there really a significant difference based on gender?

The data[3] indicates that both genders use both voices at times, but there is a predominance of care language in the reports of women. In recent work Gilligan has weakened some of her initial claims, but the ethics of care is still a legitimate voice that needs to be accounted for in a complete ethical theory. Gilligan claims that the kind of difference she is talking about can be seen in the following accounts. When asked to define morality, Ned said:

Morality is a prescription, a thing to follow, and the idea of having a concept of morality is to try to figure out what it is that people can do in order to make life with each other livable, make for a kind of balance, a kind of equilibrium, a harmony in which everybody feels he has a place and an equal share in things. Doing that is kind of contributing to a state of affairs that goes beyond the individual, in the absence of which the individual has no chance for self-fulfillment of any kind. Fairness, morality, is kind of essential, it seems to me, for creating the kind of environment, interaction between people, that is prerequisite to the fulfillment of most individual goals. If you want other people not to interfere with your pursuit of whatever you are into, you have to play the game (Gilligan, p. 98).

■ *The Men's Orientation*

Like most males Ned presupposes that moral agents are separate but equal individuals with their own goals. These assumptions fit with the concept of male maturity defined by the ideal of autonomy. Individualism and social separation are accepted as basic elements of adult life; the problem is to figure out how to live with others. Relationships are important, but they are a means for facilitating the male's "success dream."[4] Thus, morality is a game of reciprocity each must play to protect the individual right to pursue "whatever you are into." Obligations to others are defined negatively as "noninterference." The primary need of rational autonomous individuals is to be protected from external interference.

As Ned points out, on the male model the goal is to choose a conception of the "good" life where self-fulfillment is possible. To keep others from interfering, individuals need some rules to protect themselves. Morality is thus a means for supporting the right to live a private life. It is not an end in itself, it is only an agreed-upon set of negative constraints to keep people from violating individual rights. Individuals have due process rights to be treated equally before the law, and that is all equality and justice require.

The popular rugged individualist version of this approach argues that no one has a positive duty to help others satisfy their goals (unless, of course, one has voluntarily taken on positive duties of station by making explicit additional contractual commitments—like marriage). Thus, we have positive duties to feed our own children, since in having them we contract to care for them, but no one has positive duties to care for orphans. It is, of course, morally virtuous to help orphans, but that is purely charity. Each individual's choice of lifestyle will determine how charity fits in with each individual's plans. It is virtuous to choose a lifestyle that helps others, but it is not a duty to do so. Justice gives us strict duties not to interfere with others, but charity is not a matter of justice, it is a matter of virtue.

Betty Sichel argues that the following features are central to this male way of viewing ethics.[5] First, it emphasizes the abstract, the general, and the universalizable. Second, it advocates emotional detachment and viewing relationships in subject–object terms. Third, it sees moral dilemmas as primarily involving issues of autonomy and individual rights.

Men and women both share these three traits, but males are more likely than females to emphasize them. No one is saying that these are bad traits, it is only that they seem to be the dominant focus in the male gender. It seems to me that if this characterization of the male view is accurate, we can expect male philosophers to typically feel comfortable enough focusing on background abstractions that they will be inclined to write less about the foreground, which is made up of immediate concrete relations (and we could expect this tendency to grow as pluralistic cultures become less and less tribal).

■ The Women's Orientation

In contrast to the male's background emphasis on autonomous individuals who have private ends, the women's background focus is on obligations to care for others they encounter in particular relationships. Thus, Diane (a woman in her late twenties) defines morality as a sense of feeling a need to take care of the world. This leads to immediate responsibilities to help needy people she encounters. According to this conception, morality is itself a lifestyle choice, not a means to other choices. One of her primary concerns is whether she should create the ultimate relationship between mother and child in a world where relationships cannot be properly maintained.

> [Morality is] . . . trying to uncover a right path in which to live, and always in my mind is that the world is full of real and recognizable trouble, and it is heading for some kind of doom, and is it right to bring children into this world when we currently have an overpopulation problem, and is it right to spend money on a pair of shoes when I have a pair of shoes and other people are shoeless? It is part of a self-critical view, part of saying "How am I spending my time and in what sense am I working?" I think I have a real drive, a real maternal drive, to take care of someone—to take care of my mother, to take care of children, to take care of other people's children, to take care of my own children, to take care of the world. When I am dealing with moral issues, I am sort of saying to myself constantly, "Are you taking care of all the things that you think are important, and in what ways are you wasting yourself and wasting those issues?" (Gilligan, p. 99).

In general, women emphasize interventions designed to meet the different needs of unique individuals. They are more likely to feel obligated to find the best exceptions to the rules to alleviate the needs of people who are seen as unequals. Gilligan says:

> Care becomes the self-chosen principle of a judgment that remains psychological in its concern with relationships and response but becomes universal in its condemnation of exploitation and hurt. . . . This ethic, which reflects a cumulative knowledge of human relationships, evolves around a central insight, that self and other are interdependent (Gilligan, p. 74).

Women learn to define themselves in terms of a relational network, at the same time that they are being discouraged from participating as individual decision makers in a world controlled by competitive males. When we combine this competitive disadvantage with the fact that young girls model on their mothers (who seem to be selfless to the young), we get a unique "nest" experience that teaches women to think that: "The moral person is one who helps others: goodness is service, meeting one's obligations and responsibilities to others, if possible without sacrificing oneself" (p. 66).

Betty Sichel[6] argues that women's different experience changes the way they conceptualize moral issues. First, women are more likely to emphasize the uniqueness of each person. This leads to an emphasis on listening, trying to see the other person's side, and to paying attention to the particularities of the form of life within which each person is embedded. Second, this requires them to be concrete and focus on the particularities of the immediate foreground: What is the situation of "this" person right now, right here? (Someone wrote on the sidewalk outside of my office: "God is in the details." I remember thinking that the slogan characterized the approach to God and life of my female friends.) Third, since no one can ever be another person, women recognize the need to rely more on a tacit understanding of another and less on explicit public understanding. Women are more likely to listen to others with their whole being, as a mother does to her child. Fourth, since the relationship to the other is the center of focus, women focus on how to be responsive, to communicate, to avoid betrayal or isolation, and to care for the other's needs given their unique situation.

Because responsibility or duty to others is defined by the psychological logic of intimate relationships rather than the abstract logic of equality, rights and responsibilities are conceptually linked to protecting the social net on which relationships depend rather than protecting the separate status of abstract individuals. This is especially true during the Level II conventional orientation, because at that level women think those who insist on individual rights are being selfish. This way of thinking about rights, however, creates a conceptual disparity between responsibility to others and individual rights that needs to be resolved. According to Gilligan,

> . . . Women's insistence on care is at first self-critical rather than self-protective, while men initially conceive obligation to others negatively in terms of noninterference. Development for both sexes would therefore seem to entail an integration of rights and responsibilities through the discovering of the complementary of their disparate views (p. 100).

Gilligan's data indicates that about fifty percent of the female population has been historically under-represented in philosophical debates. Trying to account for the "women's voice" in ethics may give us new tasks in our search for a transcendent perspective. We should not assume, however, that their focus on concrete particular relationships means that women have no interest in transcendent issues in ethics. To focus on each person's situation does not commit us to being individual relativists. As Jaggar says:

> Feminist ethics recognizes that we inhabit a painfully prefeminist world and takes itself to be contributing to the transformation of this world into one in which the basic moral commitments of feminism have become universally accepted—and in which, consequently, feminism has become otiose. From a feminist perspective, therefore, feminist ethics in necessarily transitional. Because of feminism's essential interest in social transformation, it is hard to see how feminists could be content with the parochial conventionalism or conservatism often associated at least with the communitarian tradition of contemporary moral relativism.[7]

■ Possible Causes of Gender Differences

What causes these gender differences in orientation to the world? Perhaps they are the result of the fact that males and females typically begin life under normal but different "nesting" conditions. We do not have the space to fully explore these differences in formative early experiences, but a brief survey of some of the current literature suggests that some differences may be fairly crucial. For example, Chodorow[8] and others argue that in the first three years of their lives, when children are choosing their gender identity, both male and female children are raised by women. This is significant. Studies show that women treat little girls differently. Girls are touched more often (both at home and in the nursery), held for longer periods of time, comforted longer, and not as severely punished or rejected for expressing emotions. This teaches girls that it is safe to seek intimacy by moving toward the mother–day care–nursery school nurturers in order to bond with them. There is less emotional need to separate and individuate when it is so pleasant to be "in" relationship. Because girls are also often systematically discouraged from acting independently or autonomously, a girl's developing self is defined by her relationships, rather than by a stress on individual accomplishments. They learn that their natural task in life is to duplicate the most intimate relationship of all by becoming mothers themselves.

Traditionally in our culture, often starting with painful procedures like circumcision, boys learn early that they are on their own and that intimacy is dangerous. To become male, boys must separate early from the female nurturers that surround them. Although little boys want the same love and affection that girls get, they cannot become "males" if they model themselves on women, so the nurturers push them away. This has to happen for the boys to become men, but it hurts (perhaps we need more male nurturers so that little boys do not need to withdraw). Studies show that boys are not comforted as long, and they are more often shamed for showing the emotions that are associated with vulnerability. They are told: "Big boys don't cry." "Be tough, stand on your own two feet."

According to Gordon Wheeler's and Daniel E. Jones's 1991 workshop on male development at The Cleveland Gestalt Institute, the experience boys receive creates a shame barrier between their publicly displayed and praised, rugged individualist self and their unconscious, dependent self that wants to live "in" emotional relationship with others. Men are taught to be strong, silent, and stoical, to *do* things, to be successful, and to feel ashamed to admit (even to themselves) they might want to live in an intimate caring relationship with others. A polarity then develops between an inner, receptive, private part that must remain hidden, and an external, self-reliant, aloof self that it is safe to present to the public.

These disparate nesting experiences may contribute to the differences between men and women. One thing is clear from the survey data: in varying degrees men and women do focus on different ethical truths. It might be possible to transcend some of these differences if we can find a way to experience them, reflect on them, assimilate them, and accommodate them. The power we have to let reason critique reason itself, to turn feelings on feelings, and to make comparisons between traditions holds out the possibility that we may be able to engage in a hermeneutic search for successively transcendent ethical conceptions. A sexual heritage, a tribal heritage, and a philosophical heritage are all stages in the process of natural human development that can (and ought to) lead to new transcendent points of view. But how can we truly understand and assimilate another orientation? I will explore this issue in more detail in Chapter Eight, when I discuss Albert and Diane Pesso's theory of emotional reeducation.

■ A Mature Ethics Requires Both Genders

From the perspective of moral agency and individual responsibility, the woman's orientation may not necessarily be a positive development given the social context in which women find themselves. Because women have historically been a disenfranchised class, too often what emerges from their traditional experience "is a sense of vulnerability that impedes these women from taking a stand" (Gilligan, p. 66). The "intimidation of inequality" (p. 95) can combine with their relational orientation to make them too selfless. When this happens, it is difficult to fully exercise the right to take a place in the social world as an active, responsible moral agent. Gilligan says:

> The essence of moral decision is the exercise of choice and the willingness to accept responsibility for that choice. To the extent that women perceive themselves as having no choice, they correspondingly excuse themselves from the responsibility that decision entails. Childlike in the vulnerability of their dependence and consequent fear of abandonment, they claim to wish only to please, but in return for their goodness they expect to be loved and cared for (p. 67).

There is another side to this issue that also needs to be addressed. In a talk at the Midwest American Philosophical Association meetings several years ago, Claudia Card warned that we must approach the woman's perspective cautiously, since it is always possible that it represents what Nietzsche called a "slave morality." He believed that the downtrodden often designed moral systems as an expression of their lack of power. Slave morality convinces the oppressed that they are actually better off and superior to those who oppress them, and in this way it encourages them to keep their inferior position. Catherine MacKinnon expresses a similar worry about the ethics of care in her discussion of Gilligan[9] by reminding us that the care ethic was developed in a world of male power. But, I think a care ethic would be a slave morality only if the final conception of this voice insisted that passivity and self-sacrifice were *the* major virtues. Mature women, however, co-ordinate their emphasis on care for others with an equal emphasis on honesty and the personal obligation to become an active moral agent who exercises power.

Gilligan's research shows us that because the developmental path of men and women is different, in their respective search for transcendence they have different tasks. Men start attached to mother, learn to separate and be independent, and then have to learn how to care and be responsible for others in need. Women start attached to mother, learn to bond in a caring intimate relationship with her, and then have to learn to separate and be autonomous. What women need, then, is a social world that allows them to develop as autonomous moral agents, not by acting as men but by blending independence with their unique capacity to care. Men, in a corresponding way, need a world that allows them to care and be responsible for others without feeling ashamed and without the risk of losing the autonomy that they have already worked so hard to achieve.

It is important to be sensitive to "voice" when we interpret ethical issues. Voice has a powerful influence on the practical interpretations we give to theory and on the theoretical interpretations we give to practice.* The man's voice, with its emphasis on protecting rights, gives the principle of justice top priority. The woman's voice, with its emphasis on care, gives the principle of benevolence top priority. If there is an ethical tradition that can help both sexes transcend their respective voices by creating a social vision where both lines of development can merge without doing damage to the gains made by either sex, it would be instructive to consider it. Since males in tribal settings typically speak with a voice that places a strong emphasis on positive obligations to their community, perhaps the tendency in much liberal, individualistic philosophy to deny that we have positive duties to be benevolent is primarily a characteristic of patriarchal cultures in which males have been torn from their tribal roots. If so, to find a tradition more compatible with the woman's voice, it might be useful to consider a philosophical tradition that comes from an area with a strong tribal heritage.[10]

---

* For a fascinating discussion of yet another perspective or voice, see Bill Lawson, *The Underclass Question*. The text will be out in 1992 from Temple University Press. For a look at the voice coming out of the experience of slavery, see Howard McGarey and Bill Lawson, eds., *Between Slavery and Freedom: Philosophy and American Slavery*. This text will also appear in 1992, from Indiana University Press. The authors argue that by "listening to the voices of former slaves . . . [they] will show how the slavery experience and its aftermath can help to gain a better understanding of . . . [moral] concepts" (p. 2).

The Scottish communitarian perspective seems compatible with both the male and the female voice. Members of the Scottish Enlightenment were careful to contrast their approach with what they called the selfish school of morality behind the theories of Hobbes and Locke.[11] Since Hobbes, Locke, and Rousseau all began with an assumed background of original self-rule, they naturally emphasized the utility of having a social contract for protecting the self's interests. In contrast, theories enunciated in the Scottish Enlightenment assumed morality was based on man's social nature. For example, Hutcheson argued that all men have a "moral sense" which gives them the capacity to see and approve of benevolence. It is like an aesthetic sense in that it leads to disinterested pleasure in witnessing benevolent acts even when we are not the recipients of the benevolence.[12] Where moral sense rules, the basis for social intercourse can be a bond of affection rather than mutual gain through bargaining and contracts. Under these conditions, one will experience a positive motive to help needy others even if one is a male. Discussions of moral content need not give impartial justice center stage, as they do when the dominant focus is negative duties.

With their emphasis on universal benevolent feelings, Scottish philosophy can see the possibility for a kind of personal success that does not have to be purchased at the expense of relationships, but instead will contribute to community relations. Even their definition of individual rights places emphasis on the interconnection between self and others rather than on noninterference between autonomous beings. For example, individual rights to life and liberty are social conventions that good men insist upon, not for protection but because they are necessary prerequisites for the possibility of living a benevolent community life.[13] We can also judge other social forms—the marketplace, exchange of goods, competition, and so forth—according to how they affect the opportunities for cooperative interdependence (e.g., market relations are morally justified because, in creating a need for community, they provide an opportunity for benevolence).

The assumed right to self-fulfillment behind Ned's account of morality takes on an interdependent social connotation when viewed from the context of moral sense theory. One cannot seek self-fulfillment unless one is part of a social web that encourages the exercise of our highest faculties. Since our moral sense is the source of the highest form of pleasure, the most fulfilling life is benevolent social life. Thus, even if a person is motivated by self-fulfillment, his moral sense will moderate any natural tendencies to be greedy, since our relational self rather than our individualist self is the source of greatest pleasure.

■ A WOMAN'S VOICE INTERPRETATION OF ADAM SMITH

The Scottish Enlightenment communitarians came close to emphasizing the same virtues as the women's perspective discussed above, and yet one of them, Adam Smith, has generally been considered to be one of the champions of the liberal, negative-rights approach to duties. Could it be that this modern view of Smith is the result of male philosophers interpreting his theory with the content concerns of the male voice? It would be useful to compare the masculine, individualist interpretation of Adam Smith with a caring woman's voice interpretation.

Smith is probably best known in Western culture for his famous assertion in *The Wealth of Nations* that the best way to help a nation prosper is to allow businessmen to pursue their own interests in a competitive marketplace free of government regulation. He maintained that pursuing self-interest in a free laissez-faire market will maximize the social good just as though a fairly benevolent invisible hand were directing the outcome. Smith's apparent emphasis on the individualistic pursuit of self-interest free from government regulation seems to fit nicely with the liberal economic tradition that emphasizes protecting negative rights to economic freedom among autonomous equals. A modern statement of this practical philosophy says:

> . . . Pure laissez-faire capitalism implies unimpeded, absolute individual discretion on the part of property owners to use, trade, or sell their property without government regulation, even in emergencies, wars, catastrophes, and so forth . . . laissez-faire capitalism lets business do what it wants outside of such criminal conduct as assault, theft, and murder, and precludes the great bulk of government regulatory measures many citizens now take for granted.[14]

Is this vision compatible with Adam Smith's philosophy? There are, of course, some good reasons to give a male voice interpretation of Smith. For instance, G. R. Morrow argues that:

> Adam Smith's employment of self-interest in *The Wealth of Nations* . . . merely means that Smith was preaching, in the economic world, the same gospel of individual rights and individual liberty which in one form or another was the burden of eighteenth-century social thought. It expresses his faith in the value of the individual and in the importance of freeing the individual man from the fetters of outworn economic institutions.[15]

When "Smith was conscripted to individualist uses by nineteenth-century liberalism,"[16] however, his language received an emphasis that was far more individualistic than Smith probably intended. Certainly as a male, Smith shows the usual concern for individual autonomy and justice, but this emphasis is softened when one uses the woman's voice to refocus on those contextual elements in Smith that reflect his Scottish heritage's emphasis on the social emotions. Smith was not a strict moral sense philosopher. He thought the emotion of sympathy provided all that was needed for making sense of morality, so there was no need to hypothesize another sense. Morrow argues that there is only one Adam Smith.

. . . In his book [The Theory of] *Moral Sentiments* Adam Smith opposes the egoistic doctrine that man acts only from self-love, and exalts benevolence as the highest virtue. But there are other, inferior virtues recognized, such as prudence, frugality, industry, self-reliance. These virtues must be restrained and regulated by justice, but when so regulated they are conducive to the welfare of the general public as well as of the individual. . . . Very little is said in *The Wealth of Nations* about the principles of justice (that was to have been the subject of Adam Smith's projected work on jurisprudence); but justice is of course always presupposed as necessary for the existence of nations at all. . . . In short, unregulated self-interest is no more advocated in *The Wealth of Nations* than it is in the *Moral Sentiments*, whereas in the latter work the moral value of the inferior virtues, when properly regulated, is fully recognized.[17]

How should inferior values be regulated? R. B. Lamb claims that:

In *Moral Sentiments* as in *The Wealth of Nations* Smith makes exactly the same assertion, that he expects men to act first in accordance with their self-interest before thoughts of benevolence. Yet . . . in neither book does self-interest eliminate sympathy. The two are universal human sentiments experienced by all men. . . . They often exert simultaneously their influence upon individuals engaged in property relations. Sympathy means being able to comprehend and enter into the situation of others, especially into their property and self-interested situation and sensing and then judging our approval or disapproval of their acts.[18]

Notice that the ability "to comprehend and enter into the situation of others" is a role-playing skill that requires well-developed social abilities. A moral economic agent not only can sympathetically understand the lot of other economic agents, he can exercise "self-command," which is Smith's way of referring to the capacity to restrain selfish inclination in order to do what is right.[19] If Smith believes that economic agents do not need government regulation, it is because he assumes that they are already regulated by an IMPARTIAL SPECTATOR in their own breast. To understand the social, caring nature of this abstract-sounding concept, we must look more closely at Smith's theory of the moral sentiments.

How do moral agents develop self-command and the inner, impartial spectator? In his early works Smith indicates that we exercise self-command to gain the approval of others (like Kohlberg's stage 2 child), but in later works he says we begin to exercise it to gain the approval of our own conscience (like Kohlberg's stage 6 mature adult). Consider the following statement from the first edition of Smith's *The Theory of Moral Sentiments:*

We must imagine ourselves not the actors, but the spectators of our own character and conduct, and consider how these would affect us when viewed from this new station. . . . We must enter, in short, either into what are, or into what ought to be, or into what, if the whole circumstances of our conduct were known, we imagine would be the sentiments of others, before we can either applaud or condemn it. . . .

A moral being is an accountable being. An accountable being, as the word expresses, is a being that must give an account of its actions to some other, and that consequently must regulate them according to the good-liking of this other. Man is accountable to God and his fellow-creatures (Smith, cited in Hope, 1984, 159).

In this first edition Smith is pointing out that conscience is guided by the attitudes of fellow members in the community. It represents a fairly low level of moral development. By the time the sixth edition of his work came out, however, Smith's theory had evolved to the point where he contrasts this first primitive conception of self-command with a much more mature conception of conscience. Thus, Hope points out that "The rudimentary stage of the virtue of self-command, found in the child or the man of weak character, depends on the feelings of actual spectators. The higher stage, reached by the man of constancy, depends entirely on conscience."[20]

As we saw earlier, developmental research shows that this higher conscience develops only after people pass through two previous stages of (1) forced obedience, and (2) voluntary identification with the social order. The sixth edition's "man within" may refer to an autonomous conscience, but it is a conscience that understands and sympathizes with social existence. It is not the conscience of an autonomous, self-interested economic agent. Of course, Smith did not have access to modern developmental theory, thus, according to Hope, he was always uneasy with the elevation of the inner "impartial spectator" to the level of an *ideal observer*. He continually emphasized that ethics must be based on the sympathy felt between "real" people (which is, of course, another emphasis we find in the women's voice). Smith also seemed uncertain about how to characterize the relation between conscience and convention, having a tendency to equate the two at times, but apparently not feeling comfortable with the equation. Hope summarizes Smith's dilemma as follows:

> If conscience is conventional, the ordinary man can be conscientious, but duty is the slave of fashion. If conscience requires perfection, duty is freed from public opinion, but the ordinary man cannot be conscientious. His confusion is indicated, perhaps, by his reference in the second edition to "this inmate of the breast, this abstract man, the representative of mankind," the latter phrases suggesting someone who is not real, yet somehow epitomizes real attitudes.[21]

While this could be seen as tension that results from an attempt to accommodate both the women's contextual perspective and the men's abstract perspective, Hope chooses to give a male voice interpretation of Smith's problem. He says:

> Smith unfortunately confuses mere dutifulness with virtue, of which, indeed, it forms a part, and hence precludes the possibility of being more than dutiful. . . . He should recognize the difference between mere dutifulness and true virtue, between meeting an obligation and acting supererogatively. There is no inconsistency

between conscience agreeing with a minimum laid down by convention while advocating that more be done. How much more the individual does is up to him and his natural virtue.[22]

But, perhaps as a good communitarian speaking in a more relational caring voice, Smith did not want to make use of the male version of the supererogatory distinction. The fact that a moral spectator is impartial does not mean he is blind to the interdependent, emotional nature of social life. Smith says that a complete judgment is informed by "the whole circumstances of our conduct." To a communitarian, protecting the "relational context" of conventional social life is an important part of the circumstances. It is possible, then, that Smith may have wanted benevolence to be a duty rather than a supererogatory act. A transcendent male voice sympathetic to Smith's problem would try to explore the logic behind an ideal observer who accepts the view that we have positive duties to maintain a caring or sympathetic conventional order.

Speaking in what I would characterize as a transcendent women's voice, Onora O'Neill says that when making decisions we should ask ourselves what "rational needy beings" would choose,[23] rather than what "rational autonomous beings" would choose. It seems to me that this is the emphasis we would find in a transcendent impartial spectator from a gender-blended communitarian school. He will have a more sympathetic and caring interpretation of how to best draw the line between negative and positive duties. Is this pure speculation, or is there further contextual evidence that would support a woman's voice interpretation of Smith?

Smith claims that "The rules which she [nature] follows are fit for her, those which he [man] follows for him: but both are calculated to promote the same great end, the order of the world, and the perfection and happiness of human nature."[24] What is the "perfection of human nature"? Smith says, "To feel much for others, and little for ourselves, that to restrain our selfish, and to indulge our benevolent affections, constitutes the perfection of human nature. . . . [25] To achieve this sense of self, we need a rich moral heritage. A human is not an isolated social atom pursuing private profit and hiding from duties to care for others behind his negative rights. As Lamb says, for Smith,

> . . . Morality begins with society, the field of moral training is provided for a man in the family first, and then in society and the state; the range though not the intensity of his sense of duty expands as he finds himself rising from small groups to larger ones.[26]

Thus, it is possible to see both an individualist in Smith who might speak with Ned's masculine voice, but it is also possible to see elements of a more relational and caring voice in Smith. As a tribal being, a Scottish gentleman would be more concerned with his place in the community than with some kind of private, individualistic goal.

Although Smith gives numerous indications that self-interest is men's rational motive for their acquisition of wealth, their fundamental desire is to receive sympathy from other men for their material as well as their moral situation. They seek wealth to acquire approval. They seek dignity because this will ensure the continuous approval of other men.‎ Therefore "sympathy" rather than self-interest is the basis of property in Smith's system.[27]

Finally, Smith's focus on self-interest in *The Wealth of Nations* may just be part of his empirical approach. He is a practical man who understands how social life functions. We must express our positive duties in the way that will be most effective, by taking care of those close to us first, since we can affect them the most. But we should not forget that all the levels combine to make up a network of relations. One level should not receive all of our attention. As Hope says:

> Equality of interest does not mean, however, equality of attention by one person to others. . . . Each person should look to himself first, then to his family, friends and associates. Impartiality asks that everyone's interests are open to the same means of satisfaction, though each person gives prominence first to himself, then his family and so on. So self-interest combines with altruism under the general direction of sociableness.[28]

It seems clear that the voice one uses to interpret Smith does matter. In popular Western economics, the elements of Smith's philosophy that recognize our interdependence have been marginalized.[29] Perhaps it is due to the tendency of male writers to focus on those features of his philosophy that are of special interest to the individualist male voice. This may not be the best historical interpretation of Smith, but even more important, it is not the best prescriptive use of Smith's rich philosophy. It seems simplistic to think of Smith as a modern economic liberal focusing only on a conception of negative rights, when the impartial spectator develops out of a heritage built on human sympathy. We can get greater normative insight from Smith if we read him with a transcendent voice that incorporates the insights from both the male individualist perspective and the woman's relational, caring perspective.

If the Scottish businessman's egg has not been rolled, it will not seem "natural" to him to benefit himself at the expense of the community's good (remember the "stable nest" analogy in Chapter Four). Since his own perfection is tied intimately to his identification with the community's good, in acting on self-interest he would be regulated more thoroughly than if the government was regulating him. I think it was his faith in self-command, human sympathy, and man's need for dignity that led Adam Smith to the optimistic belief that an economy based on self-interest would serve the public good just as if it were being guided by an invisible hand. The invisible hand is really not so invisible, since it is found in the sympathetic breast of every adult communitarian businessman.

To achieve a transcendent vision, an attempt must be made to characterize abstract individuals as social, and social people as individuals. Just as some women have trouble accepting the moral responsibility that comes with the background of autonomy presupposed in the male world, some men have trouble remembering that they are obligated to care about meeting the needs of others in this relational world. A theory that could successfully unite male and female perspectives would give us an example of the kind of moral progress we should be looking for in a universal philosophy. It may not be a final theory, but it would be more enlightened than the individual heritages out of which it arose. In this regard, theories need to stimulate a proper reverence for a community of relationships at the same time that they acknowledge the individual's right to be autonomous. A world view like that of the Scottish moralists is likely to keep us focused on the necessary range of social values. Annette Baier makes a similar point when she argues that the Scottish moralist David Hume is a women's philosopher. She says:

> Hume lived before autonomy became an obsession with moral and social philosophers, or rather lived while Rousseau was making it their obsession, but his attack on contractarian doctrines of political obligation, and his clear perception of the given-ness of interconnection, in the family and beyond, his emphasis on our capacity to make others' joys and sorrows our own, on our need for a "seconding" of sentiments, and the inescapable mutual vulnerability and mutual enrichment that the human condition, when thus understood, entail, make autonomy not even an ideal, for Hume.[30]

If I have a quarrel with Baier, it is because she, like Hume, seems too willing to take an empirical approach to ethics, which makes her too much opposed to autonomy as a moral ideal. I would like to see her struggle to find a proper place for it in the moral world (which I will attempt in the next chapter). In addition, even Hume, with his emphasis on reason being a slave to the passions, did not mean to imply that the capacity to reason was useless in helping us reevaluate our passions and goals. Reason is the faculty that helps us reflect on the proper balance between passions, thus it is the source of whatever autonomy and ethical transcendence we can achieve, Hume would argue that reason needs to be pushed along by moral emotions; I would argue in return that a self-critical reason does not have to passively accept the emotions that start it on its reflective path.

In a pluralistic world, we don't have much choice but to use reason to evaluate our evaluations and to figure out how best to blend the various voices. Of course, blending voices may be a futile activity if we are looking to establish a final ultimate priority. It may be that the world is full of logically different types of moral values, so that establishing an absolute priority is impossible. Nagel argues that humans

> are complex creatures who can view the world from many perspectives—individual, relational, impersonal, ideal, etc.—and each perspective presents a different set of claims. . . . Conflicts between personal and impersonal claims are ubiquitous. They

cannot, in my view, be resolved by subsuming either of the points of view under the other, or both under a third.[31]

Obviously morality is complex, and any tradition that focuses exclusively on any one aspect of this complexity is going to be deficient. Moral education needs to focus on all the human virtues. It must provide opportunities to care for others and be cared for by others; to exercise moral judgment and think reflectively; to stimulate our moral imaginations; to hypothesize about ideals; to practice using the virtues; and so forth. The voices of men and women (and the plurality of religious and ethnic traditions) make up pieces of a complex moral world. They may represent world views that are so different that it might be impossible to unite them, but we should try. The next chapter takes up the task of trying to find room in ethics for both autonomy and relational sympathy.

■ STUDY QUESTIONS

1. What does it mean to say that men typically see morality as a means to facilitate their success dream, while women are more likely to see morality as a lifestyle question?
2. Contrast the different way that men and woman typically treat issues of charity and duty with regard to helping needy others.
3. Some people think that gender differences are caused by different nesting experiences. What kind of early experiences might cause men to focus on autonomy and rights and women to focus on relationships and care?
4. In the search for a transcendent point of view in ethics, what are the different tasks that fall on men and women?
5. Why does the Scottish communitarian tradition seem to have elements of both the male and the female voice in ethics? In particular, what is the primary virtue that humans see and approve of with their special moral sense?
6. Why does a typical modern interpretation of laissez-faire capitalism resemble a stereotypical male view of the economy? What elements of Smith's ethical philosophy might lead one to modify the masculine interpretation of laissez-faire principles?
7. Why does a plurality of voices make transcendence seem almost impossible?

■ NOTES

1. Carol Gilligan, *In a Different Voice* (Cambridge: Harvard University Press, 1982). All quotations attributed to Gilligan are from this text.
2. Virginia Held, "Liberty and Equality from a Feminist Perspective," in Neil Mac-Cormick and Zenon Bankowski, eds., *Enlightenment, Rights and Revolution* (Aylesbury, England: Aberdeen University Press, 1989), p. 222.
3. Betty A. Sichel, "Gender, Thinking and Moral Development," *ISDA Journal*, 4, No. 1, 1991, p. 13.

4. Daniel J. Levinson, *The Seasons of a Man's Life* (New York: Alfred A. Knoph, 1978), pp. 93ff.

5. Sichel, pp. 3–4.

6. Ibid., pp. 7–10.

7. Alison Jaggar, "Feminist Ethics: Some Projects and Problems," *Newsletter of the Center for Values and Social Policy*, **IX**, No. 2, Fall 1990, p. 2. The full article will also appear in Claudia Card, ed., *Feminist Ethics* (Lawrence, KS: University of Kansas Press, 1991). In her paper "Telling Right from Wrong: Toward a Feminist Conception of Practical Reason," delivered at the August 1991 North American Society for Social Philosophy meeting, Jaggar pointed out that many feminists were beginning to have doubts whether anything as simple as a male/female difference could be sustained. There are many different voices and experiences in both genders. This is of course true, and while it complicates the search for a transcendent conception of practical reason, it does not negate it.

8. In particular, see N. Chodorow, *The Reproduction of Mothering* (Berkeley: University of California Press, 1978) and M. F. Belenky, B. M. Clinchy, N. R. Goldberg, J. M. Tarule, *Women's Ways of Knowing* (New York: Basic Books, 1986).

9. Catherine MacKinnon, *Toward a Feminist Theory of the State* (Cambridge, MA: Harvard University Press, 1989), p. 51.

10. Most of the material in the next few pages is adapted from my paper "Scottish Communitarianism, Lockean Individualism, and Woman's Moral Development," in A. J. Aruaud and E. Kingdom, eds., *Women's Rights and the Rights of Man* (Aylesbury, England: Aberdeen University Press, 1990), pp. 36–51.

11. Garry Wills, *Inventing America* (New York: Vintage Books, 1978), p. 215.

12. Frances Hutcheson, "Concerning the Moral Sense, or Faculty of Perceiving Moral Excellence, and Its Supreme Objects," in Daniel Sommer Robinson, ed., *The Story of Scottish Philosophy* (New York: Exposition Press, 1961), pp. 42–53.

13. Wills, p. 213.

14. Tibor R. Machan, "Should Business Be Regulated?" in Tom Regan, ed., *Just Business* (New York: Random House, 1984), p. 204.

15. G. R. Morrow, "Adam Smith: Moralist and Philosopher," *The Journal of Political Economy*, June 1927, p. 33.

16. Wills, p. 232.

17. Morrow, p. 330f.

18. Robert Boyden Lamb, "Adam Smith's System: Sympathy not Self-Interest," *Journal of the History of Ideas* **35**, Oct.–Dec. 1974, p. 682.

19. As cited in Vincent Hope, "Smith's Demigod," in V. Hope, ed., *Philosophers of the Scottish Enlightenment* (Edinburgh: University Press, 1984), p. 158.

20. Ibid., p. 158.

21. Ibid., p. 161.

22. Ibid., p. 161f.

23. Onora O'Neill, "The Great Maxims of Justice and Charity," in MacCormick and Bankowski, eds., *Enlightenment, Rights and Revolution*, p. 306.

24. As cited in Lamb, pp. 671–682.

25. Ibid., p. 675.

26. Ibid., p. 681.

27. Ibid., p. 682.

28. Hope, pp. 164–165.

29. This term was used by O'Neill in her interesting analysis of the modern treatment of the charitable virtues (see endnote 23).

30. Annette Baier, "Hume, the Women's Moral Theorist?" in Tom L. Beauchamp, ed., *Philosophical Ethics* (New York: McGraw-Hill, 1991), p. 295.

31. Thomas Nagel, "The Fragmentations of Value," in Beauchamp, ed., *Philosophical Ethics*, p. 60.

■ CHAPTER SEVEN

Normative Ethics

■ IDEAL THEORY AND JUSTIFICATION

When Zimbardo said we have seen how a total institution " . . . could dehumanize people, could turn them into objects and make them feel helpless and hopeless," he was drawing our attention to the destruction of human values. What are human values? It is clear that everyone has values, but which of these should have the honor of being "human"? Consider the second-day rebellion in the Zimbardo experiment. They tore off "their" numbers and stocking caps and barricaded themselves in "their" cells. It was as though the rebellion was a desperate attempt to reestablish a sense of identity and personal control over their own lives. Is personal control an appropriate human ideal? Is it a moral ideal or a personal ideal? Questions such as these are fundamental in ethics. IDEAL THEORIES attempt to answer such questions 'by justifying prescriptive principles (like the five listed in Chapter One) that draw our attention to the human values that are essential to a moral life'.

■ Feelings

People occasionally ask: "Why do we need an ideal theory? Why can't we just accept the values that have been introjected into us?" The answer can be found in the following motto from philosophical ethics: "Feelings do not justify moral positions, moral positions justify feelings."[1] This slogan reminds us that a personal feeling is not an argument, that is, a personal feeling is not a reason why someone else should think they are obligated to do anything. Personal feelings need to be justified before other people will trust them to be guides for their own moral behavior.

Perhaps "personal" is the key word in this discussion. We shouldn't base public ethics on personal feelings. There are good reasons to keep public prescriptions distinct from private ones. For instance, current research on dysfunctional families shows us how children from such homes often develop desperate coping strategies to help them survive their chaotic childhoods.[2] As adults they may continue to feel very strongly that the familiar emotional responses and strategies that helped them survive the idiosyncrasies of their own childhood are right for no other reason than that familiarity makes them feel natural. But, unless there are good public reasons that can justify the way they feel, their values may not amount to anything more than a familiar prejudice or an outdated personal coping strategy. This same point applies to the personal feelings of everyone.

If personal feelings cannot serve as an ethical justification, perhaps common public feelings can be used to establish a sound foundation for ethics. On the surface, this approach seems reasonable, since feelings shared by all of us do not seem to be inappropriately personal. In fact, there is a long tradition in ethics that emphasizes how important it is for each person to share the values of their society.

One version of this tradition argues that the values embodied in the norms of a society are ultimate, not because they are necessarily the most rational but because shared norms are a necessity for saying we have a society at all. For example, Lord Devlin defined morality as nothing more than the body of common feelings and norms that hold a society together. In a famous attack on individualism, he argued that since society's standards of right and wrong have been introjected into each Englishman, morality amounts to no more than the rules that are consistent with the feelings of the average man in the street. We'll call this approach to judging values the **REASONABLE MAN STANDARD**.

> English law has evolved and regularly uses a standard which does not depend on the counting of heads. It is that of the reasonable man. He is not to be confused with the rational man. He is not expected to reason about anything and his judgment may be largely a matter of feeling. It is the viewpoint of the man in the street. . . . It is what Pollock called "practical morality" which is based not on theological or philosophical foundations but "in the mass of continuous experience half consciously or unconsciously accumulated and embodied in the morality of common sense."[3]

The strength of Devlin's approach comes from its backward look at our previous social context. The norms a society historically passes on from generation to generation are important because they embody a people's heritage. This reasonable man standard is in tune with our conventional desire to have people conform to society's norms for the good of the whole. Other things being equal, responsible people respect social traditions.

As formulated by Devlin, however, this approach to values amounts to cultural relativism. He even goes so far as to point out that because "There is no logic to be found in this" (p. 45), we should not expect rigorous standards of consistency when we establish laws to implement the feelings of the man in the street. That is, since feelings can shift, the man in the street can have different feelings about fairly similar cases. For example, Devlin says that since the reasonable man feels differently about male homosexuals than he does about lesbianism, it is not an objection to the standard that the former sexual preference is illegal in England while the latter preference is not.

This is the consequence of the reasonable man standard that bothers philosophers like John Stuart Mill, who worried that unreflective reliance on a public sentiment would stifle legitimate individual differences by imposing popular but arbitrary public feelings on individuals. He argued that

> nine-tenths of all moralists and speculative writers . . . teach that things are right because they are right; because we feel them to be so. They tell us to search in our own minds and hearts for laws of conduct binding on ourselves and on all others. What can the poor public do but apply these instructions, and make their own personal feelings of good and evil, if they are tolerably unanimous in them, obligatory on all the world? . . . The public of this age and country improperly invests its own preferences with the character of moral laws . . . until it encroaches on the most unquestionably legitimate liberty of the individual. . . .[4]

Mill preferred to use a rational, individualistic perspective as a background conceptual framework for ethical theory. Thus, he argued that ethical positions should emphasize preserving individual liberty rather than some favored communal or cultural heritage. Mill would probably ask Devlin: "Whose introjected values best represent society?" In a pluralistic culture "society" is a vague term, since it is not clear which group should get to have its preferences represent society. Furthermore, what if the dominant social feelings turn out to be no more than mass prejudices? Just because a feeling is popular does not mean it is automatically right. If it cannot be justified by sound reasoning it may still represent an evil but popular position.

Mill is working within a philosophical tradition that emphasizes rational justification. He is arguing that a proper approach to ethics must go beyond local social authorities to a RATIONAL MAN STANDARD, 'which advocates universal reasons that can stand up to cross-cultural critical public debate'—similar to the model of the jury box mentioned in Chapter Four. This kind of UNIVERSAL ETHIC is supposed to have 'principles that can apply to all people everywhere in a logically consistent manner.' That is, since all people similarly situated ought to be treated in a similar manner, arbitrary exceptions are wrong even if they are popular. Contrary to Devlin, then, Mill would insist that there must be some logic in all of this. If past standards are arbitrary, there is no reason to preserve them at the expense of individuals who are striving to live their own rational conception of a good life. The rational man standard emphasizes critical skills that are supposed to help any reasonable person map out rational, socially responsible future options. Mill makes sense to many people, because his rational individualism is in tune with the beliefs in Western pluralistic cultures that like cases should be treated alike and individuals are better off if they are free to govern themselves as they see fit.

■ *Universal Standards of Reason Reconsidered*

Universal philosophical theories try to find reasons that will support cherished human values, and help us distinguish them from personal and tribal values that may not be suitable as foundational human values even when they are popular. In the remainder of this chapter we will focus on how the concerns of both Mill and Devlin might be reasonably integrated in an ethical position suitable for a pluralistic culture. To get a better feel for what it might take for a moral agent to integrate both these traditions, let's consider the case of Socrates, a Greek philosopher whose life and philosophy have inspired people for centuries.

■ THE EXAMPLE OF SOCRATES

Two thousand years ago in Athens, people who wished to silence Socrates' criticisms of the government accused him of corrupting the youth and worshiping false gods. The plan was to undermine Socrates' prestige by embarrassing him at a public trial. He was eventually judged to be guilty and then sentenced to death by drinking hemlock—a poison. There is good reason to assume that no one really thought Socrates would be put to death. The rulers did not want to be accused of executing the leading thinker in all of Greece. They were merely trying to manipulate him into repudiating his beliefs, but, since a man like Socrates cannot be pressured or controlled by ordinary contingencies, events at the trial turned out differently from what anyone expected.

In the Athenian court, guilt or innocence was determined by a majority vote of all citizens who attended the trial. It is likely that if citizens had realized that in the end Socrates would be executed, enough of them would have changed their vote to reverse the outcome. But, there were no fixed penalties for Socrates' kind of crime, so voters had no way of predicting the eventual penalty that would be assessed. The procedure in the Athenian court was to assess the penalty after a person was found guilty. The accuser would propose a penalty and the guilty party would propose an alternative penalty. The jury of citizens would then have a second vote on which penalty to assess.

Socrates' accuser, Meletus, proposed death—a very harsh penalty for something that was not normally a capital offense. Scholars assume the jury would have been happy to assess Socrates a reasonable fine as an alternative to the death penalty, or if Socrates proposed it, they would have been happy to banish him. But Socrates continued to follow his own conscience. He could not be manipulated, and he did not choose the easy way out. Rather than ask, "What do I want?" Socrates asked, "What principle regulates this situation?" Socrates' style was always to rationally analyze what the ethical course of action ought to be, and then follow it no matter what the consequences for himself. Thus, when he was found guilty he asked, what penalty does principle dictate? What should be imposed on an innocent man who has worked hard to serve Athens? He said:

. . . If I must make a just assessment of what I deserve, I assess it at this: free meals in the Prytaneum . . . (p. 38).[5]

People who had served the city well (particularly people victorious at the Olympic Games) were commonly rewarded with free meals in the town hall. He argues that to assess some other penalty (like a fine or imprisonment) would be evil, since it would require him to violate the principle that governs just punishment. Socrates acknowledged that if he had given into the fears of ordinary men and tried to get himself acquitted he could easily have figured out how to do so, but that would require him to violate his principles. Remember, in postconventional thinking, ideal theory is the moral authority, not the fear of punishment, desire for rewards, or conventional norms. Socrates did not want to be executed, but he was motivated by a sense of duty to a universal principle rather than by subjective desires.

. . . Wherever a man has taken a position that he believes to be best, or has been placed by his commander, there he must I think remain and face danger, without a thought for death or anything else, rather than disgrace. . . . When the god ordered me, as I thought and believed, to live the life of a philosopher, to examine myself and others, had I abandoned my post for fear of death or anything else, that would have been a dreadful thing, and then I might truly have justly been brought here for not believing in the gods . . . (p. 32).

Socrates clearly showed that ultimate human values were his primary concern—values that transcend the more concrete concerns of a particular social life. Because ultimate human values governed his life, Socrates had a moral constancy even when he took on new roles or was placed in unusual situations. Situations can change, but our conscience, if guided by truly ultimate values, should be steady. Remember, in Chapter Two Jones said: "I wondered if it often happens to us, that we take a role and bend our lives to fit the role." That did not happen to Socrates. He brought his character and beliefs to his roles; he did not abandon himself. To be truly autonomous one must be capable of this kind of authenticity. Socrates said: " . . . Throughout my life, in any public activity I may have engaged in, I am the same man as I am in private life . . ." (p. 35).

Because of a religious mission that was underway (no executions during the mission), Socrates was required to spend a month in prison before he could be executed. Since no one wanted Socrates to die, including Anytus (the head of the city-state), Socrates' friend Crito was able to get Anytus' blessing for an arranged escape that would allow Socrates to go into exile. Everyone was bribed. Socrates could have walked out of the prison, but he refused. Once again he asked: "What principle regulates this situation?" The background facts are: He has been condemned (falsely), received a fair trial by Athenian standards, and been sentenced. Also, as a good citizen Socrates understood the value of a conventional system of laws and his obligation to obey them. Socrates would disobey a law only if a higher principle required it; he would not disobey only to satisfy a personal desire. Socrates refused to escape, so Lord Devlin could be proud of him for not arbitrarily disobeying social conventions to satisfy a personal desire to stay alive. But is this an inconsistent stance in light of the fact Socrates previously said he would practice philosophy even if the state told him to stop? No, because in the previous case, with higher principles justifying disobedience, he was not choosing on the basis of personal desire.

Like J. S. Mill, Socrates does not think he should always do what nine-tenths of all moralists might say he should do, that is, look inward and act on common social feelings. The man in the street would probably escape, especially since it was clear that popular feelings had changed. But Socrates is more complex. He looked inward in order to act on his conscience, but his conscience was more than his feelings, it was a prescription that had been sharpened by rational debate, an exceptional social heritage, and a mystical communion with a divine voice. Thus Socrates was governed by higher moral authority at the same time that he was governed by respect for his traditions. He recognized that there were different levels of ethical consideration, and he strived to set reasonable priorities among all the demands that were placed on him by the different levels. He asked the friends who were encouraging him to escape to imagine what the laws would say to him if he were to escape for personal reasons rather than truly universal reasons.

> . . . Both in war and in courts and everywhere else, one must obey the commands of one's city and country, or persuade it as to the nature of justice. It is impious to bring violence to bear against your mother or father, it is much more to use it against your country . . . (p. 51).

■ Ideal Moral Agents

What can we learn from Socrates' interesting blend of devotion to "duty of station" combined with a willingness to go against concrete duties of station when they come into conflict with the higher principles that govern his conscience? There are four dominant Socratic virtues that moral agents ought to model. First, he accepted responsibility for his actions. Second, the moral authority in his life was not social success; he was governed by a rational love of justice, truth, and wisdom. That is, he cared about ultimate values and dedicated his life to a rational search for the highest human values possible. Third, as a man of practical wisdom, theory and practice were one in his life. Abstract knowledge motivated him on the concrete level, and his concrete experiences informed his theoretical beliefs. Fourth, Socrates believed that the goal of normative philosophy was to attain the virtue of understanding. Motive is closely linked to knowledge in a rational moral agent. To understand what is truly good is to be positively compelled to do it—as Bernhardt said in Chapter Five, he could not shoot civilians at My Lai, for once he saw that something was right he was just positively compelled to do it. Socrates is an IDEAL MORAL AGENT, then, because he 'accepts responsibility, cares about doing the right thing, is motivated to seek ultimate values, has the concrete skills to engage in the search, understands how the theoretical and concrete should be combined, and has the courage and motivation to act on duty once he sees the truth'.

Socrates' life shows us that ideal conduct requires emotional development, moral experience, and theoretical understanding. Emotional growth comes with proper moral experience in an environment that gives us an opportunity to care and be cared for. Theoretical understanding, however, may have to be taught in a setting that encourages rational debate; it is the goal of an academic course in ethics. That is, as a discipline, ethics contributes to the intellectual side of moral agency by encouraging rational reflection and debate.

■ Philosophical Ethics Reconsidered

At this point we can define PHILOSOPHICAL ETHICS as 'the disciplined critical study of the belief systems or theories that people use to set boundaries on acceptable ways of life, to resolve social conflicts, and to make sense of moral experience in general'. When we study ethics we must use (1) research from other disciplines, (2) qualitative information gathered from our own life experiences, and (3) the sharp edge of critical public debate to reason as objectively as we can about all the available information.

Although we do not have to have Socratic ability to be moral agents, we do expect moral agents to have enough autonomy that they can be held responsible for their actions. Since autonomous people generally rely on a consciously chosen ideal theory to guide their practical decisions, in Chapters Nine and Ten we will look at five ideal theories that have been designed to guide autonomous decisions. First, however, we need to explore in more detail what it means to be autonomous. If possible, we want an interpretation of autonomy that is compatible with the voices from both genders, and although autonomy has some important ties to individualism, we will also strive for a definition that can give Devlin's concern for social heritage a proper place. As we shall see, an adequate conception of autonomy has important implications for how to interpret the five theories discussed in Chapters Nine and Ten.

■ AUTONOMY

Autonomy is a concept that was originally borrowed from political philosophy. The term referred to nations[6] that were self-supporting, self-governed, and capable of an independent foreign policy. In some sense, then, an autonomous person must also be independent. Feinberg points out that the term can be used to mean either the capacity to govern oneself, the conditions of being self-governed, an ideal character, or the authority to govern oneself.[7] The subjects in the experiments we previously examined lacked autonomy in all of these ways, since they were controlled by externals. This point, however, should not be misinterpreted. Autonomous people are not immune to the external world. It would be irrational to ignore the environment; it provides us with useful data. So, the proper perspective is to say that while autonomous people are *influenced* by externals, they are *not controlled* by them. Control must come from within, that is, from their own belief systems and values.

■ Minimal Conditions for Autonomy

Without qualification, autonomy means only "independent control of one's own life." The minimal necessary conditions for this kind of autonomy are the capacities we need to make reasonable choices about means to ends. According to R. S. Peters, a young child in Piaget's preoperational stage is not yet an autonomous chooser, because in some sense he is still the plaything of faulty concepts and external pressures. Peters says at the very least a child must possess the categorical concepts of "thing hood," "causality," and "means to an end." These enable him to think "realistically" in contradistinction to small children and paranoiacs whose consciousness is dominated by wishes and aversion.[8]

Of course, we develop the necessary skills over time, so children will possess them in varying degrees. But this characterization shows that arbitrary whim on either the personal or public level is incompatible with the usual notion of autonomy. Autonomy, then, presupposes a stable internal "I" that is in charge of decision making. This is not to imply that an autonomous agent must exercise rigid unbending consistency or exclude elements of the irrational from her internal environment. Autonomous people can have desires that are frivolous or with which they do not identify. For example, if I am addicted to nicotine, I will feel as though my desire for nicotine is a force within me. I may welcome it, or I may choose to fight it. If I choose to fight it, the desire will not feel like it belongs to the "real" me, it will feel like an alien presence. Such desires are called compulsions to distinguish them from what we "really" want. In the face of an internal compulsion (or craving), we may not feel personally autonomous. But when it does not affect public behavior in a significant way, we can still feel autonomous with regard to decisions about public relationships.

Autonomy is thought of as a virtue, partly because it concerns consistent, conscious self-control by a stable set of beliefs rather than control by arbitrary or inconsistent desires over which we appear to have little control. It is difficult to develop even this minimal sense of autonomy in a chaotic environment. Families that create inconsistent arbitrary environments where similar choices lead to contradictory self-defeating consequences are not rewarding rational choice. This characterization often fits households that are dominated by mental illness or severe drug abuse. These environments teach children that rational plans are useless at best and dangerous at worst. Since it hurts to have rational expectations squashed for irrational and arbitrary reasons, children raised under these conditions develop irrational coping strategies that will make them vulnerable to external control when they become adults[9] (more on this below). Since "rationality" is one of the components of morally responsible decision making, arbitrary households must be characterized as dysfunctional from any moral point of view that emphasizes rationality. These considerations lead to the following provisional definition of PERSONAL AUTONOMY:

> 'One is controlled by an independent will with a stable, fairly consistent set of beliefs, in contrast to being controlled by (1) biological or introjected social desires that we consciously reject, or (2) social and external forces that we consciously reject'.

■ Personal Autonomy Is Not Moral Autonomy

This minimal level of autonomy covers the prudential skills needed to evaluate habits (like smoking) or to make economic career plans. To clarify the richer notion of moral autonomy, it is useful to begin by discussing why personal autonomy (which is characteristic of self-interested economic agents) cannot serve as an adequate characterization of an autonomous moral agent. As we saw in the last chapter, a critic like Baier can ask, "Why should autonomy be a moral ideal?" By itself, personal autonomy is morally neutral; it is consistent with choosing good or bad, moral or immoral options. Because the element of caring, which is one of the characteristics of a morally responsible agent, has not yet been brought into the definition of personal autonomy, even a sociopathic personality could be considered autonomous in this minimal sense. As Feinberg says:

> It is important to emphasize at the outset that even a refined conception of autonomy will be at best only a partial ideal, for since it is consistent with some important failings it is insufficient for full moral excellence. No further analysis can be expected to rule out as impossible a selfish but autonomous person, a cold, mean, unloving but autonomous person, or a ruthless, or cruel, autonomous person. After all, a self-governing person is no less self-governed if he governs himself badly, no less authentic for having evil principles, no less autonomous if he uses his autonomy to commit aggression against another autonomous person. The aggressor is morally deficient, but what he is deficient in is not necessarily autonomy. He may have more than enough of that (p. 45).

I assume that there must be some way to refine the concept of autonomy if a genius like Kant would make it the foundational concept in his moral philosophy. So, what should be emphasized to make the concept work as a moral ideal? It may be instructive to begin by looking at a type of person who sometimes seems autonomous even though he does not make a good moral agent. SOCIOPATHS fit into this category. They are controlled for the most part by their own internal beliefs and personal desires and do not act on whim or impulse any more than the rest of us. Their problem with morality is not a lack of self-control, but has more to do with the narrowness of the self that is in control. The American Psychiatric Association's DSM-III-R manual describes this personality type as characterized by disregard for social obligations, lack of feeling for others, and impetuous violence or callous unconcern. There is a gross disparity between behavior and the prevailing social norms. Behavior is not readily modifiable by experience, including punishment. People with this personality are often affectively cold and may be abnormally aggressive or irresponsible (p. 462).[10]

Because a sociopath is not bothered by social emotions such as remorse or guilt, his life choices are simpler than the norm and can be consistently stable, under his own will, and according to his own belief system. If he is careful not to collide with external authority figures, he can even act in prudent ways to further his ends. Yet no loving parent would point to a sociopath and say to her child: "Son, when you grow up, I hope you will be just like that independent, self-contained sociopath over there." For instance, when a drifter and mass murderer like Ted Bundy makes life choices, we are unlikely to embrace his practical style as an inspiration to pursue moral autonomy. Instead we think that something has gone seriously wrong in his choice of goals and means. In fact, with Bundy something had gone wrong. He had quantitative rational skills, but according to psychologists who examined him, he appeared to have the emotional development of about a twelve-year-old. He understood punishment and rewards and could think on an abstract level, but he was morally stunted because he could not understand the emotional side of social life. When we read the following statement, we can only shake our heads in disbelief. Bundy believed

that under the correct circumstances he could select any person as a victim and that there would be virtually no attention paid to that person's disappearance. People disappear every day. It happens all the time. . . . He was always amazed and chagrined by the publicity generated by disappearances he thought would go almost totally unnoticed. There are so many people. It shouldn't be a problem. What's one less person on the face of the earth, anyway?[11]

This kind of person does not understand community. If Bundy is autonomous, his independence from external social controls is not based on human virtues but on human deficits. He lacks certain common moral intuitions that are built on the prerequisite ability to empathize with others and to understand the qualitative point of conventional life. It is difficult to think that someone can be truly autonomous in a "human sense," when he does not understand options that are obvious to any person whose egg has not been rolled. If on a fundamental level, a person cannot care about social life, how can he understand what moral choice is all about? How can he choose, in an autonomous sense, when he can't understand the most important options?

To be autonomous in a sense that is morally significant, people must have some Socratic qualitative understanding of the social nature of the moral options available to them, even if for some reason they decide not to choose any of these alternatives. A sociopath like Bundy cannot comprehend what it means to feel social commitment or respect for others, thus he cannot be said to have CHOSEN in a morally autonomous sense to exclude them. He excludes them by default, by lack of feeling, not because of independent value deliberation. He may be autonomous in a narrow sense, a banal sense, but he is not an autonomous "social" agent since he is socially blind. I am assuming, of course, that autonomous choice implies that options are available and the chooser has the capacity to evaluate them. Autonomous people are assumed to be in control of their life, and to be free to choose their own values, life plans, and principles, but their choices will not earn our respect if they are based on a deficient vision of the social world. A society of sociopaths is possible, of course, but we would need a police officer on every corner. Autonomy without some commitment to a notion of common social good leads to isolation, alienation, and meaninglessness. Without some sense of moral or social commitment, then, social life in a full moral sense is only a fantasy.

From a legal point of view society may decide to hold the Bundys among us responsible, as though they are fully developed moral agents. It is a social necessity to impose legal sanctions on such people. But it is instructive to consider why Bundy is not an example of a well-developed moral agent even if he has a kind of legally recognized personal autonomy. His autonomy amounts to no more than what we would expect to find in a clever antisocial child.

When we praise autonomy, we feel more comfortable using an autonomous person like Socrates as a model for our children. A morally responsible agent like Socrates may reject elements of his community's values, but he will reject them because he disagrees with their value content, not because he doesn't care about or emotionally understand the point of community values. This is because Socrates learned the meaning of social norms from the inside, by living them. He experienced all three major developmental orientations to social life, so he is free to make comparisons and choose between them. When he is deliberating about principles or variables that ought to influence moral choice, he gives the demands of the conventional order its proper weight. The fact that his ability to think on a "theoretical level" gave him the capacity to turn around and criticize some of the social institutions that had nurtured him does not change the fact that he understood thoroughly the social value and meaning behind rules. Socrates did not see social norms as external constraints imposed upon his impulses as is the case with sociopaths and children. He understood why certain rules have intrinsic social value in addition to their instrumental value to individuals. Peters makes a similar point when he says that to be a moral agent, a person

> must be sensitive to considerations such as the suffering of others or fairness which are to serve as principles for him. For it is not sufficient to be aware that actions have certain types of consequences; he must care about the consequences.[12]

Finally, a morally autonomous person has to choose to impose *moral* rules on himself. They must be social in nature, but they also must be authentically his; they cannot be slogans picked up somewhere. As we saw earlier, Socrates had this kind of moral authenticity. Kant's treatment of reason, discussed in Chapter Four, also emphasized authenticity. He argued that one must think for himself or he is not truly part of a rational dialogue. I agree with Kant that actions and thoughts based solely on causal factors outside of a person's rational moral will are simply not his own thoughts or moral actions. In this sense, a person is neither a rational agent nor a moral agent if he is forced to obey someone else's rules. If we want to hold moral agents fully responsible for what they do, the moral rules they follow must also in some sense be their own. As Feinberg says:

> The autonomous person is not only he whose tastes and opinions are authentically his own; he is also one whose moral convictions and principles (if he has any) are genuinely his own, rooted in his own character, and not merely inherited. . . . Insofar as the autonomous person's life is shaped by moral beliefs, they are derived neither by mindless conformism nor unthinking obedience to authority, but rather from a committed process of continually reconstructing the value system he inherited (pp. 36–37).

Again, this is similar to Kant's assertion that the authentic moral thinker must be aware that he is involved in a community activity. Communication and morality are inherently social. Even if authentic individual agents are continuously reevaluating social norms, they must not forget what it means for a norm to be social. To be in a moral choice context requires us to acknowledge its public nature. We cannot deny the logic of what we are doing and still be rational beings. Feinberg points out:

> Immoral authenticity is as real as its moral counterpart. In theory we all have a choice between the moral life and its amoral and immoral alternatives. But if we opt to govern our lives by moral principle, then insofar as our subsequent moral convictions are authentically our own, certain life policies will no longer be eligible for our choice. . . . Persons who opt otherwise, to repeat, may be thoroughly self-governing (autonomous), but in order for moral principles to be authentically their own, they must have moral principles in the first place (pp. 38–39).

■ MORAL AUTONOMY

We can use these criticisms of simple personal autonomy to develop a more adequate definition of moral autonomy. Morally autonomous people are independent in the sense that the rules they follow are self-imposed, but they are also independent in the sense that they are choosing with a full understanding of the public nature of moral rules. This means that moral autonomy is a very complex notion. It refers both to an ability to live according to moral principles (rather than live only on the basis of desires), as well as to an ability to authentically adopt or reject the principles after informed critical deliberation. Morally autonomous people have developed the advanced virtues that enable them to be critical of their own learned moral values and inclinations at the same time that they care about having moral values.

This requirement seems paradoxical. As we saw in Chapter Four, on the one hand people are supposed to be able to evaluate themselves critically (their own values, beliefs, and modes of thought), yet on the other hand every critical evaluation presupposes who they are (that is, they are already historically situated, thus they have to use the values, beliefs, and modes of thought they are evaluating to engage in the evaluation). Is this circular? Is an emancipatory kind of critical self-reflection possible, or is it only useful to think of this as a theoretical ideal?

It seems to me it is possible for people to develop certain internal virtues that can enable moral autonomy. Of course, to emancipate us in this sense, these virtues have to be both intellectual and emotional. It would be a distraction to discuss these virtues at this time, but we cannot duck the task forever. To make sense of moral autonomy we will need to explore emancipatory virtues in detail, so the next chapter will discuss at some length the emancipatory power of critical self-reflection and decentered emotional commitment. At this point, let's assume that a significant kind of autonomy is possible, so that we can proceed with the discussion.

■ Universal Social Concern and Ethics

It is important to recognize that when morally autonomous people choose or evaluate the moral principles that will guide their social life, they will judge the principles (and the rules that follow from them) with the conscious knowledge that the moral principles have a universal social purpose. That is, (1) they know that in following "moral" principles (and rules), they are supporting standards that apply to others as well as to themselves, and (2) they recognize that these others are also moral agents who, as morally autonomous beings, ought to choose their own principles and rules. This means that the norms chosen will have to have a special character.

To be ethical, moral rules need to be universal in two ways: first, in the sense that they apply to all moral agents (there are no arbitrary exceptions) and second, in the sense that it must make sense to think that at least in principle every morally autonomous agent could agree to them. Thus, in an *ideal society* filled with morally autonomous people governed by their own choices, concrete moral policies and laws would be justified only if it makes sense to say that they are the kind of laws and policies that, in principle, would have been self-imposed by any morally autonomous person. At such an abstract principled level we expect a convergence on the kinds of lifestyle options that would be chosen, since universal ethical principles place boundaries on the choices of personal values. Feinberg says:

> . . . If we opt to govern our lives by moral principle, then insofar as our subsequent moral convictions are authentically our own, certain life policies will no longer be eligible for our choice. We cannot even consider, for example, the satanic life-

principle that we should inflict as much pain as we can, or the principle that we should promote our interests at all costs to those who might get in our way (pp. 38–39).

■ A Final Definition of Moral Autonomy

Notice that the need for a social ethics requires us to strive to decenter, in order to take everyone into consideration. Egocentric and ethnocentric people cannot adopt a decentered perspective, so by default rather than by choice, local concrete concerns will dominate their decision making. They may agree that debate between all members of the moral community is important, but their definition of moral community will be excessively narrow. At the decentered level, however, human reason strives for universal conceptions that can be shared by all. Universals do not require people to stop being who they are, unless who they are on a concrete level is inconsistent with toleration of other people's right to live according to a universal moral point of view. We are now prepared to give a final definition of MORAL AUTONOMY. It means:

> 'to be governed by social principles that are self-imposed because as a caring moral agent, the chooser believes they are the kind of principles that would at least in principle be acceptable to other agents who are rational choosers of their own principles.'

This conception of autonomy does not guarantee that the principles chosen will be the best available. Morally autonomous people can make mistakes when choosing. Also, morally autonomous people do not always win (remember, Socrates was executed). It only means the choice will be morally responsible and deserve our respect. The principle does not beg any important questions, since it is compatible with reasonable disagreements between proponents of the major Western theories. However, it does imply that when we intervene in one another's life, or create new social settings, we should be paying close attention to the moral implications of moral autonomy.

■ MORAL AUTONOMY AND MORAL ACCOUNTABILITY

Remember Adam Smith's claim in Chapter Six, that "A moral being is an accountable being?" This view implies that a morally autonomous person must have a socially acceptable theory, principles, and rules that he can use to justify his interventions in another autonomous person's life. The five Western theories discussed in the next chapter represent the kind of theoretical account that morally autonomous people typically give to one another. To see why a theoretical account is often needed, we need to analyze the intimate connection between moral autonomy and moral accountability.

Accountability can mean a number of different things.[13] We can avoid certain confusions by discussing the term in general before focusing specifically on moral accountability. Accountability relationships all share a similar form: "Some agent" (A) is accountable to a "person affected" (PA) for the "activity that affects" (AA) him. Generally, the agent must be a person or agency competent to give an account of a required kind, and the person affected must be a person or agency capable of receiving and understanding the account. Obviously, the nature of the account given will depend on the capacities of both the agent and the recipient as well as on the complexity of the type of activity. The account a nuclear physicist gives to a regulatory agency may be considerably more sophisticated than the account he offers to the general public, even though the activity is the same in both cases.[14]

Accountability procedures are most useful when the standards that regulate an activity are not very precise, because the point is to allow leeway to make decisions about how best to perform the activity. When there is no leeway for choice, there is no need to give an account. The fact that an activity requires accountability means the agent is being given a degree of autonomy to act on her own.[15] In this sense, it is important to emphasize that holding people accountable is not punitive. It is a way of giving people leeway to act, while reminding them that their actions are supposed to serve certain ends or stay within certain boundaries. A call to give an account is supposed to lead to a dialogue that benefits both agent and recipient by clarifying the standards that should regulate the activity. For example, an account of how one chooses to teach should lead to a dialogue about goals and means that will clarify the teaching standards that establish boundaries on what activities are acceptable.

Accountability procedures, of course, are restrictions on liberty, since they are incompatible with complete, unregulated autonomy. Sometimes people who place great emphasis on autonomy feel that autonomy means freedom from being called to account as though their activities were totally private rather than part of a social system. For instance, some members of professions dislike being held accountable by clients. They feel it is an insult to their professionalism to have to give an account of their role behavior. The problem, of course, is that not all members of professions can be trusted to be professional, especially in contexts where the consumers of their professional decisions may be powerless to call them to account. Liability to an occasional account is not a severe restriction on autonomy; it only asks for an explanation of how a person is exercising autonomous judgment. Furthermore, this kind of restriction on autonomy is required by the logic of moral autonomy itself.

■ Moral Accountability

Moral accountability is logically entailed by the nature of moral autonomy. The ideal of moral autonomy gives people power over their own life, but *only* their own life; thus whenever our actions affect the interests of others we owe them an account of why we think our actions have stayed within the boundaries set by the ideal of moral autonomy. In ethics there is always room to act, hence there is always room for individual judgment about how to be moral. An account clarifies the principles that we are following. Moral agents need to act with an awareness that background moral autonomy implies a background of MORAL ACCOUNTABILITY as well, which stipulates that 'in principle, agents must be prepared to give those they affect an explanation that will show how their actions respect the moral autonomy of those affected'.

To refuse to give an account for public behavior is to refuse to recognize a fundamental background norm that comes with the ideal of moral autonomy, that is, that people are in principle moral equals. This background is assumed by most Western theories and is sometimes summarized by the phrase "everyone counts as one." This is also the ideal of moral equality that was referred to in the Declaration of Independence. These theories assume all people are moral equals who are accountable to one another no matter what concrete material inequalities exist.

Because the ideal of moral equality holds in principle, many people regard it as only a theoretical ideal. For them the concrete inequalities of daily life constitute reality. Because there are so many concrete relationships of inequality, it is difficult for them to stay focused on the "reality" of the abstract moral equality that comes with the ideal of moral autonomy. To make this ideal real to them, then, it would need to be implemented in actual concrete institutions by procedures that emphasize moral accountability.

A practice of moral accountability should function to encourage us to remain thoughtful about our actions, just as we would be if we knew we were being watched by a third person. We are reminded to ask ourselves, "Would I be doing this if an independent rational agent were observing my actions?" Among people who are equal in rank, this kind of third-person perspective is always present; that is, equals think of themselves as having enough status and power to be rational observers of each other. We expect our peers to be aware of what we are doing to them, so the obligation to give an account to a "real" equal is taken for granted (we can say a kind of third-person moral point of view is inherent in the nature of equal relationships). But institutional inequalities can undermine this perspective.

For example, many years ago, I experienced the way in which real inequalities in status can contribute to a type of moral insensitivity. I was a new assistant professor at my university. I made an appointment to talk to the Director of the Counseling Center after his lunch hour. I arrived at 1:00 P.M. and had to wait 45 minutes before he showed up. This was not particularly disturbing, for I assumed he was tied up with something important and would apologize (give an account) for keeping me waiting. When he arrived, however, he looked surprised to see me and said: "Oh, David. I didn't know you were my 1:00 o'clock appointment. I thought it was a student. I would have been on time if I had known it was you." There are, of course, problems with this account.* If he could have made it on

---

* By the way, I did not challenge his poor account. At the time I did not have these ideas organized into a coherent framework. I was also like the "good" guards in the Zimbardo experiment. I was morally sensitive enough to disapprove of immoral behavior when I saw it, but I had a tendency to let immoral and unpleasant behavior slide by—hoping it would soon go away. I should have encouraged him to go into more detail.

time for me, he could have made it on time for anyone, so he should have been on time. An appointment is an appointment. Alternatively, if there had been good reasons for his being late, he should have used the good reasons to give me the same account that he owed the student. I think his attitude illustrates the easy way we let real institutional inequalities in status and power begin to undermine our obligations to treat one another as moral equals. When he saw it was a peer waiting for him, he felt either embarrassed or apologetic, so he gave me the type of account that he thought a peer (who shared his status on campus) would understand. To him, his concrete institutional superiority was real and a grounds for treating people as unequal in terms of punctuality. But the ideal of our equal moral autonomy (moral equality) should have priority over these concrete inequalities. This helps explain why Socrates seems wise to so many people. He has achieved a conceptual level that allows him to see moral ideals as more real than concrete conventions. I have often wondered: if a third person had been observing the entire affair, thus giving the Director a concrete reason to believe in the reality of the ideal of moral equality, would he have been more sensitive to the equal human status of students and faculty, and thus less likely to keep a student waiting for no good reason?

Unfortunately, it is easier to focus on the reality of "the way it is" than on the reality of "the way it ought to be." Most institutions are hierarchical in design, and it is a fact of life that those high up in a hierarchy possess real concrete superiority to those below them (e.g., unequal political and economic power). This real institutional superiority daily draws our attention, especially if we are concrete operational thinkers when we judge social relations. Under such conditions, it becomes easy to forget that those below us are real moral equals.

This is a very important point. We live in a world that is filled with institutions that could be characterized as authoritarian in structure. Authoritarian social structures have a superior authority to make the important decisions that will affect the other members of the social group. The members are expected to display their respect for authority by obeying the rules passed down to them. In varying degrees this is the structure found in orphanages, hospitals, schools, the military, prisons, the patriarchal family—in short, in most caretaker institutions. The crucial feature of these institutions, as it relates to the ideal of moral autonomy, is the lack of downward accountability. Those lower in the hierarchy are to be the beneficiaries of decisions; they are not expected to partake in the decision making.

Occasionally, even philosophers have been overly impressed with such concrete inequalities. The mere existence of unequal status has been used to justify the power of kings, the subjection of groups of people, and even evils like slavery. As far back as the Enlightenment we find Rousseau criticizing the concrete moral reasoning of Grotius, Hobbes, Caligula, and Aristotle. He claimed that they made the mistake of trying to derive what ought to be from fact. He said: "It might be possible to adopt a more logical system of reasoning, but none which would be more favorable to tyrants. [The problem is, their reasoning] . . . mistook the effect for the cause."[16] In spite of his criticism, we still find that each new generation of leaders must still be reminded that "the way it is" is not synonymous with "the way that it ought to be." Unless we cure the human tendency to be distracted by an overly concrete focus, we will continue to find the arrogant assumption that those who are being cared for are simply not capable of expressing their true needs, let alone competent to participate in making decisions about how to satisfy them.[17] I think that the temptation to assert arbitrary power under these circumstances is very hard to resist.

In an authoritarian structure it will be difficult to implement practices designed to protect moral autonomy. If the practices are to be effective, they must inevitably undermine the unequal power of the "expert" authority who runs the institution and who will, therefore, be in charge of implementing recommended new practices. Whenever administrators feel superior to those in their care, enjoy the power of making decisions, and are blinded by the virtue of efficiency and of quantitative objectivity, they will be inclined to resist many legitimate changes. I am sure that most administrators in a position to care for others have high aspirations. The problem is practical, because in spite of high aspirations the implementation of recommended procedures to protect moral autonomy lies with the authority figure whose power is undermined by the new procedures. Theoretical, situational, and political forces, often combine to make administrators reluctant to implement morally indicated changes in an institutional status quo. Together, these forces help explain why we sometimes drift away from our original aspirations, until our treatment of others falls below minimally acceptable standards.

A system of moral accountability will not, of course, stop all activities that unjustifiably harm those in whose lives we choose to intervene. Other forces are also at work. But by focusing our attention on (a) variables that affect moral autonomy, (b) moral autonomy's special status as a moral value, (c) the accountability structure of institutions, and (d) our obligations to give an acceptable account to the moral equals we affect, a system of accountability can help us lower the number of instances in which we are genuinely surprised to discover that we have harmed someone despite our good intentions. Stop for a moment and think about some situation where you did something that made you feel ashamed or guilty. Would you have been as likely to do it if some third party had been observing you? Ideally, we should develop to a Socratic level, so that we carry a rational third-party peer around in our heads—a conscience to whom we feel accountable. Zimbardo must have arrived at a similar conclusion, since after analyzing his experiment, he concluded:

> In the future, we will insist that students, or representatives of the population being studied, be part of the University Committee to pass on the ethics of human experimentation. We will encourage that committee to send an observer to, or secure recordings from, a pilot session of any "potentially unethical" research. We will ourselves in the future incorporate a metaexperimenter in the role of unbiased monitor with "detached concern." His/her task will be to assess the impact of the treatment on the subjects as well as the impact of the progress of the experiment on the researchers.

Such a person should also have the authority to intervene on behalf of the subjects if necessary. [18]

Zimbardo's use of a "detached observer" is innovative and in the spirit required by the concepts of moral autonomy and accountability. His recognition of the need for an outside observer to whom he would naturally feel accountable might be traceable to the fact that it was an outsider who caused him to finally halt his experiment (that is, someone who was not participating in the actual experiment). Although he reports he was planning on stopping the experiment anyway, he was jolted into action when his fiancee (who had accompanied him to his mock prison) looked through the observation hole at the end of the hall and tearfully told him: "It's awful what you are doing to those boys."[19] This contact with criticism external to the research setting helped him bring moral reality back into a situation where concrete inequalities had taken control of all of the participants.

■ SUMMARY

It should be clear by now that ethical theories can have a fairly practical impact if we will let them guide our decisions. Theoretical ideals are transcendent moral realities that can become actual in our lives when we allow them to influence our actions and when we build them into the structure of our institutions. In pluralistic cultures, of course, we can become confused about how to proceed. Recommended ideals are not always consistent with one another, and even a consistent set may not always be uniformly implemented in the day-to-day rules by which we live. Under conditions of pluralism, transcendent norms have to be constantly rediscovered for each new generation. We have to make a continuous, conscious effort to keep evaluating them and to keep rebuilding them into the structures of our concrete daily existence.

This is the task facing morally autonomous agents. Moral autonomy leaves considerable room for individual lifestyle differences and unique emotional attachments, but it does make a significant normative claim: Promoting the enabling virtues for moral autonomy should have the highest priority in any caring, individualistic tradition that recognizes our right to be independent agents with a capacity to feel social responsibility. So, we need to ask: "How can we promote enabling virtues? And, what if people who lack autonomy do not want to develop them?" To answer such questions, the next chapter will need to address a number of practical and conceptual problems that arise when we try to implement the concept of moral autonomy.

■ STUDY QUESTIONS

1. Clarify the statement "Feelings do not justify moral positions, moral positions justify feelings."

2. What is the difference between a private feeling and a public or common social feeling?
3. According to Devlin, what is the reasonable man standard? What is its primary strength as a principle? What is the major logical weakness of this principle?
4. Why does a universal ethics insist on standards of logic when formulating ethical principles?
5. Socrates is supposed to be a good example of an ideal moral agent. Why?
6. What are the minimal criteria that we need for a "value neutral" conception of individual autonomy? Why do people think of autonomy as a virtue?
7. Why is personal autonomy not the same as moral autonomy? What is missing?
8. Why does the definition of moral autonomy have to be so complex? Explain why each major term in the definition is needed.
9. Discuss the two ways moral principles that are compatible with moral autonomy would have to be universal.
10. Why does the concept of moral autonomy imply the need for moral accountability?
11. Why does the fact of concrete real inequalities make it useful to implement real accountability procedures in actual institutions?
12. What do we have to do to make theoretical ideals function as actual realities?

■ NOTES

1. Ronald Dworkin, "Lord Devlin and the Enforcement of Morals," in Richard Wasserstrom, ed., *Morality and the Law* (Belmont, CA: Wadsworth Publishing Co., 1971), pp. 63f.
2. In recent years there has been an explosion of literature on the effects of dysfunctional family life, especially in families dominated by drug dependence. The more traditional literature is summarized in R. S. Peters, *Reason and Compassion* (London: Routledge & Kegan Paul, 1973). For a fine introduction to the substance abuse literature, see Jane Middleton-Moz and Lorie Dwinnell, *After the Tears* (Pompano Beach, FL: Health Communications, 1986) and Janet G. Wortitz, *Adult Children of Alcoholics* (Health Communications, 1983).
3. Lord Patrick Devlin, "Morals and the Criminal Law," in Wasserstrom, ed., *Morality and the Law*, p. 38.
4. John Stuart Mill, "On Liberty," in Wasserstrom, ed., *Morality and the Law*, p. 19.
5. I have taken the Socrates quotations from the translations of the "Apology" and "Crito" by G. M. A. Grube, *The Trial & Death of Socrates* (Indianapolis: Hackett Publishing Company, 1975), pp. 27–47.
6. Joel Feinberg, *Social Philosophy* (Englewood Cliffs, NJ: Prentice Hall, 1973) p. 15.
7. Joel Feinberg, *Harm to Self* (New York: Oxford University Press, 1986), p. 28. For a very clear and thorough discussion of autonomy as it is used in legal contexts, see Chaps. 18 and 19.
8. Peters, p. 36.
9. See the text by Middleton-Moz and Dwinnell.
10. *Diagnostic and Statistical Manual of Mental Disorders, DSM III-R* (Washington: American Psychiatric Association, 1987).
11. Stephen G. Michard and Hugh Aynesworth, *The Only Living Witness* (New York: Signet, 1983), pp. 310–311.
12. Peters, p. 99.

13. The discussion of accountability that follows makes use of many of the distinctions developed at the October 12–14, 1979 conference on accountability by the American Section, International Association for Philosophy of Law and Social Philosophy (AMINTAPHIL) at the University of Texas, Austin.

14. Michael D. Bayles, "Accounting for the Variables in Accountability: A Commentary," paper prepared for the AMINTAPHIL conference (see endnote 13).

15. J. Ralph Lindgren, "The Costs of Accountability," paper prepared for the AMINTAPHIL conference.

16. J. J. Rousseau, *The Social Contract*, in Sir Ernest Barker, ed., *The Social Contract: Locke, Hume, Rousseau* (London: Oxford University Press, 1968), p. 171.

17. A good account of this tendency can be found in Kai Nielsen, "True Needs, Rationality and Emancipation," in Ross Fitzgerald, ed., *Human Needs and Politics* (Rushcutters Bay, Australia: Pergamon Press, 1977). Pearl S. Buck also argues persuasively that even severely retarded people are quite capable of expressing their needs if not implementing them. See her book about her retarded daughter, *The Child Who Never Grew* (New York: J. Day Company, 1950).

18. Philip Zimbardo, "On the Ethics of Intervention in Human Psychological Research: With Special Reference to the Stanford Prison Experiment," *Cognition* 2 (2), 1974, pp. 254–255.

19. Philip G. Zimbardo, "Transforming Experimental Research into Advocacy for Social Change," in M. Deutsch and H. A. Hornstein, eds., *Applying Social Psychology* (Hillsdale, NJ: Lawrence Erlbaum Associates, 1975), p. 44.

CHAPTER EIGHT

Practical and Conceptual Problems with Moral Autonomy

■ MORAL AUTONOMY AND HUMAN VIRTUES

As mentioned in the previous chapter, to even talk about autonomy seems a bit paradoxical. What evidence supports the idea that people can develop virtues that will enable them to act in an autonomous fashion? To understand the positive side of an issue, it is often instructive to compare it with its opposite. So, as a way of getting started, I'll review some literature[1] that explains how certain family structures inhibit the development of those virtues that enable autonomous choice. At this point, we will define a family as DYSFUNCTIONAL FROM THE MORAL POINT OF VIEW when 'it produces children with such extreme personality styles that they cannot function as morally autonomous adults on either the rational or the caring dimension'.

Claudia Black[2] argued that dysfunctional family relationships are usually characterized by three rules: (1) don't talk, (2) don't trust, and (3) don't feel. Family structures that lead to such cautious inhibition can have devastating effects on family members, especially those who are still struggling with developmental tasks. For instance, when a family inhibits the ability to develop intimate personal relationships, by extension it will inhibit one's ability to function as a caring member of a community. As adults, members of such families may choose to go along with community norms for prudent reasons, but they may not ever be able to feel loyalty or commitment to community norms.

We can see this most clearly if we look at two extremes on the caring dimension: first, the sociopathic personality, and second, the relational co-dependent personality. Studies of sociopaths teach us the importance of a consistently supportive family or tribal heritage in the background of moral agents. If an abusive home life forces separation and autonomy too soon, it destroys or inhibits the development of an ability to care about social life. Marshall and Barbaree point out that

[With regard to etiology] The same disturbed family interactions and parental mismanagement are observed whether the offender is from a lower-class, middle-class, or

> upper-class background. . . . Not only do the parents . . . use inconsistent discipline, they almost exclusively employ harsh punishment . . . [which makes] feedback irrelevant to the budding psychopath, [and] it also fails to endow the parents (and by generalization other people) with reinforcement value. . . . [The sociopaths] learn by observation to be self-interested and aggressive, and they fail to experience affection, and are not provided with models whereby they might acquire appropriate emotional concern for others. . . . Psychopaths enter an adult world prepared to look after themselves in an exaggeratedly self-interested way.[3]

Children need social support early in life to lay down the foundational structures on which later moral development depends. Once developmental stages are missed, it can be very difficult to undo the consequences. Thus to deny early nurturance is to make a decision that might morally sterilize a segment of the next generation. While an emotionally abusive environment may still allow children to calculate and manipulate, it will not teach them to feel normal human sympathy for others. Without sympathy their calculations will be grossly one-sided. The tragic fact is that because sociopaths (what Marshall and Barbaree call psychopaths) are emotionally flat, they are

> far less responsive to stimuli or events that are emotionally provocative to others, and consequently, psychopaths . . . experience boredom more frequently than others. Boredom, of course, leads individuals to seek excitement, and so we would expect psychopaths to be stimulus seekers. . . . [In studies they] showed a greater preference for frightening and dangerous experiences than did normal subjects. . . .[4]

Unless we solve this problem as a society, we may have to contend with more horrendous examples of sociopaths trying to alleviate their boredom—for example, consider the frightening manifestation of the inability to feel concern for others that is provided by the example of the youths who sought a good time through "wilding," a brutal assault on an innocent victim for no apparent motive other than to relieve boredom (*Time*, May 8, 1989, p. 20). It sometimes seems to me that we excel as a society at producing conditions that promote sociopathic tendencies and then at acting startled when those the culture has abandoned show us how well they have learned.

At the other extreme are co-dependent persons who care so deeply for another (or are so needy) that they lack the ability to make independent decisions. As we saw earlier in Chapter Six, Gilligan's research shows how the unique circumstances of the average woman gives her a strong need for intimate relationships. This might explain why relational co-dependence appears to be more common in women. For my purpose, the following definition from Wegscheider-Cruse's book *Choicemaking* adequately clarifies the general issue. She says that co-dependence is

> a specific condition that is characterized by preoccupation and extreme dependence (emotionally, socially, and sometimes physically) on a person or object. Eventually,

this dependence on another person becomes a pathological condition that affects the co-dependent in all other relationships.[5]

I'll clarify the moral significance of this disorder by discussing it in the context of a common type of shame-based co-dependence. Just as "sociopathic disorder" seems to be primarily a male characteristic, H. Lewis[6] argues that " . . . women's greater sociability and lesser aggression, together with their second-class citizenship in the world of power, increases their tendency to experience shame. . . . Shame is the affective-cognitive state of low self-esteem" (p. 191), and if it is the kind of low self-esteem produced in dysfunctional families it can become so strong as to be maladaptive from the moral point of view. Lewis states:

> Shame is one of our species' inevitable responses to loss of love, whether in early childhood or in old age . . . In order for shame to occur, there must be a relationship between the self and the other in which the self cares about the other's evaluation. . . . This special position of the self as the target of attack makes shame a more acutely painful experience than guilt. . . . Shame is about the self; it is therefore global. Guilt is more specific, being about events or things. Adults regard shame as an "irrational" reaction that is more appropriate to childhood, especially if it occurs outside the context of moral transgression. . . . [S]hame involves a failure of the central attachment bond. This failure evokes rage, as does the painful experience of lost attachment because one is unable to live up to the standards of an admired image. It is the feeling state to which one is more susceptible when one has fallen in love. The "other" is a prominent and powerful force in the experience of shame. . . . In this affective tie, the self does not feel autonomous but dependent and vulnerable to rejection (p. 191f).

When a child is rejected by a parent, the child may develop a vulnerability to shame reactions that are so severe that even in adulthood the reactions will still seem like childish reactions—thus the name "adult child" seems appropriate for some of those who suffer from shame-based co-dependence. To avoid the acute pain of humiliation, and also the guilt that is induced by fits of humiliated rage against the loved person, shame-based co-dependent persons will do almost anything to avoid rejection by a significant other. Their effort to please may overwhelm their ability to maintain moral responsibility. The shame-based co-dependent appears to be extremely vulnerable to charming people with sociopathic personalities who do not hesitate to take advantage of the co-dependent's extreme vulnerability to manipulation (which is due to their immense need to please the sociopath). Sociopaths and the shame-based co-dependents who love them are two extremes on the caring dimension who are capable of uniting in a lethal alliance (for instance, as when the mass murderer Charles Manson teamed up with his emotionally starved runaway girls).

Of course, the discussion so far has been about human traits that we all possess to some degree. There will be times when all of us find it difficult to care about other people, and there will be times when most of us care very much. But when normal human traits are carried to an extreme, they become psychological disorders that can interfere with moral function. Sociopaths and co-dependents both suffer from character disorders that make them reactors rather than autonomous choosers. It is difficult for them to stick to principled conduct, especially in situations calling for intimacy and commitment. They are either cold, uncaring citizens or driven by extreme unreflective needs for affection. Helfer[7] (who works with adults who were abused as children) points out that he has to consistently remind his clients that childhood comes first. Until they go back and master the developmental tasks of childhood and learn to care in a reasonable manner, they cannot expect to break their dysfunctional style of relating to social groups. Unless they learn to rework their past (see the discussion of emotional reeducation below), they will not be prepared to enter adulthood as morally autonomous agents.

It is clear that when certain normal human virtues are missing, it is hard for people to function as autonomous adults. Piaget and Erik Erickson discuss these virtues in depth in their psychological and clinical work.[8] We have already discussed Piaget's theory of cognitive development. (He characterizes the highest intellectual virtue as "thinking about thinking.") Erickson studied the development of emotional virtues. He argued that those that are "basic" develop in the following order: trust or hope, willpower, purpose, competence, fidelity, love, care, and wisdom. When we combine Piaget's cognitive virtues with Erickson's emotional virtues we have developmental achievements that give a person the intellectual capacities to create his own principles as well as the motivation and existential courage to act on them. Acting together these virtues are *emancipatory* when they help people become Socratic in their ability to care about social norms, gain theoretical understanding, and yet critically evaluate both of them.

Hampshire[9] argues that one of the most important of these emancipatory virtues is critical self-reflection. It provides vital skills for resisting both internal and external pressures that interfere with independent, rational moral action. It is irrelevant that this emancipatory virtue may be causally or historically related to a particular kind of socialization, because once acquired it enables persons (with the help of other like-minded persons) to reflect back on, criticize, and then build on their own previous socialization.

Adina Schwartz[10] pointed out that autonomous people not only must choose the *means* to their goals but also must be able to choose the *goals* themselves. But is this possible? If goals involve ultimate foundational feelings, can we really choose them? Do we have to give up our emotional selves, who we are, to become impartial presocial abstract agents who are somehow supposed to be choosers of foundational values? These questions raise some fascinating issues that force us to stop and pull back even further, to take a fresh look at the relationship between feelings, cognition, and autonomous choice.

Schacter and Singer conducted a seminal experiment designed to study the relationship between thoughts and emotions.[11] They told a group of subjects that they were going to be injected with a substance that would improve their vision. After the injection they were asked to wait in a room for about twenty minutes while they filled out a form. In actuality Schacter had injected them with a form of adrenalin that would create a visceral reaction (an emotional state). One group went to fill out their form in a room where a research assistant was waiting with instructions to act like a very happy person (call it the joy room). In another room (the anger room) a person was waiting who was instructed to act very angry. There was also the usual control group. Predictably, depending on which room they were in, the subjects interpreted their reaction to the adrenalin as either joy or anger. This looks like a pure case of situational control. None of the subjects consciously chose the quality of their feelings—they simply reacted first to the drug and then to the cues planted in the environment by the actor. On the basis of this preliminary data, one might conclude that people cannot choose their emotions; they can only have them.

Schacter conducted his experiment again, however, and added a new variable. He told the subjects part of the truth—that the injection would have a visceral side effect, that they would feel hot, a faster heartbeat, jitters, perhaps feel like walking around, and so on. He advised them to ignore the symptoms. This time when the subjects went into the joy and anger rooms they seemed rather immune to the emotional cues planted in their environment. Instead of imitating the quality of emotion displayed by the actors, most of them reported that they were feeling the side effects they were told to expect. Simply by changing their background cognitive state—their beliefs about what they were going to experience—Schacter was apparently able to change the foreground, that is, the quality of their felt emotions.

They were, of course, still subject to situational control because they did not have accurate information about their world, but notice what this means. Schacter's experiment clearly demonstrated that emotional "reactions" to the world are determined by previous history, biology, and current stimuli. But, he also shows that insofar as we can "control how we feel" about our environment, it will be directly correlated with (a) the background belief system we use to interpret the significance of stimuli, and (b) the extent of the knowledge available to help us reflect on our current situation. If we can increase our knowledge and ability to reflect, we can increase our choice of how to feel. If we can also learn to choose our own beliefs, we can then begin to control the quality of our emotional responses. With this greater understanding comes increased freedom to choose emotional states and alter original foundational values (we return to this issue later in the chapter). Again we see that the extent of knowledge is closely correlated with responsibility and moral agency. The need for accurate information and knowledge increases the importance of gaining moral experience and of living in environments that promote honest communication.

■ PERSONAL AUTONOMY AND MORAL AUTONOMY RECONSIDERED

It would be a simple social world if we were all like Socrates. Moral autonomy and personal autonomy would be almost synonymous, so it would be easy to reach universal agreement on how to live. But, full autonomy requires a very complex set of traits that take time to develop. To achieve the kind of personal autonomy that allows us to choose who we want to be, we need abilities that enable us to criticize our own personal preferences. To achieve moral autonomy, we need capacities that enable us to conceive of and care about abstract principles and ideal states of affairs. Since these capacities are all developmental achievements, people will always have differing degrees of both personal and moral autonomy. We will, therefore, always have to live with conflicts between factions that have different opinions about what kind of rules to impose on members of the community. It seems that actual universal autonomous agreement must always remain an ideal.

■ *Political Issues*

The fact that there will be disagreements raises a question about the relationship that ought to exist between lawmakers who are guided by an ideal of moral autonomy and people who, as *legal adults*, have a right to be treated as though they are autonomous even if they are not. Can a notion like moral autonomy be made compatible with a principle of personal autonomy, designed to give legal adults the freedom to choose their own conception of the good? What do we do when there is conflict between the theoretical ideal of moral autonomy (what in theory all rational, caring autonomous people would agree to as principles and rules to regulate their interactions), and the actual choices made by legal adults who are using a principle of personal autonomy to choose their lifestyles?

This contrast is sometimes characterized as a conflict between a theory of value and a theory of obligation. A principle of personal autonomy concerns the right of legal adults to choose their own theory of value. They are free to characterize the good life as they please, that is, choose their own lifestyle, hobbies, relationships, and so forth. On the other hand, the principle of moral autonomy is part of a theory of obligation. It is a principle that places moral boundaries on our other value choices. The question is, how tight or strict a boundary does moral autonomy place on the individual autonomy of legal adults? Which has priority, the principles that follow from the ideal of moral autonomy, or the actual choices of autonomous individuals concerning their own conceptions of the good? What if a legally autonomous adult makes a lifestyle choice that appears to contradict how we think morally autonomous people would ideally act (e.g., what if he wants to commit suicide, or take heroin, or smoke cigarettes, or get drunk every night, or gamble, or watch football all day)? What else can respect for autonomy mean if it does not mean I can choose my own good, even if foolishly?

When a choice of the good life affects other people, the choice needs to be measured against the obligations that come with the concept of moral autonomy. Moral autonomy is a virtue that is conceptually linked to humanity's social nature. It does not refer to a kind of anarchistic autonomy that says each person is an island or law unto himself who can do whatever he wants no matter what. Thus, social and legal compulsion of autonomous individuals may be justified when there are good reasons to believe the legislation ought to be consented to by all moral agents. Each case would have to be decided in context, but as a general rule we can say: "Legislators do not have the right to infringe on the choices of legal adults, unless they can show their intervention constitutes the kind of boundary infringement on choice that would be universally consented to by morally autonomous agents who were living in that social context."

This rule acknowledges that there are instances where it will be justifiable to interfere with a legal adult's actions even though he disagrees with the intervention. For example, legislators can insist that people obey a 55 mph speed limit or be taxed on gasoline if such policies are consistent with what morally autonomous people might agree to during an energy crisis to protect mutual autonomy for all. Obviously, most of the moral dilemmas we are concerned with arise precisely because reasonable people can occasionally disagree about what constitutes a lifestyle compatible with moral autonomy. If nothing else, a principle of personal autonomy for legal adults puts the burden of proof on those who want to interfere with the choices adults are making.

Even if autonomous people agree on an initial policy, we still will have problems. For example, what do we do if an apparently autonomous person changes her mind and contradicts her first choice? Do we follow her first declaration or her second one? At the parole board hearing in the Zimbardo Prison Experiment, all but two of the prisoners said that they were willing to forfeit all the money they had earned in order to buy a parole. Why didn't they just quit? Zimbardo said "they could not [quit] because their sense of reality had undergone a transformation. They did not have the power to choose to leave the experiment because it was no longer an experiment to them." Who do we listen to, the original rational volunteer, or the prisoner desperate for a parole?

This draws our attention to a very important issue. Someone capable of giving autonomous consent at one point in time may not give the same consent at another point in time. What do we do? Do we assume his old self is authentic or his new self? Since subjects in an experiment have a right to withdraw, Zimbardo should listen to the most current wish. But many situations are not this simple. For example, what if I sign a document saying I do not want to be put on a life support respirator but then demand to be put on one later? What if I agree to a lasting marriage, and then change my mind after trying it out for a few years? We are unable to answer these tough questions here, but they can make us aware that showing respect for autonomy will not make ethical dilemmas disappear. Ideals are only guides to conduct; they cannot tell us ahead of time what to do in each particular case. Decision makers will have to deal with each case in context, being guided by the moral principles that seem most enlightened at the time.

Although the concept of moral autonomy cannot tell us exactly what to do, it does focus our attention on relevant human values that should play a role in decision making. In addition, this norm makes at least one thing explicitly clear. In this theoretical framework, moral autonomy is not just another value; given that we are required to live in pluralistic cultures, it seems to be essential to responsible moral choice and should have the highest priority (assuming we do not want to return to tribal forms of existence). Respect for moral autonomy helps us focus on some of the worst harms that ought to be avoided at all costs—harms that either destroy (e.g., like starvation or brainwashing) or inhibit (e.g., like learning deprivation or indoctrination) the development of the capacities for moral autonomy.

■ Paternalistic Interventions

Even if a morally autonomous person can decide issues for herself, she must still ask, "How should I treat other people who are dependent on my decisions but who do not themselves have complete moral autonomy?" (because they either lost it or didn't develop it in the first place). That is, what obligations do those with high degrees of moral autonomy have to those who are low in capacity?

When dealing with agents who are not legally autonomous (e.g., children or the mentally impaired) most people agree that a fair degree of PATERNALISM is justified. Paternalism means that 'we make decisions for others, for their own good, even if they do not agree with our intervention on their behalf'. While paternalism is in direct conflict with a principle of individual autonomy for legal adults, nonetheless, practical considerations often require us to decide for other legal adults (perhaps they are ill, temporarily insane, in a state of ignorance or duress, etc.) When we decide for either group (children or adults), we should not forget the ideals expressed by the background notion of moral autonomy.

One way to do this is to ask what would they consent to if they could give morally autonomous consent. The same idea was expressed by Dworkin when he said we should use an idea of "future oriented consent,"[12] that is, what would they consent to in the future when they better understand their position? When I was working as an ethicist in a hospital, a physician told me that the idea of consent was farcical, because he could get a patient to consent to anything. But his power over the patient is not the main issue. The issue is: does he take a background right to give consent seriously as an ideal? If he does, then he will see it as placing boundaries around his professional interventions. He would then also strive to make it work rather than play games with it. The point is, when practical necessities require us to be paternalistic with people who are dependent on us, we must always make our decisions on the basis of "what the person will come to welcome, rather than on what he does welcome now."[13]

Even with this kind of guiding background conception, however, it is still not easy to make the right choice for those who are not autonomous. For example, do I decide for them on the basis of their current preferences and project into the future what I think they will want, that is, what they would come to want if they were rational autonomous persons but were starting with their current preferences? (But wouldn't they have different preferences if they were rational autonomous people?) Or should I try to do for them what I think any rational autonomous person would want done, whether they currently prefer that or not? (Let's set aside for the moment that in complex cases, it is possible that morally autonomous people might not be able to agree in any case. Sometimes continued debate is the only option.) It seems to me that I must do both. I must take account of their current preferences (and leave them alone if they are not immoral or insane), but I must also ask idealized questions about their future as well, that is, what their preferences would probably look like if they were autonomous, or will look like once they become autonomous. Of course, it is presumptuous on the one hand to assume we could know what people would consent to, but in many caretaking contexts we don't have much choice. Practical life requires us to presume we know what they would want.

If an intervention might change a person's preferences (developmental effect), the change ought to be for the better from the point of view of moral autonomy. After we are certain of this point, we can rely on a theory of the good in order to fine-tune our interventions. We have to ask, based on a theory of human needs, preferences, and cultural conditions, "How would they want to be treated now, if they could make the decision for themselves? When I'm done educating, raising, giving therapy, rehabilitating, or experimenting, will they be left with preferences that are compatible both with who they are now as well as with the ideal of moral autonomy? If not with who they are now, is that because who they are now is immoral or clearly insane or maladaptive? If not, then maybe I should not intervene." None of these questions are easy to answer, and of course particular cases would need to be historically situated. However, although the whole approach is very abstract, it is conceptually coherent to ask the questions, and trying to answer them in an honest, committed way can make us more sensitive during our interventions into one another's lives.

■ SQUARING AUTONOMY WITH PERSONAL HISTORY

As we saw above, the concept of autonomy is fraught with difficulties. Can the concept of autonomy (on either the moral or personal level) ever serve as more than a hypothesized, idealized abstraction that presupposes an individualistic conception of human nature? If there is not some way to make the concept relevant to our concrete life experiences, then we cannot expect people to take it seriously.

Chapter Four briefly discussed Gadamer's claim that all human conceptions are bounded by historical prejudice. He is primarily arguing that systems of knowledge grow out of previous historical contexts. His main point, which is well worth making, is that there is no transcendent, objective perspective outside of history that can give us a fresh perspective on our own tradition. This position also has a clear implication about the limits of individual autonomy. Because individual beliefs, indeed, our whole way of thinking, are a product of historical context, individuals (by themselves) can never step outside of their historical moment to achieve an independent perspective. Every change in consciousness will only be an event caused by the historical forces at work at that moment. Since we do not choose or control these forces ourselves, we cannot be autonomous in any significant sense. This means that individuals are events, historical moments, rather than actors in history. Gadamer says:

> In fact history does not belong to us, but we belong to it. Long before we understand ourselves through the process of self-examination, we understand ourselves in a self-evident way in the family, society and state in which we live. The focus of subjectivity is a distorting mirror. The self-awareness of the individual is only a flickering in the closed circuits of historical life. That is why the prejudices of the individual, far more than his judgments constitute the historical reality of his being.[14]

A "flickering" of self-awareness does not leave much room for autonomy. According to this conception, history makes decisions for us, like a parent who welcomes a child into an already fully formed social context. It would be absurd for a parent to tell a child to make fully formed, wise decisions for herself about who she wants to be. The child has little to work with, so parents socialize her to have skills that will help her function as a member of a historical tradition—family, religion, community, nation. A child cannot get outside of herself to become her own parent. Gadamer is pointing out that adults also cannot get outside of themselves to become their own history. We cannot be more enlightened than who we historically are. There is a strangeness, then, to the idea that an autonomous person is going to make decisions about who he is going to be, as though he could function as his own tradition. Thus, a historically determined perspective is helpful like a parent, since it provides the background tradition that chooses for the less enlightened or historically incompetent.

For Gadamer, the question "Who do I want to be?" can't be answered by looking into the future and searching for an ideal conception of the good life. Wallulis argues that Gadamer's method is retrospective and reconstructive. Even if we do look into the future, how we look will be determined (not just influenced) by where we have been in the past. With respect to a philosophy of consciousness, Gadamer's whole approach emphasizes a "happening or event" structure for man rather than an "action" structure.[15] That is, the structure of consciousness is like something that happens to us; it is not like something that is a matter of choice or something we achieve. To become self-conscious is to become aware of the human predicament of historical determination. This means self-consciousness is a consciousness of human limitation, as was the first phase in Schacter's experiment where the people were reacting to the joy and anger rooms.

On the other hand, Habermas argues that there is an active agency structure to consciousness, since once a self-reflective observing ego develops, it becomes possible to achieve a measure of personal emancipation from historical origins. Habermas's thinking is still in the process of evolution, and it is not clear what his final position will be. In his early work *Knowledge and Human Interest,* [16] he argued that Freud's theory of psychoanalysis provided a good practical example of self-emancipation through awakened self-understanding. During therapy the client remembers repressed material and develops a new reflective self-understanding that allows him to reappropriate a part of his life history that had been lost to his conscious self because of repression. This contributes to self-emancipation, since it eliminates unconscious controls that inhibit his ability to live a self-directed life. In the working alliance that develops between client and therapist there is a strengthening of the capacity for self-determination or autonomy on the part of the client. Habermas is arguing that the self-conscious appropriation of our past by our reflective observing ego can be part of a process of developmental enlightenment. In a clever restatement of Freud, Wallulis summarizes Habermas's position as: "If Freud says, 'Where id was, there ego shall be,' the famous statement may be reformulated to read, 'Where a disturbed process of socialization and of personal self-formation was, there successful socialization and independent personal identity shall be.' "[17]

Gadamer, of course, explicitly argues against Habermas's faith in the power of self-reflection. He believes the consciousness of history is not an achievement of our surpassing our history through critical self-reflection, but rather an experience that reveals our human finitude. It simply increases our awareness of being conditioned by history.

In response to such criticisms, Habermas turned to Piaget's developmental work. The concept of formal operational thinking shows how we can think about thinking, evaluate our mode of evaluation, and formulate a hypothesis about our own modes of living. Habermas was impressed with the emancipatory implications of this ability to form a hypothesis about the human condition, so he introduced hypothetical thinking into the social, interactive realm as a crucial breakthrough in human emancipation. In particular, it makes room for moral autonomy, because we can *hypothesize* what it would be like to live in a society with universal moral ideals. [18]

Of course, a person's historically determined past will influence the individual's hypothesis, but this influence itself gets focused on, so that it in turn becomes a topic that is critically, self-reflectively discussed in interactions with others. In this way we are self-consciously created over again in and through self-conscious social interactions. Notice that to build a new self we have to be engaged in social interactions, but the self does not have to be seen as an event in social history. As an active conscious participant in its own social development, the self-reflective ego creates the new social interactions on purpose.

How might this work? As we saw in Chapter Three when we discussed tribal ethics, normally an individual unconsciously builds the social content in his identity by introjecting the collective historical identity that makes up the content of his social tradition. In this way, the social tradition functions as a dominant "established objectivity"[19] that is introjected into each person. But under conditions of pluralism and reflective honest communication, it is possible that a new self-conscious ego identity can arise that can achieve a degree of detachment from these prior introjected historical roles. This allows for a new, higher level of social interaction, which is inherently self-reflective and thus self-critical. The "ego" identity of an adult reaches greater degrees of maturity and acknowledges itself by exercising its ability to construct or hypothesize new ideal social identities for itself.[20] At the same time the observing ego simultaneously integrates the hypothesized ideal options with its past historically socialized sense of identity. Because it is built on the formal conditions of rationality, this new ego identity can serve as the basis for a new universal social identity.

A social identity that is built on universal content cannot be articulated in the contents of any particular historical world view, since it by definition is universal and therefore transcends particular contexts. Habermas says that a new universal social "identity can also no longer be that of association or memberships," because membership is itself shaped by the local conditions of a particular group, and the new ego identity is conceived of as belonging to a universal community.[21] But because a universal community is only a formal concept (due to practical limitations of reality and thus experience), this new universally oriented ego identity can only be conceived of by looking into the future and hypothesizing it as the "new identity of an as yet emergent global society."[22] (As we shall see in Chapter Ten, this is very similar to the way in which Kant uses the notion of a "kingdom of ends" as a regulatory ideal to help us judge current historical social arrangements.)

At the highest level of ego development, then (in a situation of interactive honest communication with the observing ego of reflective others), choices of moral values are not to be made on the basis of a union with a past tradition but on the basis of a projected future universal community. This is the source of our capacity for moral autonomy. In ethics we are governed by the logic of "ought," which is future-oriented. The intellectual transition that takes place represents a movement from being someone with an ego that has been structured by a concrete, historical role identity to being someone with an ego that can realize its own moral identity insofar as it can hypothesize transcendent ideals. This carries with it a change of orientation from the past toward the future, and so, at least where moral choice is concerned, we do have a significant kind of moral autonomy.

According to Wallulis, however, Habermas's recent work shows he has some doubts about the concept of personal autonomy. Because a person has a literal past, personal autonomy does not make as much sense as does moral autonomy. That is, a person is living a history, she is not a hypothesized ideal interactive community. Habermas says:

> At the level of ego identity a person understands himself in a different way, namely, by answering the question, who or what kind of person he wants to be. In place of the orientation of the past, we have an orientation to the future, which makes it possible for the past to become a problem. . . . An autonomous conduct of life depends in turn

on the decision—or on successively repeated and revised decisions—as to "who one wants to be." . . . In any case, the answer to the question, who does one want to be, cannot be rational in the way that a moral decision can. . . . There is an indissoluble element of arbitrariness in the choice of a life project. This is to be explained by the fact that the individual cannot adopt a hypothetical attitude toward his own origins and background, that he cannot accept or reject his biography in the same way as he can a norm [moral principle] whose claim to validity is under discussion.[23]

This latter point seems to make room for Gadamer's emphasis on our being limited by our history. Habermas's explanation for the impossibility of adopting a hypothetical attitude toward our own past depends on his background assumption that "the life conduct of an individual is entwined with the life-form of the collectivity to which he belongs."[24] The choice of a lifestyle is not, then, a moral question about ideal principles that ought to regulate ideal communities, it is an evaluative question about the particularities of a specific life with its tastes and goals and desires. These particularities are not accessible to rational discussion; they are determined by having lived in a tradition. Hence the hypothetical attitude of the universal moral reasoner seems to be both impossible and inappropriate. Habermas says:

> Whether the life-form of a collectivity has turned out more or less "well," has more or less "succeeded," may be a general question we can direct at every form of life, but it is more like a clinical request to judge a patient's mental or spiritual condition than a moral question concerning a norm's or institutional system's worthiness to be recognized.[25]

We cannot judge the nonmoral value of a way of life we have not lived. We are outsiders if we didn't live a way of life, since what is past is past. That is, we cannot give ourself the historical experiences that would have made us members of a tradition we did not live, nor can we change our own past to become a different historical product. The past is a problem for autonomy, since it makes it nonsense for a person to ask "who do I want to be" in any sense of having options that are not already provided by his own lived historical context.

A theory of obligation (morality) can be saved from relativism by its universality, the hypothetical nature of "ought," and the human capacity to use formal operational thinking to hypothesize ideal moral relations. This capacity makes it possible to engage in meaningful cross-cultural moral judgments if they are based on hypothesized universal ideals. But a theory of value about what constitutes a good life, about what I might personally want to be in nonmoral contexts, can only be asked in a form determined by my own historical and cultural context. It looks as though we are stuck with Gadamer's happening structure. There is a basic limitation on personal self-consciousness and choice of nonmoral values, because we can't hypothesize in any significant sense a new past for ourselves. Our past is over with, it is impossible to live some other heritage so as to give ourselves a different history.

■ *The Possibility of Emotional Reeducation*

Since it appears that the only way to judge the nonmoral value of a way of life is by making a kind of clinical judgment about whether it seems satisfactory to those who have lived it, I will end this conceptual debate by drawing on a clinical model that suggests there may be other options. The work of Albert and Diane Pesso has led to a method of emotional reeducation that can enable people to take up a hypothetical perspective toward their own past. Their work suggests that people can choose to be other than who they historically are if they can create a setting that will enable them to redo their socialization in a way that creates new memories of the past. This sounds absurd. What kind of setting are we talking about?

It would have to be a setting that could help an ego choose to alter the physical, emotional, and intellectual effects created by its own past. Insofar as personal development also depends on social interaction, the setting would have to allow the ego to control new social interactions with significant others. Because this latter step would require others to give up their own autonomy in order to be of service to someone going through emotional reeducation, the setting would require the immoral use of others unless it was part of a voluntary community designed for this purpose. Finally, the setting would have to activate the formal operational thinking capacities the ego needs to take charge of the setting. Therapists usually refer to this state of consciousness as having an active "observing ego." But the ego has to do more than observe, it must also remember, compare and contrast, experience, judge, hypothesize, and choose. A trained leader could facilitate the process, but out of respect for autonomy a leader would have to follow the lead of the person doing the work and never impose a personal agenda.

Pesso's therapeutic design satisfies all of these conditions through an artfully constructed social, emotional, learning laboratory called a structure. Participants volunteer to take turns making themselves available to one another's self-critical reflective ego. This allows each of them to have a turn controlling the process that facilitates their own emotional reeducation. We do not have space to outline the details of a structure, so I will only highlight the main purpose behind this clinical model.

> A structure is a controlled, organized psychotherapeutic/symbolic event that includes the restructuring of past emotional reactions and expressions during significant historical moments which resulted in the creation of important life channeling patterns (filter and gate biases [in the nervous system]). In a structure, all the unprocessed energy (information) that has been stored in the central nervous system (and therefore in the body) as symptoms are given access to conscious experience and expression, are given names, and allowed to have significance and meaning attached to them. Further, a structure includes the creation of a new symbolic event to provide those kinds of essential, countershaping interactions via the use of role-playing ideal

figures who provide antidotal behavior to counteract the toxic behavior of the original negative figures.[26]

The agenda for the first two-thirds of a structure is to get in touch with the kind of personal historical material emphasized by Gadamer. All the genetic and historical material stored in the individual is brought to the surface and externalized, (with the aid of others who role-play historical voices from the person's past). Once the past is externalized, the self-reflective ego can easily contemplate it. A structure always ends with an attempt to antidote any negative material that has been revealed during this initial exploration of the past. A proper antidote is arrived at by hypothesizing alternative pasts to see what kind of experience would have led to a more satisfying personality constellation. When a hypothesized antidote is chosen, the ego then selects ideal figures to role-play elements of the hypothesized past. This allows the ego to have a literal, affectively loaded symbolic experience of the hypothesized alternative past, creating synthetic memories that antidote the emotional effects of previous memories stored during our personal history. An antidote does not eliminate previous memories, it merely creates new synthetic memories that compete with old memories for our attention. This provides us with new options so that we do not have to feel or behave in the same old way that was determined by our literal history.

At this point a brief example may help. Suppose that someone had been physically abused by her father. Suppose this early experience created a general mistrust of adult males. Must this person live with mistrust (or hatred) for the rest of her life? The goal of much traditional counseling is to stimulate emotional relief and new insight through talk, with the hope of teaching new, nonmaladaptive ways to deal with the pain and anger. If public talk and guidance can reduce tension caused by having denied the past, this is a good first step. But it is not the same thing as taking autonomous control of one's being. If a person could control a setting that would allow her to go back and symbolically reexperience a new relationship with an ideal father, then she would be liberated to an even greater degree from her real personal history. For her to entertain this idea, she will have to begin a process of speculation about what an ideal father would have been like in her actual past. This will require a hypothesis about a past possibility that if experienced would help create a new self. When the idea is sufficiently formed, the ego chooses ideal figures to creatively structure (with the aid of the leader) the conditions that will enable her to symbolically experience the alternative ideal father, so as to create new synthetic memories that can serve as the foundations of a new chosen self. Of course, her initial hypothesis about an ideal father will itself be a reflection of her personal history. But this is true only in the initial experience of a structure. Having new synthetic memories can open up new possibilities for a second and third round that will be determined by her own evolving aware ego. Pesso insists that attempts to create synthetic memories must be done with ideal figures. An antidote is not an attempt to reexperience the actual past or redo the experience with the actual father to make the real father conform to the ego's wishes. The point is to get on with a new life, not spend energy trying to fix the people from the old one. Pesso says:

> The combination of support and care offered by the therapist and the group (combined with the techniques) lend themselves to the creation of a level of consciousness where the memory and affect [emotion] of past conditioning events can be made alive and visible in the room. It is a kind of symbolic time machine that allows clients to visit the past, live it out fully, and then provide themselves and their memory systems with a synthetic piece of memory. This synthetic memory will be laid down in the psychic domain beside the memory of the original events. This provides the client with an alternative set of "facts" to create new views and attitudes toward the outside world and of the self. Thus when new present events are met which evoke the inhibition causing memories of the past, the new symbolic memories created by the structure will also be evoked, because they have been placed beside the earlier ones and they too will have an effect on the filters and gates [in the nervous system that determine] performance and selectivity. It is as if their observing ego as an adult is in an alliance with the therapist and the group to provide the child with experience of this new more satisfying, more validating interaction. [27]

Since this clinical approach shows us a technique that we can use to experiment with different ways of being, it gives us a background clinical context from which to say that one can choose to alter the threads of the social tradition that made one. Again, in a structure,

> . . . while the old event is made visible so that unfinished affect [emotion] and expression can finally take place, a parallel counter event takes place which would allow those developmental needs to be satisfied which might not have been satisfied in the first place. . . . [Past experience] having given rise to an image of the world and the self that is negative and life suppressing, [it] is recorded in the memory and affects the functioning of the filters and gates [in the nervous system] now and in the future. That image is called a map, which others may call the memorized Gestalt. The new ideal image creates a new map which is laid down, so to speak, beside the old one. . . . With the new map (expanded filters and gates [which the self created]), new experiences become more possible and more parts of the self are expressible. Belief in the future— hope and anticipation—is enhanced. [28]

Pesso's work shows how our personal historical situation does not have to be out of reach of our autonomous control, because it is possible to experience a hypothesis about our past—increasingly so as we become more skilled with the method. If symbolic interaction can alter the places where the past is stored in the body and in memory, then in this way, the guiding self-reflective autonomous ego (that was a mere Gadamerian flicker in the face of history) can become a bright flame of autonomy illuminating possible pasts and futures. Of course, in most clinical uses of the Pesso process, one is not going this far, one is instead trying to help clients experience satisfaction of old needs so that they can begin to function in a different way in their current life. I am only suggesting that the logic of the method suggests that there is no reason one cannot use the technique to explore radically new options in life. Acceptable new options, of course, must fall within the ethical boundaries set by the prior notion of moral autonomy. Pesso's system has considerable ethical integrity since it has moral constraints built into the procedure itself. [29] Because of the social nature of the process, and the moral rules on how to proceed, one cannot use the techniques to construct an immoral personality constellation without first choosing to intentionally abuse the process.

The new affectively loaded memories are of course synthetic in the sense that they are not literal past experiences. They happened under the gaze of the observing ego with the aide of helpful others who suspended their own historical agendas for a time. But the symbolically created memories play the same role in our life as those laid down by a literal history, thus even though they are synthetic they are a functional remapping of our history. However, this time our memories are laid down on purpose, after engaging in formal operational reflection on hypothetical alternatives. That is, the memories that help determine our choice of lifestyle are a result of our own choice. Because history can be suspended in this clinical setting, we create a possibility sphere that is not as historically determined by outside forces as is an actual community, giving new meaning to the concept of personal autonomy.

The fact that people can do this sort of thing if they choose is morally significant. It enhances the respect and awe we feel for the power of individuals to become someone of their own making. Since it is done with the help of others, it also increases our appreciation for the interdependent, social nature of even autonomous humanity. It adds fuel to the desire to create conditions that will further not only moral autonomy but also the personal autonomy that makes lifestyle choice an option.

Since transcendent moral and personal ideals are discovered (or created) during theoretical discussions, some people say they are only abstractions and not real. What a philosophical orientation to values helps us to remember is that all ethical norms were once merely part of someone's ideal conception. It is by acting on theoretical ideals that we improve and modify the actual concrete environment. They become concrete reality when people live them, but to live them consciously we have to understand the role they play in moral life. Philosophical theories help us to transcend concrete situational variables that can trap us into living unreflective, institutional lives. Without the intellectual possibilities generated by philosophical theories, there would be no freedom, moral autonomy would be fantasy, and Socrates' life could not inspire us to seek greater understanding. In the next two chapters, we will analyze the theoretical context of five major principles that have been advocated by autonomous people in Western cultures.

■ STUDY QUESTIONS

1. Why do people from morally dysfunctional homes often lack emancipatory virtues?
2. What are the two extreme poles on the caring dimension? Why does each represent a moral character disorder?
3. What are emancipatory virtues? Why are formal operational thinking skills crucial to emancipation?
4. What is the significance of Schacter's experiment about the relationship between cognition and emotion?
5. Why is there potential for conflict between personal autonomy and the ideal of moral autonomy? What is a plausible way to establish priorities on this issue?
6. When dealing with paternalistic decisions for those who lack autonomy, what kind of guiding questions should we be asking?
7. What is the major disagreement between Gadamer and Habermas with regard to the human situation?
8. Why does Habermas believe we can have moral autonomy but not personal autonomy?
9. In what way does Pesso's clinical theory suggest that there may be a solution to Habermas's doubts about personal autonomy?

■ NOTES

1. Much of the material in the following pages is adapted from David Cooper, "The Dysfunctional Family, Ethics, and the State," in Robert C. L. Moffat, Joseph Grcic, Michael D. Bayles, eds., *Perspectives on the Family* (New York: The Edwin Mellen Press, 1990).

2. Claudia Black, *It Will Never Happen To Me* (Denver: M.A.C., 1981).

3. W. L. Marshall and A. F. Barbaree, "Disorders of Personality, Impulse, and Adjustment," in S. Turner and M. Hersen, eds., *Adult Psychopathology and Diagnosis* (New York: John Wiley and Sons, 1984), pp. 422–429.

4. Ibid., p. 422.

5. Sharon Wegschneider-Cruse, *Choicemaking* (Pompano Beach, FL: Health Communications, 1985), p. 2. For a psychoanalytic discussion of this disorder, see Timmen L. Cermak, *Diagnosing and Treating Co-Dependence* (Minneapolis: Johnston Institute Books, 1986).

6. H. B. Lewis, "The Role of Shame in Depression in Women," in R. Furmanch and A. Gurian, eds., *Women and Depression* (New York: Springer, 1987), p. 191.

7. Ray Helfer, *Childhood Comes First* (East Lansing, MI: KEMPE National Center, 1978).

8. Erick Erickson, *Childhood and Society* (New York: W. W. Norton & Company, 1963), p. 274. Also see Jean Piaget, *Six Psychological Studies* (New York: 1968), p. 63.

9. Stuart Hampshire, "Prediction, Decision, and Freedom of Action," in Leslie Stevenson, ed., *The Study of Human Nature* (Oxford: Oxford University Press, 1981), pp. 297–310; and the recent text by Jerald Wallulis, *The Hermeneutics of Life History: Personal Achievement and History in Gadamer, Habermas, and Erickson* (Evanston, IL: Northwestern University Press, 1990).

10. Adina Schwartz, "Autonomy and the Workplace," in Tom Regan, ed., *Just Business: New Introductory Essays in Business Ethics* (New York: Random House, 1984), pp. 129–166.

11. S. Schacter & J. Singer, "Cognitive, Social and Physiological Determinants of Emotional State," *Psychological Review*, 69, 1962, pp. 379–399. What causes human emotion is a complex issue, and Schacter and Singer have their critics. But, it seems to me that they have demonstrated clearly that the quality of our emotional states is linked also to cognitive variables and not only to physiological variables.

12. Gerald Dworkin, "Paternalism," in Richard Wasserstrom, ed., *Morality and the Law* (Belmont, CA: Wadsworth Publishing Co., 1971), p. 119.

13. Ibid.

14. Hans-Georg Gadamer, in Garrett Barden and John Cumming, eds., *Truth and Method* (New York: Seabury, 1975).

15. Wallulis, Chapter One. Much of the following account of the evolution of Habermas thought is taken from Wallulis's interpretation.

16. Jürgen Habermas, *Knowledge and Human Interest*, transl. by Jeremy J. Shapiro (Boston: Beacon Press, 1971), Chapter Ten.

17. Wallulis, p. 52.

18. Jürgen Habermas, *Communication and the Evolution of Society*, transl. by Thomas McCarthy (Boston: Beacon Press, 1979), pp. 100–101, 109–111, and Chapter Two.

19. Wallulis, p. 80.

20. Jürgen Habermas, in R. Dobert, J. Habermas, and C. Nunner-winkler, eds., *Die Entwicklungdes Ich* (Cologne: Kiepenhever & Witsch, 1977), p. 11, as cited in Wallulis, p. 75.

21. Jürgen Habermas, "On Social Identity," *Telos*, 19 (1974), p. 99.

22. Ibid., p. 100.

23. Jürgen Habermas, *The Theory of Communicative Action. Volume Two. Lifeworld and System: A Critique of Functionalist Reason*, transl. by Thomas McCarthy (Boston: Beacon Press, 1987), pp. 106 and 109, as cited in Wallulis, p. 83b.

24. Ibid., p. 110, as cited in Wallulis, p. 84.

25. Ibid., p. 109, as cited in Wallulis, p. 86.

26. Albert Pesso and Han Wassenaar, "The Relationship Between Pesso System/Psychomotor Therapy and a Neurobiological Model," in Albert Pesso and John Crandell, eds., *Moving Psychotherapy* (Cambridge, MA: Brookline Books, 1991), p. 38.

27. Ibid., p. 40.

28. Ibid., p. 40.

29. See my paper, "Professional Ethics and Pesso System/Psychomotor Therapy," presented at the First International Meeting on Pesso System/Psychomotor Therapy, Amsterdam, Holland, June 10–13, 1992, published in *Pesso Bulletin*, 2nd Vol., Summer, 1992 (Oosterbroek 5, 9761TG Eelde, Holland).

CHAPTER NINE

Ideal Theory: A Consequentialist Background

The five major theories mentioned in Chapter One divide into two types—consequentialist theories and nonconsequentialist theories. This chapter discusses the consequentialist approach, the next chapter the nonconsequentialist approach. Keep one thing in mind during our review of these theories. Philosophical frameworks are very complex. Thus, our discussion will only scratch the surface of the technical aspects of these theories. However, the discussion should be adequate enough to give the reader a good idea about the kind of background context that is provided by each theory.

The best way to understand an ethical theory is to study how it develops its major principle. A principle focuses our attention on relevant variables that ought to serve as a reason for acting. Efficiency, power, rights, glory, self-interest, wealth, justice, agreements, benevolence, love, hate, profit, friendship, respect for persons, duty, happiness, and envy are all variables that can influence action. Which are the most relevant variables for guiding ethical judgment? Theories want us to give priority to the variables that follow from their foundational principles.

■ CONSEQUENTIALISTS NEED A THEORY OF VALUE

Egoism and utilitarianism are called CONSEQUENTIALIST theories, because 'what ought to be done is determined by looking at the various options to see how much nonmoral value or "good" is promoted by each option'. These theories need to develop a THEORY OF VALUE that can 'clarify what is good in life, determine what goals should be pursued, and help us pick the best means to the goals'. On this approach, morality is a means to an end. It is a system of principles and rules designed to help facilitate the pursuit of those things that the theory of value indicates are worth pursuing. This means the theory of value has logical priority over the theory of obligation, since we can't develop a complete theory of obligation until we know what goods to pursue.

Theories of value turn out to be quite complicated. Even if I try to stay simple and assert that "good" means any consequence that satisfies my interests, complications immediately arise. It does not take much experience to realize that "what we have an interest in" is not necessarily the same as "what is in our interest." Children often have no interest in school, but with our broader understanding we know it is actually in their interest to go to school. It is always possible for people to be mistaken about what is good for them, thus before we can design moral systems to further our interests, we need to discover what is actually in our interest.

■ Prudence

A PRUDENT person 'makes wise decisions about how he should live'. Because he is interested in his *best* interest, he will search for a useful theory of value that can give him a perspective about how to establish priorities and resolve conflicts when his interests conflict.

HEDONISM is one very common theory of value. The hedonist claims that 'above all else, people want to be happy. Since pleasure is the essential constituent property of a happy life, we ought to pursue it'. Each pleasure is like a moment of happiness and all of them together make up a happy life. There is no obvious reason we can give for saying why we value pleasure. Its value is simply an obvious fact of experience. Something of this nature is called an INTRINSIC GOOD, because 'it is valued for its own sake'. There is no way to prove intrinsic goods; the proof is in the experience of the thing itself. "Pleasure is good," the hedonist will say, "and that is just the way it is." Likewise, experience tells us directly that pain is intrinsically bad. It is not bad because it is not useful (in fact, a little pain may be very useful when it tells us what to avoid); it is experienced as bad on an immediate intuitive level, and that too is just the way it is.

On the other hand, EXTRINSIC GOODS are 'those things we value because they are useful for getting other things that we value'. It is easy to give reasons why an extrinsic good has value—we simply point to the other goods that it brings us. Pleasure is intrinsic, and something like money is extrinsic (we want money for the sake of something else, e.g., the pleasure it can buy).

Consequentialists say extrinsic goods have UTILITY. Utility is 'the quality in a thing that contributes to its value; for example, if we are hedonists, the utility of an object depends on how much it contributes either to pleasure or to the avoidance of pain'. In theory we can calculate a thing's extrinsic value by adding up how much utility it has. In a similar manner, DISUTILITY refers to 'the properties in a thing that either create pain or deprive us of anticipated pleasures'. The more pain produced, the more disutility the object has. The prudent consequentialist will, therefore, try to maximize utility and minimize disutility.

How do we measure the amount of utility? Profit and loss calculations are often very rough, since there is not always a clear quantitative standard (like money) that can be used to guide judgments about utilities. We have to rely on personal experience, intuition, and the meaning system of the relevant group. We must also decide: should we delay gratification and strive for long-term utility, or should we design institutions to bring immediate rewards? Another complication: should I make tradeoffs between kinds of goods, for example, like a trade between freedom and money? The prisoners in the Zimbardo experiment did this. All but two of them regretted it. Would they give freedom more utility after this experience or give the other values less?

Such calculations are difficult because there are qualitative differences between kinds of pleasures. The quality of a thing's value shifts depending on how central it is to our way of life. How much weight (both in terms of intrinsic pleasure and extrinsic money) should I give to something like my love for my child? For most parents, a child is so important in their life that it seems ridiculous to even think in comparative utilitarian terms. These thorny issues can complicate calculations that look relatively simple. Consequentialists will need a sophisticated theory of value to help them deal with these issues. Economists sometimes duck these difficult issues by leaving choice of values up to consumer preferences. But are the things consumers have an interest in always in their interest? The question remains: "How should a prudent consequentialist measure utility and balance different kinds of utilities in order to construct a good life plan?"

■ Standards for Choosing Our Best Interests

What standard should a prudent consequentialist use when making choices about value? For instance, the Federal Trade Commission,[1] in order to deal with practical problems about value choices in the real marketplace, has vacillated between using a "rational man standard," a "reasonable man standard," and an "ignorant man standard" for judging the appropriateness of advertising. As we saw earlier, the best way to understand the difference between reasonable and rational standards is to contrast "the man in the street" with "the man in the jury box." A man in the street often acts on introjected feelings and standardized social norms. Since he does not thoroughly investigate all the details of a decision, he may need protection from unscrupulous advertising. A person on a jury, however, can take the time to deliberate and can make use of expert testimony. If everyone acted according to the rational man standard, then perhaps no one would make foolish tradeoffs like those between freedom and money. We would only need a few protective rules in the marketplace. On the other hand, the IGNORANT MAN STANDARD tells us to be very cautious in designing our institutions; because ignorant 'people who make careless and foolish value choices need to be protected from themselves'.

How much care consequentialists use in designing policies to promote utility will probably depend on both their confidence in people's abilities to reflect and how crucial various decisions are to their overall well-being. REAL WILL THEORY tells us to 'design institutions so that they reflect the way real people do in fact choose to satisfy their interests'. How do real people choose? When ultimate values like life are at stake, they will want the rational man standard used (as in a jury trial). If it is a matter of taste of some importance (such as choosing a new car), they do not have to be so cautious, thus they can calculate like a reasonable man and merely read

Consumer Reports or go with popular trends. If they are buying prescription drugs, they may feel so ignorant they will want someone else to decide for them (like a doctor or a federal agency). We could continue the general discussion about the complexities in establishing an adequate theory of value, but it will be more useful at this point to examine how egoist and utilitarian theories would develop their *theory of obligation* if they were using this general theory of value as a background.

■ ETHICAL EGOISM

The egoist's theory of value is straightforward. What is good is what brings me pleasure by satisfying my interests. The theory of obligation naturally follows from the theory of value. We are obligated to promote as much personal good as possible. This theory looks easy to use, it seems so uncomplicated. But, before we can even begin, we have to confront an immediate problem. At what level do we apply the foundational principle? A major principle, by itself, is already fairly abstract. If we focus on it, we are looking past the immediate foreground made up of the rules within which we live. Are we supposed to skip the intermediate levels and apply the principle directly to each of our actions? Or are we supposed to apply

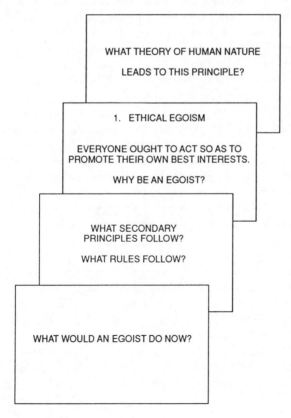

WHAT THEORY OF HUMAN NATURE

LEADS TO THIS PRINCIPLE?

1. ETHICAL EGOISM

EVERYONE OUGHT TO ACT SO AS TO
PROMOTE THEIR OWN BEST INTERESTS.

WHY BE AN EGOIST?

WHAT SECONDARY
PRINCIPLES FOLLOW?

WHAT RULES FOLLOW?

WHAT WOULD AN EGOIST DO NOW?

the principle at the intermediate level of rules, and then as individuals just follow the rules the principle justifies? Which approach is more apt to be in our interest?

Now we begin to understand why major principles seem confusing. To apply even a simplistic principle requires us to have already made a number of theoretical assumptions. The impulse behind the egoist principle is straightforward. Do whatever will promote your own interests. But, even this simple command is not easy to carry out in a social world. One of the first questions that has to be answered is: "How do I know if the ethical egoist principle itself is in my best interest?" Because theory can be confusing, it may be useful to begin on a concrete level by exploring how one would have to modify Kohlberg's Instrumental Relativist stage to try to turn this egocentric egoist orientation into a Level III philosophical theory that could conceivably convince a morally autonomous person that the egoist's principle is in his interest.

■ Personal Egoism Is Not Ethical Egoism

We have to live in institutions. What should a stage two instrumental egoist focus on when designing institutions? In the first place, he wouldn't have to worry about others, since he defines human values egocentrically as "my values." A person who takes this approach to all questions about "what ought to be" is called a PERSONAL EGOIST. The principle that governs his behavior can be stated as follows: 'I ought to always do whatever will promote my own best interests'.

An egocentric person cannot understand another person's point of view, but a philosophical egoist must be able to understand others. So, our first move in making a stage two orientation philosophical will be to decenter. We will have to assume that the instrumental egoist has developed beyond egocentrism. He must have some public reasons for choosing his principles; he should not adopt them by default because of a psychological inability to understand other options.

Although a philosophical egoist can understand other people's interests, from his perspective there is no inherent ethical reason to value satisfying them. In short, other people have extrinsic value for an egoist, but they do not have special intrinsic moral status of their own. However, let's assume that our personal egoist wants to go public with his principle so that it will begin to function as a social rule. The fact that he must live with other people will give him sufficient reason to modify the principle.

To make his principle public, he would have to make it universal so that everyone is given the same duties, even if the theory of value remains the same. Thus, if the theory of value says "What is good is what is in my best interest," the theory of obligation should say "Everyone ought to promote what is good, that is, my best interests." Now the principle is universal, but is it sufficiently public? Why should all of us work to satisfy one other person's interests?

A prudent personal egoist must ask himself: "Is it wise to publicly lobby for institutions that only satisfy me?" He cannot constantly be on guard against attack from those who would like to modify institutions so that they benefit others. If he wants security he will have to change the principle. Furthermore, what if an egoist would like to have friends? He will have to convince others to voluntarily adopt his principle by convincing them that it is also in their best interest. This means he will have to decenter to a greater degree and modify the theory of value so that it includes powerful or useful others. A modified principle would read: "Everyone in my group ought to act to promote their own best interest."

In this limited form, the principle becomes an aristocratic or "club" principle. It gives special privileges and duties to a restricted group. Because aristocratic principles (that pretend to be ethical principles) arbitrarily exclude groups of moral agents from the benefits of the social order (often as a hidden agenda), it is very difficult to think of them as principles of a rational ethics.

A rational ethical system treats like cases alike. People who are excluded are going to expect a rational account that clarifies the criterion or criteria for exclusion (for example, as when we give empirical reasons for excluding amoral babies from blame). In addition, as we saw in Chapter Two, an ethical principle guides the resolution of ethical disputes. It seems illogical to prescribe duties that exclude members of the dispute from consideration. There must be good reasons given before any affected party can be excluded from equal consideration by an ethical principle. The problem with aristocratic principles is that they exclude certain parties in a domain for reasons that seem arbitrary from the moral point of view.

Personal egoists may think the rational concern for consistency and universal application is irrelevant to their chosen way of life, but that is just one reason why their position is rejected in most philosophical literature. Before egoism will be taken seriously as an ethical principle, it must satisfy the criteria of the moral point of view. This is the goal of those who advocate a philosophically based ethical egoism. They modify the principle to make it universal and general. The final version of philosophical ETHICAL EGOISM says: 'Everyone ought to act so as to promote their own best interest'. This universalized, generalized principle now has the form we expect an ethical principle to have, so a morally autonomous person can now at least legitimately consider it as an option. But, are there sufficient reasons to assume this principle is compatible with what rational, caring people would choose?

■ *Psychological Egoism*

We need to be careful not to confuse this normative theory with the descriptive theory called PSYCHOLOGICAL EGOISM. The psychological theory says: 'People in fact always do act in their own self-interest'. Sometimes psychological egoism is used to argue for ethical egoism, but the wise ethical egoist has to be careful about accepting a theory that purports to describe human nature. For instance, suppose a psychological egoist argued that since ethical egoism is the only theory that does not contradict what people are capable of doing, it is the only theory that can be empirically recommended. A normative egoist would not find much comfort in this defense, because it conflicts with the logic of his own ethical principle. Psychological egoism makes it redundant for the ethical egoist to tell people that they ought to act on self-interest. Why do we need an ethical principle to tell people to do what they will naturally do? If psychological egoism is a true description of human nature, the ethical egoist principle appears to be reiterating nature; it is not really giving prescriptive advice.

As a prescriptive theory, egoists have to explain in what sense it is possible for people to act contrary to their principle—making it necessary to give the prescriptions. There are two ways they might do this. First, they can reject psychological egoism and assert that people can in fact act in ways that will sacrifice their own interests (e.g., for the social good, for the good of someone else, or for the sake of a higher principle). This egoist position would agree that altruistic behavior is possible, although it argues that altruism is morally wrong. An egoist believes sacrifices for the social good are right only if somehow the sacrifice will lead to a benefit for the egoist. This is a key point on which to focus. On a fundamental level, egoists challenge any moral point of view that requires us to care about principle, the tribe, or others as much as we care about ourselves.

A second way to deal with psychological egoism is to accept it, but point out that it does not necessarily negate ethical egoism. Psychological egoism says that people always try to act on their own self-interest, but it does not say they are always successful. Because people can fail to act on their true self-interest, an egoist prescriptive theory could be used to encourage them to stay true to their nature. The ethical principle would remind us to look for the best alternative (in this way, the "rational man" standard can be used in ethical egoism). Of course, if psychological egoism is true, once we know our best interest we will have no choice but to act on it. Further prescriptions become redundant when there are no temptations to overcome.

The major problem with psychological egoism is that it just seems to be a poor descriptive theory of human nature. There are countless counterexamples of people who seem to act in selfless ways for others, for principles, for nations, and so forth. (David Hume argued that we only need to think about motherhood to find a perfect counterexample to psychological egoism.) Psychological egoists often defend themselves by asserting that there are hidden self-interested psychological motives behind such counterexamples. But of course, if we allow theories to appeal to hidden evidence, then they can never be falsified and any belief can be defended no matter how absurd. We can leave this issue here, since even if the descriptive theory could be proven, it would not help the ethical egoist's position.

■ Problems with Ethical Egoism

The toughest question for the ethical egoist is: can it really be in our self-interest to live in a world governed by a universal principle of self-interest? So long as we are social beings who must live in a social context, it is not going to be easy to implement an egoist principle. Will we be able to trust anyone? Will we have to change the connotations for ethical terms, so words like "loyalty" and "friendship" refer to people who are "saps"? Egoism tells people not to care for others unless they can get a reward for caring. Would you want to marry such a person, or have one for a parent?

Can egoism ever be in the best interest of enough people to make it work as a social theory? If a person is really rational, he will see that a life governed by egoism cannot be in his own interest unless he can maintain a favored economic slot (and data clearly shows that there are no guarantees for most of us). Would a rational egoist want some kind of social insurance policy to protect himself against the possibility that he too might slip into the ranks of the poor due to accidents, assaults, the harsh whips of inflation, unemployment, and declining welfare programs? What about slipping into the ranks of the aged? If we live long enough, membership in this group is guaranteed. Can we trust the next generation to help us out when we begin to lose our faculties if they have been told to live like egoists? Why would an egoist help anyone who cannot pay him back? Can someone who is only self-interested really be committed to any principle at all—even an egoist principle?

These questions create a practical problem for the egoist. In a competitive society, how can he get enough people to support his program? Too many people will look at the consequences of such a life and say, "I just don't want to live that way. There are more rewarding ways to live." People with religious convictions often feel this way, as do those who believe tribal loyalty and duty of station are essential to having a good life (these concepts presuppose a level of commitment that might require a person to sacrifice himself).

■ Enlightened Ethical Egoism

To respond to these concerns, egoists sometimes advocate something called enlightened ethical egoism. They argue that a rational egoist will take all of the above into consideration. She will understand that the good life requires love, charity, and social commitment. These options will not be left out, since they are extrinsic goods that should be part of a rational person's lifestyle choice. Once everyone is educated to understand how humans get the richest pleasures, things will work on a social level since rational egoists do not make self-defeating choices. Ancient Greek philosophers often talked like this. Everyone seeks their own happiness, but since humans are social animals, the only way to be happy is to have friends, a city-state to support, and a just soul that will bring you rewards in an afterlife.

The critics of egoism argue in return that enlightened egoism pretends to represent the moral point of view (by being impartial, caring, universal, general, prescriptive, etc.), when in fact it represents the opposite perspective. If someone is truly enlightened he will probably not be an egoist at all. Egoism not only has trouble with caring, it also glorifies being partial in opposition to a truly enlightened point of view, which advocates impartiality in ethics. A primary dilemma in moral life concerns the problem of how to get a judicious balance between being self-interested and being disinterested, that is, balancing concerns for self with concerns for people and principles. Ethical egoism glorifies one at the expense of the other, and does not give very good arguments for its priorities.

There are also certain logical or conceptual problems with egoism. First of all, the theory is weakest as an ethical theory precisely where we expect ethical theories to do their best work. When there are major conflicts of interest to be resolved, ethical egoism becomes practically useless. Assume you are an ethical egoist who wants to live, but Joe will benefit if you die. Assume Joe is in a position to either save you or let you die with no penalties to Joe. Your principle of ethical egoism obligates both of you to act on your own self-interest. But is it in your interest to tell Joe this? If he asks you what he ought to do, are you going to tell him he has a duty to act on his own self-interest and allow you to die? Or are you going to do your duty as an egoist and act on your own self-interest and lie to him (tell him he is obligated to save you)? Ethical theories tell us how we are supposed to act. Surely we should be able to advocate them openly and with pride without betraying the theory or ourselves. It is a strange ethical theory that requires a moral agent to keep quiet about the ethical theory in order to act according to the theory.

This latter point is not a strong argument against egoism until we tie it back to the overall consequences that follow from living in an egoistic world. It just shows us once again that egoism implies it is in our self-interest to be deceitful or at least shrewd and calculating. Ethical egoism has trouble explaining why anyone should do his duty when he knows no one is looking. If it is in his interest to carefully break promises, contracts, and other rules, then an egoist ought to do so. When duties are merely an extrinsic means to self-interest, doing your duty has no intrinsic worth; for example, a promise should be kept only when keeping promises is in our own interest.

The enlightened egoist will argue that it is not prudent for egoists to promote a society that may allow them to be cheated. Honesty protects egoists as well as others, so they will advocate punishing dishonesty in general. This response does not satisfy the critics, however. They worry that the shrewd consistent egoist will tell other people to be honest, but she will only pretend to be committed to her own duties and will violate them when it is in her interest to do so. There will always be times when an egoist can get away with violating her duty, so it is hard to see how we can convince her to respect (in a full sense) standard ethical notions like duty, loyalty, devotion, or commitment. The egoist will develop these character traits only if she thinks they will benefit her, and she will feel justified in ignoring them when it serves her purpose to do so. An occasional violation of a duty or promise will not bother the committed egoist, but it should bother others who have to live with her.

One final point: enlightened ethical egoism is supposed to work as a social theory because enlightened egoists understand that it is in their best interest to have a community of trusted fellows. But this argument presupposes that egoists are socially sophisticated beings who can understand the long-range social implications of their and other people's behavior. To be truly enlightened, they would need to understand the qualitative social meaning of community norms. For this sophistication to develop, children need to pass through the kinds of moral stages studied by Kohlberg. That is, in order to know how to function at a Socratic level of self-interest, people need to experience what it is like to live a Level II Conventional orientation to social norms. If we explicitly teach egoism throughout childhood, people may well fail to develop the conventional capacities that underlie the enlightened egoist's world view. The egoist cannot teach people his theory until after they have gone through their conventional training, where they learn that egoism is wrong. This objection is not crucial, but it does seem strange to advocate an ethical theory that cannot be openly taught in childhood.

■ UTILITARIANISM

Most people who favor a consequentialist approach that focuses on satisfying interests adopt some version of UTILITARIANISM. Traditional utilitarian theories adopt the same theory of value as egoism, but they depersonalize it. That is, they agree that pleasure and satisfying self-interest is good, but they point out that this is true in general, so everyone's pleasure counts equally. Thus, the utilitarian theory of obligation says it is our duty to promote as much good as possible for everyone. We should evaluate all alternatives, then act on the one whose consequences will make for the greatest amount of happiness.

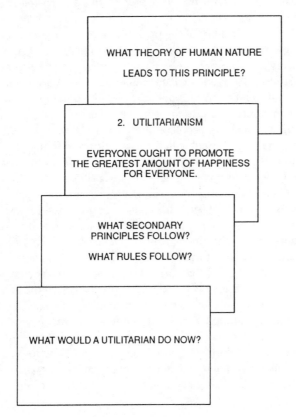

It is important to keep this point in perspective. Some critics of utilitarianism assume utilitarians are interested in maximizing pleasure, period, as though it were some kind of entity that exists independently of agents. If this were the case, a creature who could experience an infinite amount of pleasure would be an embarrassment to utilitarian theory, for it would then make sense to distribute all the extrinsic goods in such a way as to feed the pleasure monster. This is absurd. The original point was to make all *people* happy, not promote pleasure for its own sake. So utilitarians start with a background theory that says: what is important is people in general and how they are feeling. It is right to promote people's good feelings, and wrong to promote their bad feelings. The ideal is to make everyone happy. It is good to have lots of happy people. It is bad to have any unhappy people.

How do we promote happiness? Can we just send out happiness shares in the mail? Of course not. Just as we saw in egoism, happiness is an intrinsic nonmoral value. To increase it, we must distribute extrinsic nonmoral values (like money, prestige, honors, and liberties) in ways that make people happy. Extrinsic goods have utility, so the more utility promoted the more happiness promoted. Thus, the utilitarian principle can be stated in a number of different ways: *"Everyone ought to always choose that act that will create the largest number of happy people."* Another version: *"Always choose that act that will promote the greatest amount of utility."* Another version: *"Always choose that act that will create the greatest good for the greatest number."*

What all of these versions of the principle have in common is the emphasis on maximizing extrinsic and intrinsic values so as to maximize general happiness. Utilitarian theory is completely decentered, so it is a mistake to apply it in an ethnocentric fashion. Everyone's good is supposed to count in social calculations. Since every moral agent counts for one, the pleasure or happiness of a king is no better than the pleasure of a peasant. The happiness of people in Asia is just as important as the happiness of people in the United States. The we/they approach to social problems is inconsistent with the major thrust of utilitarian theory. However, insofar as ethnocentric concerns bear on people's happiness, these concerns will also have to be taken into consideration since they amount to interests.

Because of the emphasis on maximizing pleasure or happiness, critics of hedonistic forms of utilitarianism once charged that it was a philosophy for pigs. They argued that if pleasure is the greatest value in life, we might as well sit around and scratch our itches. John Stuart Mill responded to this kind of argument by pointing out that the "type of agent" experiencing the pleasure is important. He said that it was unfortunate that these critics were only acquainted with pig pleasures. As for himself, Mill believed that humans received the greatest pleasure from things that exercised the higher human faculties,[2] such as pleasures of the intellect, of imagination, of moral and spiritual sentiments, and so forth. The sensual pleasures of the body (which we share in common with animals) are legitimate pleasures, but humans do not focus only on these lower pleasures.

Mill was making the point that there are higher and lower pleasures in life that are INCOMMENSURABLES. As we saw in Chapter Four, types of things are incommensurable when 'they have properties that are so radically different that there is no way to weight the properties of one set against the properties of the other'. A popular way to express this is to say "you cannot compare apples and oranges." They are different in kind or quality, not just different in degree or quantity. For example, Mill believes that freedom is one of the higher values. The pleasure we get from sensual joy is different in kind and not just degree from the pleasure we get from being free. Beyond a certain necessary minimum (e.g., avoiding starvation), no amount of the sensual (pig) pleasures can compensate for the loss of the higher pleasure that humans get from being free. Mill summarized this point by saying: It is better to be Socrates unsatisfied than to be a fool satisfied.[3] (If you don't understand this, Mill would suggest that you need training in the higher pleasures. He thought that only a judge who has experienced both types of pleasure can properly choose between pleasures that are different in quality.)

By making a distinction between higher and lower pleasures, Mill greatly complicates utilitarian calculations. What is the legislator to do? If Mill is right about human nature, it is probably a mistake in the long run to trade off lower pleasures for higher ones (e.g., spending money to promote drinking, eating, dancing, and football is not as likely to maximize happiness in the long run as spending money on activities that promote intellectual virtues). So, in redesigning institutions we have to do more than figure out how to satisfy the current interests of all the people involved; we need to decide as well if their interests are tied to higher pleasures or lower pleasures. If two interests conflict and one is higher, other things being equal, we should always take the higher.

It is important to remember that, as an ethical theory, utilitarianism is a philosophy about the way we should live while in pursuit of the good. Utilitarians do not have to passively sit by and accept whatever interests some person wants to champion. They can use the utilitarian agenda to judge interests. Some interests are easier to promote, last longer, are more apt to lead to additional pleasure, have greater intensity and greater quality, and so forth. A utilitarian can also legitimately judge on the basis of maximizing utility in the long run. A child may want a lollipop now, but the tooth decay in the future will also affect a utilitarian parent's decision. A country may want to cut down its rain forests now, but a utilitarian will balance the next generation's interests against the interests of those who will benefit immediately from turning the forest into farm land.

Because of their willingness to judge the utilitarian value of various pleasures, it is a mistake to think of utilitarianism as a majority rule principle. The majority will not always rule; it depends on what the majority wants. From a utilitarian perspective, what the majority has an interest in may not be in the interest of everyone. When evaluating public policy or legislation, it is not enough to simply ask: "How many people want this?" A utilitarian also has to ask: "Should people want this, what intrinsic values are involved, what extrinsic values, are they higher or lower pleasures, and what are the long-range consequences for human happiness?" In short, utilitarianism is not an economic theory where we simply try to efficiently maximize people's preferences; it is an ethical theory that calls upon us to judge preferences as well as everything else that needs to be judged from the moral point of view.

A different kind of problem concerns the clash between pleasures that are pro-utilitarian and those that are anti-utilitarian. What has more value, the John Wayne guard's interest in humiliating others, or prisoner 416's interest in deciding for himself when he is going to eat? Granted that everyone counts for one, but does it really make sense to give the John Wayne guard's sadistic pleasure the same weight as 416's interest in pleasing himself? Narveson argues that sadistic pleasures should not be given any weight at all. They are by their nature anti-utilitarian. First, they cannot be satisfied except by creating pain in another, thus they cancel themselves out with the disutility used to purchase them. But Narveson claims there is a second objection that is even stronger. He says there is no reason why a utilitarian should have to give positive weight at all to an interest that is known to be opposed to utilitarianism.

> There is a sense, of course, in which the internal character of a desire is irrelevant to the utilitarian. . . . But it is one thing to say that the particular character of the desire is irrelevant because all desires should be considered, and quite another to say that no desires of any sort should be rejected, upon consideration. The most obvious consideration there could possibly be for rejecting a desire in any system of ethics is that it is a desire for the exact opposite of the aim of the system. . . . A desire to inflict harm on another person is the very paradigm of this kind of desire the utilitarian is out to control.[4]

According to Narveson, then, to acknowledge a principle is to recognize that we must inhibit desires that conflict with it. A desire to harm others is illegitimate since the utilitarian principle says people have a duty to promote pleasure. It follows, therefore, that we all ought to inhibit desires that make us want to inflict pain. The sadist takes pleasure in doing the opposite of what utilitarians ask of us. Thus, if anything, the sadistic individual should be punished for not being a good utilitarian rather than rewarded by having his pleasure treated as though it is equal in merit. These considerations further complicate utilitarian calculations, because it is not always easy to tell the difference between a motive that is anti-utilitarian and one that is merely self-interested. If pushed far enough, would self-interest itself be anti-utilitarian, as some of the relationship-oriented women in Gilligan's study seem to think?

Because it is not easy to calculate how to maximize happiness, and because it is easy to rationalize and think that our own pleasure counts more than the pleasure of other people, utilitarians often recommend an artificial device to help people remain impartial, decentered, and yet caring when they calculate utility. They say we should calculate utility in the same manner as an IMPARTIAL BENEVOLENT SPECTATOR would calculate it.[5] This is similar to the emphasis we find in the jury box conception of rationality with its emphasis on impartiality, reasoned debate, and reflective equilibrium by caring peers. The utilitarian calculation is impartial when it treats like cases alike (so everyone counts as one and everyone affected is included in the calculation). It is benevolent when the calculation expresses concern or sympathy for the people involved (the calculator cares, she can empathize and properly weigh the pleasure and pain involved). And it takes the view of a spectator when it imitates the moral agent on the jury who has a proper balance between interest and disinterest (a disinterested interest in judging right from wrong should have priority over the interested view of a biased participant who simply wants his own side to win).

The use of this device of reason provides a good example of how modern theories have tried to stay focused on the mainstream philosophical point of view that has evolved in Western philosophy. The theory also acknowledges that a morally responsible decision involves more than purely intellectual skills. By emphasizing benevolence, utilitarian theory acknowledges that both rationality and caring are important. This is, of course, a very sophisticated moral point of view. Imagine the complex set of traits needed to fully grasp and utilize this ideal spectator device. Egocentric children cannot be impartial, benevolent, or disinterested enough to function like an ideal utilitarian agent. Once reason develops one may well develop the capacity for impartiality, at least in the sense of intellectual neutrality, but benevolence or caring can only be learned through social intercourse. As we saw in Chapters Six and Seven, respect for persons and principles is probably a capacity that comes from generalizing the love we learned to feel for family and tribe. Of course, this is not an all-or-nothing dimension. Each of us will experience degrees of caring, and it is quite possible that our capacities may fluctuate during life's transitional phases and situational crises. But, as Erickson[6] argued, unless children learn trust in a family that protects them during periods of vulnerability, they may not learn to love or care for others. This may inhibit their ability to be good utilitarians, who can use this device of reason. If we cannot feel respect for distant others, how can we calculate utility as a fully developed utilitarian?

■ Problems with Utilitarianism

Does the principle of utility allow us to break our agreements when it will promote more utility to do so? Can we trust ordinary people to calculate in a disinterested way? Attempts to answer these questions have led utilitarians to emphasize different ways to apply the utilitarian principle. ACT utilitarians argue that 'we should apply the principle of utility to individual actions'. At any given moment, act so as to promote the greatest amount of happiness. But does this mean we don't have to obey rules? Not quite. Act utilitarians think that rules should definitely be considered when we are making our calculations, but we should treat them as guidelines or rules of thumb, not as unbreakable absolutes. For instance, although rules should generally be obeyed, there will always be cases where the spirit of the rule cannot be served by strict adherence to the letter of the rule; that is, more pleasure for everyone can be promoted by breaking a rule than by following it. For example, the general rule of thumb is that one should not lie, but in some cases it is right to tell a lie if lying will promote more happiness, for example, lying to save a life, or lying to your senile grandfather to spare his feelings. Even when an act is covered by a rule, the act utilitarian may apply the principle of utility directly to the act itself, rather than just obey the rule.

This willingness to suspend rules bothers some utilitarians. They think that rules should be more than simple rules of thumb. They worry that if we allow people to choose for themselves whether or not to follow a rule, they will too often break rules for self-interested reasons. These utilitarians argue that real will theory indicates too many real people do not or cannot calculate utility like impartial benevolent spectators. With so many Meadlows and Calleys (see Chapter Five), act utilitarianism cannot work properly in an average community. If all moral agents could think and act like Socrates, maybe we could allow everyone to be act utilitarians, but until then, it might be better to apply the principle of utility only to the system of rules, and those of us who are not Socratic can then follow the rules. This approach is called RULE utilitarianism since it says that 'individuals should always obey the rules that will bring the greatest happiness'. Rule utilitarians are arguing that if individuals will stay consistent with the levels of justification and apply the principle first to rules, in the long run more happiness will be promoted. We should apply the principle of utility to actions only if a rule does not already cover the situation.

Whatever level they focus on, both act and rule utilitarians have a formidable task. To judge the rightness of an act they must be able to look into the future and predict with some degree of reliability the consequences for everyone who will be affected by a decision or rule. Then they must prescribe actions or rules on the basis of their predictions. But imagine how difficult it is to accurately predict utility in a pluralistic society. Even if we rule out preferences that are not right (e.g., sadistic ones), the diversity in preferences will still be considerable. People with different value programming will be made happy by different things in different amounts. Should these individual differences be taken into consideration? Giving everyone a lump sum of money would be easy, but everyone is not made equally happy by the same amount of money. As Aristotle pointed out 2,000 years ago, because Milo the wrestler has nutritional needs that are different from the average person, an equal distribution of food won't maximize happiness.

To help simplify our task, utilitarians argue that we should use supplementary principles such as the PRINCIPLE OF DIMINISHING MARGINAL UTILITY to help guide our calculations. This principle says that 'the more goods a person has, the less utility a person gets out of an additional unit of the goods'. Five dollars does not mean as much to a millionaire as it does to a person who is broke, so if you have five dollars to distribute give it to someone who is poor. A loaf of bread to a welfare mother creates more utility than it does in a home where people have cake. Other things being equal, then, adopt policies that will distribute extrinsic goods in a broad-based manner rather than allow them to accumulate in certain wealthy localities or social classes. In the long run, in a utilitarian society there should be a tendency toward equalizing the distribution of extrinsic goods.

There are two serious problems with the utilitarian approach to ethics. First, notice how much it demands of us. Whether we are act or rule utilitarians, each time we act (or judge a rule) we must always do whatever will make the most people happy. This entails a heavy moral burden. For instance, in making a decision about how to spend my time, I have to consider all who will be affected by my decision. What right do I have to play a round of golf? My time could be used to promote much more utility if I worked to help the poor. I may feel thirsty and be inclined to spend a dollar on a beer. This will promote my utility, that is, quench my thirst and create a slight pleasant numbing of my nerves, but wouldn't it create much more utility to drop that dollar in the church poorbox? The principle of utility is clear. So long as there are people within range of my actions, I have a duty to choose the act that will maximize all our utility. Where do I draw the line between utilitarian duty and utilitarian charity? Is there any room for individual choice in these matters?

One response to these concerns is to point out that people are happier when they decide issues for themselves. The general duty is to do what you can, but you decide how much you can do. Furthermore, since utility is promoted by letting people have a private life, they should also get to decide how much of their time they will spend in private pursuits. This makes sense, since no theory can determine ahead of time the extent of all of our moral actions. All theories rely on individual conscience in situations that require judgment. The problem still remains, however, am I or am I not always duty-bound to maximize everyone's happiness? The fact I have freedom to make the calculation myself does not change the extent of the burden.

The second major problem concerns the moral status of special duties. People make decisions on the basis of legitimate expectations they have about the way the world runs. If I take on special duties by signing contracts or making promises, how long do they last? Should we nullify existing contracts and special commitments whenever doing so promises to create more utility? How would we decide when it is appropriate to nullify a contract? On the basis of utilitarian calculations, of course, but these calculations involve the touchy issue of changing the rules. Thus, we would also need some due process procedures and appeals procedures to help us avoid hasty calculations. Wouldn't this be hopelessly cumbersome and, perhaps, interfere with utility maximization by taking decision-making power away from individuals?

Furthermore, the principle of diminishing marginal utility seems to imply that we should design institutions so that there is periodic redistribution of goods. Those who are worse off will always be able to experience greater utility from periodic judicious redistributions, so society ought to periodically take extrinsic goods away from one group and redistribute them to other groups who have less. Those well off will complain, but so long as the redistribution is kept within limits their complaint would be offset by the gain in utility for those worse off. The graduated income tax is based on this notion. This seems unfair to some people. They claim utilitarian theory makes them sacrifice some of their legitimately earned income for the good of others who haven't earned it. (Is this the kind of complaint that a good utilitarian would make?) More to the point, some critics argue that redistribution violates fundamental property rights. Is it fair to require some to give up their hard-earned property even if it will promote the general happiness? What about the policy of eminent domain, where the state can confiscate property for the sake of the public good? Is it fair to take old people's homes from them (against their will) to build public buildings that will benefit a larger segment of society?

These concerns lead many utilitarians to favor some form of rule utilitarianism that gives extra weight to special duties. They argue that once you sign a contract, maximum utility is promoted in the long run by a rule that says you are bound by the contract no matter what calculations you make in the future. But act utilitarians argue that contracts are only a means to utility. They can serve as rules of thumb (general guidelines) but they are not absolutes. They should not be allowed to stop the progress toward maximum happiness. But what about the contractee's right to have the contract enforced? Is it just to nullify a contract, even if it is for the social good? All of these considerations lead some critics to charge that utilitarianism is fundamentally flawed, since it cannot adequately account for commonsense notions of justice.

■ The Problem of Justice

For our purpose we can say that a person has a MORAL RIGHT to something 'when a person can make a legitimate claim to it' (it is legitimate when justified at the proper level by an agreed-upon ethical theory). So, to have a right is to have the liberty to do or receive something because it is our "due." Just how extensive or inviolable are rights? Utilitarians say all rights are extrinsic goods justified by their role in promoting utility, so there are no rights that are more fundamental than the principle of utility itself.

Utilitarian critics, however, say that this is exactly the attitude that violates our sense of justice. They claim that utilitarians refuse to acknowledge that some rights are so important that they are indefeasible—such as rights to life, liberty, and equal opportunity. INDEFEASIBLE is a legal term meaning that "a right cannot be defeated or voided by other social considerations." These critics say that any theory is unjust if it would allow the indefeasible rights of individuals to be violated in order to promote general happiness.

Is utilitarianism an unjust theory? There is a whole series of strange "lifeboat" examples that are supposed to show that utilitarians will, at least in principle, sacrifice the rights of individuals in order to maximize social utility (e.g., if a boat will only hold 10 people and there are 12 on board, should we throw the least useful people overboard to maximize the good of the whole?). The most famous of these lifeboat scenarios is the claim that utility could be used to justify punishing an innocent person to control crime by deterring others.[7] This would clearly violate individual rights, since an individual should not be punished unless she is guilty of some crime. If utilitarianism would allow such practices it would seem to be defective.

I am not going to discuss each of these esoteric criticisms here. I agree with Narveson[8] that all of the lifeboat examples are generally weak arguments. Utilitarians are advocating a world in which everyone is happy in the long run. Individual decisions are always made against that background. The lifeboat examples are taken out of context and treated as though they are cases existing in a social vacuum, which distorts the utilitarian agenda. In addition, lifeboat cases are so problematic that it will not be clear what should be done no matter what theory we are using. Any solution will wind up violating someone's intuition, so all theories will have problems with these tough cases. With regard to punishing an innocent person, utilitarians respond that the example has to presuppose that people will be willing to favor an absurd policy of allowing governments to promote general happiness with secret manipulations such as using innocent people at the discretion of the government. Why would any utilitarian favor such policies? If anything, the general fear of arbitrary punishment that such a policy would create would produce disutility rather than a sense of safety.

The point at issue here does not, however, turn on the adequacy of the examples used to criticize the utilitarian agenda. We can forget about lifeboats and simply ask: Is it permissible at all to set aside an individual's fundamental rights if it will promote general happiness to do so? Most utilitarians will say yes, since there are times when conditions might call for this. The critics argue that any decision that would violate a fundamental right is wrong and conflicts with our sense of justice.

John Stuart Mill argues that utilitarians would never allow people or agencies to "violate" individual rights. Now and then, conditions may require us to OVER-RIDE a claim that is normally legitimate, but only 'when a higher moral claim takes precedence'. Overriding is not the same as violation. Violating a right is done for some nonmoral reason (such as private gain), but overriding is done for moral reasons. When we override a claim that is normally legitimate, it is because the claim does not have the same moral status in extraordinary circumstances. Mill also thinks critics of utilitarianism are confused about the status of rights.[9] They seem to think that there are ABSOLUTE rights when, in fact, there aren't any. An absolute is 'universally binding in all contexts and has unconditional value'. But, according to utilitarianism, there are and can only be two absolute rights: (1) the right to have the principle of utility used to make decisions, and (2) the right to have your interests considered when utility is calculated (this is required by logic, since utility cannot be accurately calculated unless all relevant interests are reviewed in the calculation).

Mill argues that all rights are actually PRIMA FACIE rather than absolute (prima facie means 'other things being equal, or on first appearance'). People have rights in the first place because they promote utility. If a new situation arises that destroys the utility of particular rights, then the rights are not being violated if we implement new policies for the sake of reestablishing conditions that will promote everyone's happiness. All extrinsic goods, including rights, have value only because they promote utility. When they stop contributing to happiness, they lose their utility, or value. Some conditions are so important for promoting utility that it is hard to think of a time when they would lose value or need to be overridden. To recognize their special status we give people a right to them (e.g., such as a right to freedom). But these rights are prima facie rather than absolute. We only have them other things being equal, that is, so long as they continue to function as a means to overall happiness.

The consequentialist approach to morality is not the only approach that can be taken. Many philosophers think that morality has its own special status; it is not only a means for promoting other values. These philosophers argue that moral rights and duties logically precede, and are independent of, any particular theory of value. An approach to ethics is called NONCONSEQUENTIALISM when it argues that 'the status of moral rights and duties does not depend on the consequences they lead to, because there is some other more fundamental "right-making" characteristic that is independent of consequences.' In fact, nonconsequentialists argue that one function of ethics is to place boundaries on what can legitimately be considered under a theory of value.

To know what these boundaries should be we need a THEORY OF OBLIGATION that 'prescribes moral rights and duties'. A theory of obligation logically precedes any theory of value, since a particular theory of value cannot be completed until we figure out the moral boundaries. For instance, some pleasures may look good to us at first glance, but once we see that they are temptations that might make us violate our duty, we appreciate that they are not really good after all. Apparent goods lose their value when they conflict with a theory of obligation. Nonconsequentialists argue that a mature moral agent reverses the historical order of things (most of us begin our moral life as consequentialists who see ethics as a necessary evil) and opts for a more abstract logical order (where we understand that right or duty comes before the choice of lifestyle). But we cannot know how to reverse the priority until we first develop a theory of obligation. The three theories we will look at in the next chapter all assume (in varying degrees) that some form of nonconsequentialism is the only legitimate approach to ethical inquiry.

■ STUDY QUESTIONS

1. Why does a consequentialist need a theory of value before a theory of obligation?
2. To a hedonistic consequentialist, what kind of value does "money" and "morality" have?
3. What is the difference between the rational man standard, the reasonable man standard, and real will theory when it comes to choosing rules for social life?

4. What do you have to do to the personal egoist principle to make it an ethical principle?
5. Why do many critics think that ethical egoism fails to satisfy the conditions of a moral point of view?
6. In what way are egoists and utilitarians the same? In what way do they differ?
7. Who are we supposed to make happy, according to utilitarians?
8. Why does the existence of incommensurable pleasures make it more difficult to calculate utility?
9. Why is the principle of utility different than a majority rule principle?
10. Why do utilitarians advocate the impartial benevolent spectator device of reason?
11. How do utilitarians deal with charity, special obligations, and human rights?

■ NOTES

1. For a good discussion of the way the FTC vacillated between the reasonable man standard and the ignorant man standard, see Ivan L. Preston, "Reasonable Consumer or Ignorant Consumer? How the FTC Decides," in Tom Beauchamp and Norman Bowie, eds., *Ethical Theory and Business* (Englewood Cliffs, NJ: Prentice Hall, 1979), p. 485ff.

2. John Stuart Mill, *Utilitarianism* (New York: Bobbs-Merrill Co., 1957), p. 11ff.

3. Ibid., p. 14.

4. Jan Narveson, *Morality and Utility* (Baltimore, MD: John Hopkins Press, 1967), pp. 161–166.

5. For a very good account of this perspective, see Roderick Firth, "Ethical Absolutism and the Ideal Observer," *Philosophy and Phenomenological Research*, Vol. 12 (1952) pp. 317–345.

6. Erick Erickson, *Childhood and Society* (New York: W. W. Norton & Company, 1963), p. 274ff.

7. G. E. M. Anscombe, "Modern Moral Philosophy," *Philosophy* 32 (1957), 16f.

8. Narveson, Chapters 2 through 7.

9. Mill, Chapter 5.

■ CHAPTER TEN

Ideal Theory: A Nonconsequentialist Background

■ NATURAL RIGHTS THEORY

The foundational principle of the NATURAL RIGHTS theory states that *everyone ought to act in accordance with universal inalienable (indefeasible) rights*. As a theory of obligation it logically precedes, and places boundaries on, all theories of value. This means it is a nonconsequentialist orientation, since natural rights have special status as boundary conditions that place constraints on any subsequent decisions about good consequences. Because natural rights are more than a means to some other end, they have their own intrinsic moral worth.

Contemporary natural rights theory is usually discussed under the label "human rights."[1] For rights to have this status they must be

1. universal (since all humans have them);
2. moral, not civil (so they do not depend on the actions of any government);
3. natural (in the sense that we have them just because we are human);
4. equal (in that we all ought to have them to the same degree no matter what our cultural context);
5. fundamental (in the sense of being inalienable and indefeasible—INALIENABLE means that 'the rights are so important to our nature that we cannot be separated from them as we can be from extrinsic values');
6. self-evident (which means they do not have to be proven; that is, they are self-justifying, since to hear about them is to immediately recognize their validity); and
7. a legitimate basis from which to make moral claims against governments and other people.

The United Nations' Universal Declaration of Human Rights was inspired by this kind of theory, as was the Declaration of Independence and the U. S. Constitution's Bill of Rights. For example, it is instructive to think of the Declaration of Independence as the kind of account a group of morally autonomous revolutionaries would give to the rest of the world, if they were using a natural rights theory to justify their actions. Jefferson thought such an account would make sense to the reason (or moral sense) of all free people.

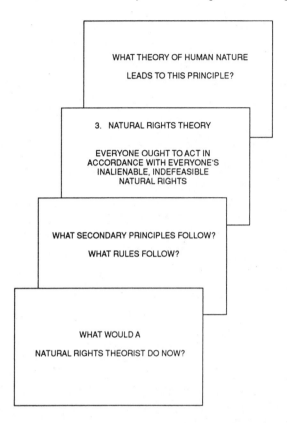

When in the course of human events, it becomes necessary for one people to dissolve the political bands which have connected them with another, and to assume among the powers of the earth, the separate and equal station to which the laws of nature and of nature's God entitle them, a decent respect to the opinions of mankind requires that they should declare the causes which impel them to the separation. We hold these truths to be self-evident, that all men are created equal, that they are endowed by their Creator with certain inalienable rights, that among these are life, liberty, and the pursuit of happiness—that to secure these rights, governments are instituted among men, deriving their just powers from the consent of the governed, that whenever any form of government becomes destructive of these ends, it is the right of the people to alter or to abolish it, and to institute new government, laying its foundation on such principles, and organizing its powers in such form, as to them shall seem most likely to effect their safety and happiness.

Although this seems like a fairly straightforward approach to ethics to many of us today, it is not an approach emphasized in ancient civilizations. There were, of course, historical trends that set the stage for this individualistic approach to Western ethics. Hebrew and Christian philosophy contributed the idea that all of nature was created by God. Since we are all part of God's purpose, we are all individually equal in the eyes of God. The Roman Stoics then elaborated on the Greek idea that nature follows rational patterns or norms that can be known by anyone if he will use human reason to interpret events. Once Roman law was literally imposed on all the different cultures in the known Western world, it helped people accept the idea that norms could in fact apply cross-culturally. As long as local customs were not inconsistent with the Roman law they were allowed to flourish in their own context, and this gave rise to the idea that local communities could have freedom to choose a way of life so long as it was compatible with the boundaries established by universal law. It is a fairly straightforward step from these historical trends to the modern conception that individuals have universal human rights that ought to be protected in any society.

B. J. Diggs[2] argues that John Locke should be given credit for making the logic behind the natural rights tradition perfectly clear. Locke explicitly states that the sovereign in a legitimate state can only be the universal rational will of the people. He believed mankind possessed a divine light of reason that enabled them to know about inalienable natural rights to things like life, liberty, health, and property.[3] Since these natural rights are sacred even for people who live outside the boundaries of a state, the natural condition of man is to be a free, equal, self-governing moral being.

But if people are free, rational, social beings with natural rights, why would they ever agree to give up this natural status and submit to a civil authority? Locke argued that the state was a necessary means for protecting individual rights. While people have a natural right to punish those who violate natural rights, because individuals and families are biased they cannot properly do the job. When they seek retribution against those who violate rights, they will overstep the boundaries of fair punishment. Friends of the punished individual will then seek retribution in return. They too will overreact, and eventually natural social life will degenerate into a state of war. To avoid this, Locke argued that rational people would agree to enter a social contract for the purpose of choosing a government that can be trusted to impartially protect their natural rights. Notice that natural rights logically precede legal arrangements, thus government is conceived of as a means for protecting them. This gives natural rights priority over all contingent social arrangements. One of Locke's major contributions to Western moral theory is his argument that no one is obligated to obey any law that is not compatible with the dictates of universal human reason. It follows that governmental institutions lose their legitimacy when they cannot be trusted to protect the natural rights of individuals.

Locke's theory is developed against a background individualism that leads to a negative rights conception of the state. In a manner similar to a night watchman whose job is to protect the store, government's main function is to stop people from infringing on the rights of individuals. As we saw in Chapter Five, this kind of background assumption leads to the idea that all contributions to the general welfare are charity, that is, supererogatory acts that go above and beyond the call

of duty. At one point, Robert Nozick was a most impressive contemporary advocate of this approach. He argued that, while it is immoral to violate the natural
rights of others, no one (including the state) has a positive duty to help others satisfy
their rights.[4]

■ Problems with the Natural Rights Theory

The major weakness with this theory is methodological. Natural rights are supposed to be self-evident, but different people see different lists as self-evident.
Whose list is right? Why should we trust a list of rights just because it feels self-
evident to someone, when we know how introjection can influence feelings? What
if the judgments that seem self-evident are only common local prejudices? Furthermore, how should we interpret the content of a particular right? For instance, the
United Nations list of human rights gives everyone "a right to meaningful work."
Is the proper interpretation of "meaningful" self-evident?

Even if we could agree to a formal list of rights, can we agree to a list of
priorities about how to resolve conflicts between the rights on the list? Is the rich
man's right to property violated if we tax him to feed young children who have a
right to life, or a right to health care, or a right to education, or a right to—where
does the list stop? All theories have to solve such PRIORITY PROBLEMS, but the
natural rights theory has special difficulties since each right is inalienable and
cannot be defeated. Such vexing questions lead some theorists to argue that the
moral world is by its nature complex. They argue that we have to accept the fact
that pluralism in absolute rights is a fundamental fact. When conflicts arise we will
just have to settle them case by case with a direct appeal to intuition.

Finally, what makes natural rights so special? The mere fact that something
is natural does not make it right. Many natural things do not appear to be right.
It is natural to die of disease but we try to prevent it at every step. It is natural to
feel emotions like jealousy, envy, revenge, and hatred, but are these emotions
moral? Whatever the right-making criteria are for natural rights, it does not appear
to be enough to merely point out that rights are natural.

Early versions of natural rights theory did not worry about such questions
because natural rights were supported by *divine command theory*. Ethical systems that are based on religious foundations say that "the right-making characteristic in ethics is God." It is moral to obey God, immoral to disobey. Since God
created nature, if something was natural then of course it was right. We do not
have space to discuss divine command theory here. In any case, it would not end
the questions, since pluralism in religious traditions is also confusing. I am not
saying that religious ethics is unimportant, but rather that we can only do so much
in a short text.

To make room for religious freedom, philosophers generally strive for a
secular theory that can help those from different religions figure out how to live
together in peace. Each member of a particular religion, as a responsible moral
agent, will have to figure out how to make her religious convictions compatible

with the dictates of secular ethics. If a rational, secular ethics gives her duties that are incompatible with her religious convictions, her religion and the secular society will have a social dilemma to solve. Such conflicts must be worked out on a case-by-case basis.

■ SOCIAL CONTRACT THEORY

In secular ethics, it is not clear if there is any advantage to be gained from calling rights natural. Maybe it would be more useful to simply ask: "What rights would rational beings be willing to agree to—whether they be natural or not?" This question avoids metaphysical questions about nature's prescriptive status by focusing on the conditions for a set of conventional rights that would be fair to all. Moral rules would be legitimate only if in principle they could have been chosen by all who are required to follow them. According to contemporary SOCIAL CONTRACT theory, it is irrelevant whether or not principles are natural. What matters is that 'they are the kind of principles that *would* be chosen by free and equal, rational, needy people entering into a social contract to establish a community'.

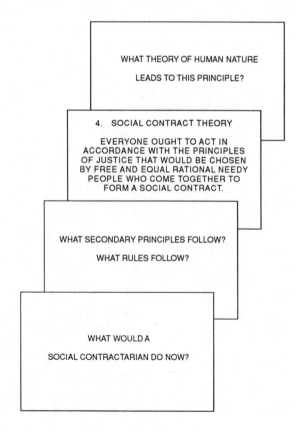

WHAT THEORY OF HUMAN NATURE

LEADS TO THIS PRINCIPLE?

4. SOCIAL CONTRACT THEORY

EVERYONE OUGHT TO ACT IN ACCORDANCE WITH THE PRINCIPLES OF JUSTICE THAT WOULD BE CHOSEN BY FREE AND EQUAL RATIONAL NEEDY PEOPLE WHO COME TOGETHER TO FORM A SOCIAL CONTRACT.

WHAT SECONDARY PRINCIPLES FOLLOW?

WHAT RULES FOLLOW?

WHAT WOULD A

SOCIAL CONTRACTARIAN DO NOW?

There is nothing natural about a social contract. It is a purely hypothetical abstract device of reason designed to guide our ethical intuitions by helping us think like hypothetically rational, autonomous agents who care about having a social existence. Rather than assuming with Locke that there *are* natural rights that need to be protected, it asks: What *would* have been chosen *if* people got together to choose rights? The goal is to find principles that could in principle receive universal consent, because they would be ideally suited for regulating social and political institutions that distribute social goods.

Many critics of social contract theory fail to understand the point of this hypothetical abstract perspective. For instance, the empiricist David Hume claimed that governments are founded on "utility" and "habitual" obedience to a prince who has come to power through "conquest or usurpation."[5] He argued that those who say obedience to a system of government is or ought to be based on consent are simply mistaken.

> But would these reasoners look abroad into the world, they would meet with nothing that, in the least, corresponds to their ideas, or can warrant so refined and philosophical a system.
> . . . It is strange that an act of the mind, which every individual is supposed to have formed, and after he came to the use of reason too, otherwise it could have no authority; that this act, I say, should be so much unknown to all of them, that over the face of the whole earth, there scarcely remain any traces or memory of it.
> . . . [One problem is that] this supposes the consent of the fathers to bind the children, even to the most remote generations, . . . besides this, I say, it is not justified by history or experience in any age or country of the world.[6]

The proper response to this kind of criticism is to say "So what?" The entire argument misses the point, since it confuses the logic of a descriptive exercise in social science with the logic of a normative theory about what ought to be. Social contract theory is not about how people in fact develop the habit of obedience or why there is utility in accepting whatever social forms happen to be imposed on them. Instead, it invites people from any generation to speculate on how things ought to be. Future generations are no more bound by their fathers' speculations than we are by ours, since we are not talking about a concrete contract, but an ideal that can justify forms of social existence. Rousseau very clearly emphasized this point when he criticized philosophers like Hobbes, Grotius, and Aristotle for being too empirical. He said their

> invariable method of arguing is to derive Right from Fact. It might be possible to adopt a more logical system of reasoning, but none which would be more favorable to tyrants.[7]

Rousseau is well aware that people can give obedience out of utilitarian necessity and habit, but he argued that duties that stem from these motives amount to no more than prudence and should not be considered moral duties.

To yield to the strong is an act of necessity, not of will. At most it is the result of a dictate of prudence. How, then, can it become a duty? (Rousseau, p. 172)

In order to make sense of the fact that we have moral as well as prudential duties to our fellow citizens and to just governments, Rousseau says we must assume that the social contract functions implicitly everywhere we find a legitimate form of government. It does not matter that it was never explicitly stated; it should have been (and will be as soon as people come to understand it). It is an ideal background condition against which to measure the legitimacy of institutional structures. He says that even if the principles of such a contract ". . . may never have been formally enunciated, they must be everywhere the same, and every-where tacitly admitted and recognized" (Rousseau, p. 180).

A hypothetical original social contract would have to be fair to everyone at the start. It is hard to imagine what a beginning position of fairness would be like. For example, if you ask, "How is the migrant farmer equal in bargaining power to a Rockefeller?" you are being far too concrete. Such questions focus on irrelevant contingencies, just as did the writer who wrote Ann Landers complaining that the Founding Fathers were wrong when they claimed "all men are created equal." A social contract is a hypothetical contract, not a real one. We are speculating about what *would* be chosen *if* everyone was agreeing *before* they had real social advan-tages and disadvantages or, in short, before they were somebody. (It seems to me that from a developmental perspective the question should be framed as: What kind of ideal institutions would we each choose to be born into if God gave us general information and the capacity to reason before we were born?)

In his seminal book A *Theory of Justice,* [8] John Rawls tries to clarify what it would be like to think on such an abstract level. He says we should imagine what it *would* be like to have to choose our principles from behind a VEIL OF IGNORANCE. This veil would 'cloud our memory to allow each of us to forget particular details about who we are'. We would know general things about human-ity but would not know personal things about ourselves. We wouldn't know if we were rich or poor, male or female, black or white, old or young, and so forth. All personal knowledge about the self would be gone, yet we would still have to choose social arrangements. This is why I said above that social contract choosers have the state of mind of a rational fetus. They are abstract beings, pure moral potentiality, since they are going to choose the society that will mold them into social beings.

To make this abstract decision procedure more concrete, let's apply it to the Zimbardo Prison Experiment. Zimbardo could have created some aspects of a veil of ignorance if he had said to the subjects in his experiment: "I am going to assign you to slots in an experimental prison community. Before I do that, however, I want you to sit down and draw up rules for the community." What would a rational agent choose under these conditions, when facing the possibility that she might have to occupy any role, office, or station that is created? If Zimbardo also had the power to say: "and you won't know if you will be guard or prisoner, staff or visitor, rich or poor, old or young, male or female," he would have imposed a complete veil of ignorance. In this way, all voices must be taken seriously, since they could turn out to be yours.

Some critics claim we should not portray contractees as rational self-interested, autonomous beings, but as rational interdependent, needy beings, or beings that have normal human emotions. I think the veil of ignorance takes care of this concern. Since contractees could turn out to be anyone, they will evaluate all the emotional options and choose the one that will lead to the most fulfilling life no matter who they turn out to be. Thus, the method does emphasize caring and concern about interdependent relationships. It is true that Rawls says contractees would be self-interested and want the best for themselves, but the veil of ignorance converts self-interest into universal concern; that is, by stepping behind a veil we move in one step from being wholly self-interested, with only particular interests, to being decentered enough to have general interests that lead us to care about every social position. If a self-interested person could wind up occupying any role, then his own self-interest would lead him into giving every role a fair hearing. This is exactly what Rousseau wanted to emphasize. He said that particular interests lead to privilege and conflict of interest, while general interests lead to equality and can serve as a basis for a just society.[9]

This approach can be used to clarify some of our most basic ethical intuitions. For example, it clearly shows that institutions like slavery are inherently wrong—not because slavery violates some natural right or leads to bad consequences, but because no rational, self-interested being would ever voluntarily establish the institution of slavery if he thought there was even the smallest chance he would have to be a slave himself. If we are not willing even in principle to choose slavery for ourself, then how can we ever be justified in imposing it on someone else without violating their status as a rational, self-interested being? Slavery obviously is based on particular interest and so turns a subjective inclination into a special social privilege. It is not an expression of the general interest that always leads to equality before the law. Thus any law that permits slavery can only be unjust.

Social contract theory rests on a background assumption that mankind's moral nature is equal at the start (all men are created equal). All inequalities are either accidents of nature or the result of conventional choices that need to be justified. From behind a veil of ignorance, if one free and equal, self-interested, rational being would reject slavery, so would all of them. Slavery is inherently unjust, because it is the opposite of what people would choose from an original position that fairly represented their moral nature. In this way, intuitively appealing rights like freedom, equal opportunity, and equal treatment can be justified by showing how they are compatible with social contract theory's major principle, which is: *"Everyone ought to act in accordance with the principles that would be chosen by self-interested, free and equal, rational, needy people who come together to form a social contract."*

Social contract theory is, then, a fully decentered abstract postconventional theory. Rawls's veil of ignorance is a device of reason to help us conceptualize the logical consequences of conceiving of humans as *morally* autonomous beings. Theoretically, what one contractee would choose would be compatible with what all morally autonomous people would choose, if they had similar information and opportunity for public debate. The amount of information available is crucial. As new information becomes available to mankind, we will have to rethink what we believe would be chosen from behind a veil of ignorance.

We can see the importance of adequate information to the fairness of a contract, if we consider the New Jersey court ruling in the recent Baby M. surrogate motherhood case. Mrs. Whitehead signed a contract in which she agreed to give birth to a baby after being artificially inseminated with Mr. Stern's sperm. She agreed to financial compensation for giving up the baby to the Sterns, who would then raise it as their own. Mrs. Whitehead changed her mind, however, and sued in court to keep the child. She eventually lost her case because of intervening variables that led the court to believe that it was in the best interest of the child to live with the Sterns. For the same reasons the appeals court agreed the child should stay with the Sterns; however, this court also ruled that the original surrogacy contract was invalid. They argued that this type of contract presupposed someone could obligate themselves before they had access to information crucial for making a rational decision. Carrying a child to term creates new pressures and experiences that ought to figure into a rational, caring decision. The court ruled that surrogacy contracts that do not allow a surrogate mother to change her mind in light of this new information are invalid.

> She was guilty of a breach of contract, and indeed, she did break a very important promise, but we think it is expecting something well beyond normal human capabilities to suggest that this mother should have parted with her newly born infant without a struggle. Other than survival, what stronger force is there? We do not know of, and cannot conceive of, any other case where a perfectly fit mother was expected to surrender her newly born infant, perhaps forever, and was then told she was a bad mother because she did not. We know of no authority suggesting that the moral quality of her act in those circumstances should be judged by referring to a contract made before she became pregnant. . . . If we go beyond suffering to an evaluation of the human stakes involved in the struggle, how much weight should be given to her nine months of pregnancy, the labor of childbirth, the risk to her life, compared to the payment of money, the anticipation of a child and the donation of sperm? . . . We have found that our present laws do not permit the surrogacy contract used in this case. Nowhere, however, do we find any legal prohibition against surrogacy when the surrogate mother volunteers, without any payment, to act as a surrogate and is given the right to change her mind and to assert her parental rights.[10]

This idea that valid contracts presuppose not just consent, but consent informed by sufficient information, is crucial to social contract theory. It means the general information available behind the veil of ignorance would have to be qualitative as well as quantitative. It would have to contain case studies as well as broad theory. We can even hypothesize that contractees might role-play situations to get the feel for the ways of life they are going to have to judge. And, although they are trying to choose final principles, they must have the opportunity to change their mind when reflection on new experiences teaches them about better ways to look at the world. Eventually, after all the debate and reflection, Rawls believes it makes sense to suppose that people entering into a social contract would in fact choose a system that emphasizes the three central virtues of the eighteenth-century Enlightenment period: liberty, equality, and fraternity. For some reason fraternity is often ignored by Rawls's critics, but this relational term plays a central role in his theory. Overall, Rawls's contractual theory would give people positive duties to promote social welfare for everyone. Thus, there would be unanimous consent to three major background principles, which would be used to judge the justice of the institutions that distribute social goods.

1. A Liberty Principle: *Everyone ought to have an equal right to the most extensive basic liberty compatible with a similar liberty for others.* This principle would have top priority. It establishes a boundary on the distribution of other social goods. Other calculations cannot be considered until after a system of liberties is established that will maximize freedom for everyone (liberties such as voting rights, freedom of the person, citizenship rights, etc.).
2. An Equal Opportunity Principle: *Inequalities are unjust unless they are attached to offices open to all under conditions of fair equal opportunity.* This principle makes equal opportunity the second most important boundary on judging institutional arrangements. Only after equal liberty and equal opportunity are guaranteed is it appropriate to distribute other social goods like wealth, power, prestige, rights and duties of station, and so forth. An unequal distribution of these goods might be permissible, but everyone has to have a fair equal opportunity to compete for any social advantages that are allowed to enter the system.
3. A Difference Principle: *Inequalities must be to the advantage of everyone in the society (the bottom class must also benefit from the inequalities).* This principle is based on the assumption that free and equal rational agents would want to keep their equal status in life, unless allowing inequalities to exist would benefit them. The only way to be certain you will benefit is if the inequalities benefit everyone.[11] For instance, perhaps differences in salary would be allowed if they lead to an increase in productivity so there would be more for all of us to share in the long run. This principle is very "friendly" in that it looks like the kind of consideration that would be chosen by people in a relational net where all of them are concerned about the well-being of the others. This is why Rawls thinks that his method emphasizes the virtue of fraternity.

Generally, social contract theories lie halfway between consequentialist and nonconsequentialist traditions. On the one hand the social contractees are trying to make choices that will maximize their conception of the good, and this makes it look like a consequentialist approach to ethics. But on the other hand, it is nonconsequentialist in that there are strict restrictions placed on the initial choice conditions. The contractees are forced by the veil of ignorance to adopt a moral point of view that is impartial, rational, universal, and caring—regardless of what adopting this formal perspective does to their particular conception of the good. In this way, the form of their choice logically precedes, and puts boundaries on, the conception of the good they can choose.

Rawls points out that in the initial contractual situation, contractees can only have a "thin" theory of the good; that is, they can only know that no matter who they turn out to be, they will want to maximize their share of the primary social goods that are a prerequisite for having any kind of life at all. These are goods distributed by all societies—things like wealth, power, prestige, rights and duties, equal opportunities, freedoms (such as the freedom to form their own conception of the good), and even self-respect—insofar as it is affected by social relations. Before they can know the details of what they will personally value, they need a theory of obligation that specifies the moral boundaries placed on the choice of any full theory of the good. The theory is, then, basically a nonconsequentialist approach to ethics, since the main focus is on the theory of obligation.

■ Problems with Rawls's Social Contract Theory

Rawls's A *Theory of Justice* is probably the most influential text on social justice in this century. It has revitalized normative ethics and stimulated wide and intense critical debate. The details of the debate are too extensive to summarize here, but most of the criticisms can be divided into two types. The first type accepts Rawls's methodology but disagrees with his conclusions about what would be chosen. Critics argue that contractees would not choose such egalitarian principles, but instead would take greater risks by choosing less cautious principles, perhaps something like a principle that would promote the average utility of society. The second group of critics attack the method itself. They argue that it is far too abstract and unrealistic (How can we get guidance by thinking about how people might think when they don't know who they are?), and is basically circular (since by carefully structuring an original contractual position ahead of time you can generate any kind of principle that you want). Although I agree that Rawls's theory is abstract, I view that as a virtue, not a liability. He clearly acknowledges the type of background assumptions any theory must adopt if it is going to clarify the institutional prerequisites for developing and maintaining respect for our moral nature.

Recently, Michael Sandel[12] accused Rawls of formulating a version of the social contract that is actually biased in favor of certain conceptions of the good over others. Sandel argues that the veil of ignorance is not really neutral toward lifestyle choices (conceptions of the good) since the desire to maximize wealth, power, individual rights and liberties, and so forth, favors choosing principles that would support atomistic individualism rather than dedication to community. There is not sufficient space to refute this criticism here, but I believe it is based on a misreading of Rawls's text.

Rawls argues[13] that he is conceptualizing the logic of just political choice, not advocating an individualistic metaphysics. There is nothing anti-communitarian about wanting a large share of wealth in the original contractual situation. Without personal information, the desire is neutral with regard to lifestyle choice. From behind the veil it can lead only to principles designed to protect everyone's rights to an equal share of social goods. Thus, it is not at all inconsistent with someone's choosing to dedicate themselves to a community. If one has a larger share of goods than is needed, one can always turn one's share over to her community if that is the conception of the good one chooses. In addition, with his emphasis on moral development and the importance of fraternity, I believe that Rawls's theory of justice would welcome anyone who cares to read it with a communitarian voice. The approach shows just how inherently social moral nature has to be. Those who are impressed with Rawls's approach are busy constructing rebuttals to these kinds of criticisms, so the literature on Rawls's theory is still unfolding. We will not pursue these matters here, because they would lead us into further metaethical concerns and away from applied ethics.

■ DUTY ETHICS

There is a tradition in ethics that is eloquently stated in the works of the genius Immanuel Kant. He argued that all consequentialist theories of ethics are misconceived, because they distract us from those variables that are truly essential in ethics. Kant believes the *form* of an action is more important for judging the moral worth of the act than the consequences that follow from it. He asks: When do we praise people for their moral behavior? Do you feel like giving praise when someone says they did their duty in order to promote their own happiness? Probably not. Kant agrees that acting to make yourself happy is not immoral, but it is also not a morally praiseworthy act. Moral actions are unique; they can be used to clarify the difference between human moral agents and other animals. Animals can act on self-interest and instinctual social drives, but they cannot act as moral agents. So what is it that humans can do that animals can't?

Humans can choose to do their duty for duty's sake. They can choose duty even in circumstances where doing their duty leads to bad consequences for themselves. For example, in certain circumstances soldiers can intentionally choose to die in support of a cause. They do not die because they expect to gain personally from dying. They do it because, under the circumstances, it is their duty to die (animals that sacrifice themselves for their tribe, flock, or pack have no choice in the matter; their apparent dutiful behavior is an instinctual reaction). Anytime we act for duty's sake, rather than to advance a personal goal, we are acting morally (remember Socrates' devotion to duty even in the face of death?).

'The willingness to do what is right even if it hurts' is a sign that a person has a GOOD WILL. I think that Kant's conception of a good will comes close to emphasizing the same notions of rationality and caring that are essential attributes of responsible moral agency. In Kant's theory, the caring side of responsibility is developed through the notion of reverence for moral law as such. The reverence for moral law felt by a person of good will comes from intellectual understanding

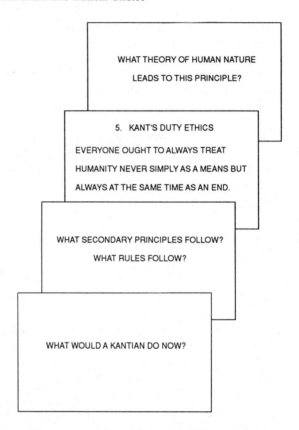

of moral law; therefore, it is caused by rational reflection. This means reverence is not an ordinary emotion, since it is not like a desire that might cause us to adopt moral beliefs. Kant says

> Now an action done from duty has to set aside altogether the influence of inclination, and along with inclination every object of the will; so there is nothing left able to determine the will except objectively the *law* and subjectively *pure reverence* for this practical law, and therefore the maxim of obeying this law even to the detriment of all my inclinations.[14]

In a footnote at the bottom of the page Kant clarifies what he means by reverence for the law. He says:

> . . . Although reverence is a feeling, it is not a feeling received through outside influence, but one self-produced by a rational concept, and therefore specifically distinct from feelings of the first kind, all of which can be reduced to inclination or fear. What I recognize immediately as law for me, I recognize with reverence, which means merely consciousness of the subordination of my will to a law without the

mediation of external influences on my senses. Immediate determination of the will by the law and consciousness of this determination is called "reverence," so that reverence is regarded as the effect of the law on the subject and not as the cause of the law. Reverence is properly awareness of a value which demolishes my self-love. Hence there is something which is regarded neither as an object of inclination nor as an object of fear, though it has at the same time some analogy with both. The object of reverence is the law alone—that law which we impose on ourselves but yet as necessary in itself. . . . All moral interest, so-called, consists in reverence for the law.[15]

Why does Kant insist that reverence must be "self-produced" rather than influenced by something outside of the person's moral will (such as genetic predispositions, introjected values, or threats of punishments and rewards)? Because Kant believes that actions and feelings that are truly moral have to be autonomous. If our moral will is going to be independent (rather than a means that serves the agenda of some other faculty), then the principles and feelings associated with it have to originate from within it, alone, free from control by "inclination" (Kant's term for all the physical desires that control the establishment of prudential goals). Our body is external to our moral will, so a morality developed to satisfy the body's inclinations (or society's introjected values) is not an autonomous morality. Kant characterized the difference by saying that "actions controlled by forces from without" are *heteronomous*, rather than autonomous. Thus, obeying the law because it satisfies a desire is to act in accordance with an authority external to the moral will rather than the authority of my own autonomous reason. Reverence is the feeling that explains our subjective caring for the moral law (a law formulated independently by pure reason). Reverence must be caused by reason's own contemplation of moral concepts rather than be a prior feeling that causes contemplation of moral law.

Developmentally speaking, I wonder if a person can be capable of reverence if the person has not had the prior opportunity to become a social being. Could a sociopath learn reverence purely through rational contemplation? Or would he first have to be taught how to care about something other than himself? Learning to care is developing a capacity, and it may require outside influence. If this were the case, it would not necessarily be incompatible with Kant's notion of reverence. Perhaps the feeling of reverence has to make use of normal emotional structures that have previously developed, just as the development of recursive formal reason has to use cognitive structures that were previously developed by outside forces. The point is that reverence and rational self-criticism build on prior structures, but they are not controlled by them.

Kant uses the term PURE REASON to refer to the 'capacity to exercise the intellect without letting it be controlled by the body's heteronomous inclinations'. Kant believes that the only way to make sense of morality, which is a practical necessity, is to assume people are free. It is therefore a practical necessity to believe that moral agents have the capacities for pure reason, since it is a necessary prerequisite for autonomy. Autonomous reason is, then, a regulative concept that guides how we must think about humans when we take up the moral point of view. Kant believes that we cannot prove we are actually autonomous in a metaphysical sense, we can only assume it. We will not pursue this issue here. In Chapter Eight, I tried to make a case for the fact that a significant kind of moral autonomy may be possible, but Kant's discussion of these issues is much more cautious.

To show respect for our autonomous nature, then, we must always treat people according to ethical principles that could be derived from their own exercise of pure reason. This is the source of moral duty. That is, duty can be defined as acting on MAXIMS (principles or intentions) that are consistent with pure reason's contemplation of moral law. Since pure reason is free from influence by subjective inclinations, its maxims are appropriately universal. That is, the moral law is the same for everyone who acts on reason. In principle, then, all creatures using pure reason ought to be able to communicate on the level of moral law. If we will act only on pure reason when we intervene in the lives of others, we will always be in a position to give them a moral account that will make sense to anyone who uses pure reason. Of course, concrete contingencies of social life will make it difficult in practice to act only on pure reason, but the ideal behind rational moral communication is clear.

How can we tell when our actions are motivated by duty for duty's sake rather than inclination? It will depend on the form or type of principle we are acting on, not the consequences of the act. The act must be based on a CATEGORICAL PRINCIPLE of autonomy, not a CONDITIONAL PRINCIPLE of heteronomy. Principles that have a conditional form say: "IF (*some inclination*) THEN (*some 'ought' command*)." Conditional principles give ought commands that only make sense if we are feeling some previous inclinations; for example, if *you want to be successful,* then *you ought to be honest.* This command makes honesty a means to satisfying a personal want (a theory of value precedes the theory of obligation). A categorical principle, on the other hand, applies universally no matter what the local inclinations; for example, *you ought to be honest, no matter what you are inclined to do.* Kant argued that all moral maxims are categorical in this way, since they are not justified by subjective or heteronomous conditions.

Although it can be stated in different ways, Kant claimed that there was only one categorical imperative: "Act only on that maxim through which you can at the same time will that it should become universal law" (p. 88). How are we supposed to interpret this universalizability criteria? I think it is important to stay focused on the fact that for Kant the universalizability test represents a social boundary on moral actions. That is, a maxim must not only be internally consistent, it must also function as a consistent, prescriptive social maxim for everyone who is going to live the type of life it recommends.

There are two ways in which maxims can fail to be universalizable. First, some maxims are simply conceptually incoherent. For example, Kant says if you make a promise with the intention of breaking it, the maxim on which your action rests cannot be turned into a universal law without contradicting itself. The maxim of a false promise is: Everyone should break their promises whenever they want. If this were the categorical principle behind the institution of promising, the institution itself would collapse. No one would believe any promise made, so the usefulness of making promises would be nullified and the act of making promises would die out. The maxim behind a false promise is conceptually contradictory, because it destroys the possibility of the act itself.

There are many immoral maxims, however, that do not seem to lead to this kind of straightforward logical contradiction. What do we do with an immoral intention that is not logically inconsistent? Kant says that these maxims fail the universalizability criteria in a second manner. They cannot be consistently "willed" as social maxims because we cannot consistently live them on a practical level. These amount to "contradictions in the will" rather than "conceptual contradictions." Their inconsistency follows from the fact that to will an end is to will the means to that end. The following interpretation of Kant's ethics closely follows Onora O'Neill's analysis in *Constructions of Reason*[10] (quotations from O'Neill are from this text). O'Neill says:

> Willing, after all, is not just a matter of wishing that something were the case, but involves committing oneself to doing something to bring that situation about when opportunity is there and recognized. Kant expressed this point by insisting that rationality requires that whoever wills some end wills the necessary means insofar as these are available. . . . This amounts to saying that to will some end without willing whatever means are indispensable for that end, insofar as they are available, is, even when the end itself involves no conceptual inconsistency, to involve oneself in a volitional inconsistency. It is to embrace at least one specific intention that, far from being guided by the underlying intention or principle, is inconsistent with that intention or principle. (pp. 90–91)

For example, the normal principle of beneficence says we ought to help others, and it is easy to universalize without inconsistency. But what if we try to universalize its opposite? To universalize the maxim to never help others, we would have to say "no one should ever help anyone else." But according to Kant, this is "volitionally incoherent." There will always be times when an agent is going to need help to achieve his goals (humans are interdependent, needy beings). It would be irrational to refuse available means to achieving your goals, so it is inconsistent with your ends to refuse the help you need when you need it. Thus, no one can consistently will that "no one should ever help anyone else," at least not as long as we remain interdependent, social beings.

The universalizability criterion behind the categorical imperative seems very abstract. It is difficult to use such an abstract imperative without practice. To help clarify the practical side of his principle, Kant gave another version of the categorical imperative that says:

> Act in such a way that you always treat humanity, whether in your own person or in the person of any other, never simply as a means, but always at the same time as an end. (Kant, p. 96)

This principle was stated in simple form in Chapter One of this text as: "Always treat people as ends unto themselves, never use them as a means only." It follows from Kant's belief that "Rational nature exists as an end in itself. This is the way in which a man necessarily conceives his own existence . . . it is also the way in which every other rational being conceives his existence. . . ." (Kant, p. 96)

O'Neill argues that all versions of the categorical imperative mean that it is unjust to involve human beings in relationships that use them as a means to satisfy someone else's purposes, unless of course it makes sense to say that in principle, rational ends would have chosen to be used in such a manner.[11] "Ends in themselves" are autonomous beings, that is, beings that ought to control their own lives with their own principles, so they never think of themselves as objects to be used by others. O'Neill points out that the injunction to never use another person as a means gives us "perfect duties" (O'Neill, 1980, p. 288). These are primarily negative duties of justice that are strict in the sense that they do not allow for individual discretion about how to carry them out. They obligate us to refrain from treating people in ways that do not give them their due as autonomous beings.

Positive duties are conceptually linked with the injunction to treat humanity (ourself and all others) always as an end. O'Neill argues that treating people always as an end requires us to act benevolently, which is "to seek others' happiness, therefore to intend to achieve some of the things that those others aim at with their maxims" (p. 288). Kant says these are imperfect duties, because the exact behavior required cannot be set out ahead of time. People want too many things, and we only have so much time, so O'Neill says, "It follows that we have to be selective" (p. 288). We do have positive duties to help others, but there is room for personal discretion and conscience in deciding who to help and how often. We will return to this issue below.

Once again we see the same theme emphasized by yet another Western theory. The categorical imperative reminds us that we must treat everyone as though they are rational moral agents who have their own ends expressed in their own practical maxims or intentions. So long as their intentions are an expression of their autonomous nature, we must respect their choice of lifestyle. This is a principle that seems perfectly fitted for pluralistic cultures, where people have to give one another room for coexistence.

This is a nonconsequentialist theory, since theory of obligation logically precedes theory of value. We don't treat people as "ends unto themselves" because it benefits us under our conception of the good to do this; we treat them that way because as rational human beings we know we are obligated to do this no matter what we value individually. We do it as a matter of duty whether or not it promotes our favored lifestyle. Because we don't have to focus on the *content* of the consequences of moral behavior but only on the *form* of the moral action (is it based on a universalizable maxim), Kant's theory is simpler to use than utilitarianism. That is, we don't have to predict future consequences for everyone's happiness, we only have to focus on doing our duty by always treating people as ends and never using them as a means only. The principle also specifies background foundational boundaries for institutions. A particular rule can look moral or immoral depending on the background. So we have to proceed in a logical manner by also judging institutions with the categorical imperative.

To properly apply the categorical imperative on any given occasion we must pay attention to how it bears on the rules that establish the immediate context of people's lives. This means that duties of station ought to be compatible with the categorical imperative. Thus, when Eichmann claimed at his trial that he was a Kantian because he did his duty for duty's sake without worrying about the consequences, he was showing that he did not understand how to apply Kant's principle to the various levels of ethical consideration. The categorical imperative applies first to foundational maxims that define a way of life. These are the maxims that must be universal, and they always have priority over the concrete laws and duties of station of a local tribe. The Nazi institutions were not designed to treat the people in the death camps as ends unto themselves. Therefore, Eichmann should have become a revolutionary rather than carry out the concrete duties of a morally corrupt station. I think O'Neill states this point well in *Constructions of Reason:*

> Intuitively, Kant's claim is that the underlying principles of a life (and perhaps of a tradition) are morally unworthy if they cannot be shared. Surface intentions, by contrast, may be unsharable without threatening the possibility of community. The demand for universalizability is a demand that the deepest principles of our lives not preclude the possibility of community. (p. 156)

Kant says that 'a society composed of autonomous people all of whom use the categorical imperative as their foundational moral maxim' would be a KINGDOM OF ENDS.[18] What shape would such a society take? I think it would be a mistake to give it a rugged individualist interpretation. For instance, if every person in the kingdom is assumed to be autonomous, it might appear that our only obligation is to refrain from violating the rights of these autonomous others (children could be protected by their autonomous parents). But the implications of Kant's concepts are not this simplistic, especially when applied to individuals who have not yet achieved autonomy. Kant's theory can easily be interpreted to account for the insights from both the male and female orientations to ethics that were discussed in Chapter Six—especially if one uses a more realistic developmental interpretation of Kant's concepts. To see how a developmental analysis would work, let's apply Kant's concepts to a small social unit like the family.

■ Kant and the Family: Implementation

On the Kantian conception, all family members are to be thought of as "ends unto themselves," but we should not confuse being an "end" with having the actual capacity to live like an autonomous moral agent (a being governed by a will that makes law for itself). Too many individualistic commentators ignore what an extreme individualist like John Stuart Mill remembered. In concrete cases, liberty principles only make sense when they are applied to people of "ripe" years with "the ordinary amount of understanding."[12] Since no one is born ripe, even "ordinary" moral understanding is impossible unless people experience at least some form of a supportive family (or tribal) heritage. It would not be functional from the moral point of view for families to treat all their members as rugged individualists. Instead, families must nurture in their dependent members the virtues that make moral autonomy possible.

Insofar as all moral agents have an obligation to promote humanity's end, they have an obligation to support the development of the necessary means for moral agency in all moral agents. As we saw earlier, Kant is clear: "To will an end is to will the means to the end." If we believe a kingdom of ends is an acceptable ideal, then we are being volitionally inconsistent if we do not form social policies that provide the means to this end, that is, policies that help people develop the virtues needed for moral autonomy. We must remember that autonomous moral saints do not reject their social heritage; they universalize it to include all of humanity. What would a Kingdom of Ends look like? Would it be a place with negative rights only, or would there also be universal positive rights? In the first place, when acting on pure reason we would simply do what the moral law requires of us. As Kant says:

> . . . As regards meritorious duties to others, the natural end which all men seek is their own happiness. Now humanity could no doubt subsist if everybody contributed nothing to the happiness of others but at the same time refrained from deliberately impairing their happiness. This is, however, merely to agree negatively and not positively with *humanity as an end in itself* unless every one endeavors also, so far as in him lies, to further the ends of others. For the ends of a subject who is an end in himself must, if this conception is to have its *full* effect in me, be also, as far as possible, *my* ends. (p. 98)

Because the capacities for moral autonomy are a necessary means for realizing humanity's end "as an end in itself," and because we cannot intend the end without intending the means, the means to humanity's end should also become my end if the categorical imperative is to have its full effect in me. Therefore, a developmental interpretation of Kant's concepts gives all of us positive duties to promote a world that nurtures the development of universal moral autonomy. To be properly nurtured, we must each get the proper life experiences in the proper sequence. It becomes especially important, then, to support institutions like the family. Families can be conceived of as the first vital link in a supportive network designed to create the conditions for a Kingdom of Ends.

But the family can fulfill its moral role only if it can support those "ends in themselves" who are not, as yet, morally autonomous. Some "ends" need more nurturance and protection than others, and some families need more outside social support than others. All autonomous agents have an imperfect duty to help families in need. There is room for personal discretion on how to carry it out, but it is a positive duty rather than only a supererogatory act of charity.

■ Problems with Nonconsequentialism

Many people think nonconsequentialism is excessively abstract. It is well and good to tell us to do our duty, but what is our duty? It would be nice to have more concrete guidance about how to live in actual institutions. For instance, what should we do if two universal duties conflict? That is, what if telling the truth conflicts with being kind? Should we always tell little old ladies that we think their hats are ugly, or is there room for a white lie? When considered outside of any particular context, Kant seems to imply that we must always tell the truth. This seems rigid to his critics. Why can't we universalize the maxim "When a small lie will spare an old man's feelings we should lie." Would this nullify itself, since no old man will believe us? What kinds of rules does the categorical imperative require in specific situations?

Because he is largely quiet on these matters, some of Kant's critics say his theory is purely formal and empty of practical advice. But Kant has good reasons for not giving much guidance about how to settle these issues. Autonomous agents are supposed to reason their own way through these conflicts. He assumes that reverence for duty and pure reason will be enough to guide our moral intuitions about how to establish proper practical priorities. In addition, practical problems are tied to a context, and Kant is only providing a background against which we can judge the deepest formal elements of all contexts. Practical solutions to specific conflicts need to be worked out through acts of conscience and public debate. Individuals who have experience with a way of life will have to make the final detailed decisions. All the theories eventually reach this point. O'Neill summarizes the problem quite well in *Constructions of Reason*. She says:

> [Kant] . . . offers an ethic of principles, rather than one specifically of virtues, and that principles can be variously embodied—both as virtues of individual characters or of institutions and also in practices and even in decision procedures. (p. 162)

> . . . and he does not see human reason as merely calculative. His modernity lies in his rejection of a conception of human nature and its telos that is sufficiently determinate to yield an entire ethic. . . . Kant offers us a form of rationalism in ethics that . . . does not generate a unique moral code, but still both provides fundamental guidelines

and suggests the types of reasoning by which we might see how to introduce these guidelines into the lives we actually lead. (p. 161)

■ SUMMARY

It is not my purpose in this text to try to solve the philosophical disagreements between the five competing theories. That would take me far beyond the scope of the text. It might be wise for a concerned moral agent to use insights from all of these theories when confronting moral dilemmas. My own favored approach should be fairly obvious by now. I accept certain Kantian assumptions about our autonomous moral nature, so I look first to see if social structures are using people as a means only. I also check to see if they have been designed to respect people as ends. I like to use Rawls's veil of ignorance to guide my thinking about concrete duties of station, that is, to establish specific rights and duties that should not be transgressed under any foreseeable contingencies. I often use utilitarian calculations to make detailed decisions if the side constraints leave several options open. If other people are not going to be affected by my decisions, I may occasionally use egoistic prudential calculations as well. But except for explaining why the text takes the shape it does, my approach should not be your concern. Basically, every moral agent is responsible for choosing her own theory. I hope the kinds of considerations that we have been discussing will be considered relevant in helping us choose the best theory.

The approach to moral issues that I most oppose is expressed in the skeptical statement: "Well, that is just the way it is." Stop and think about the consequences for social life if the great moralists in human history always approached ethical issues by saying: "Well, that is just the way it is." What would have happened to the United States if the Founding Fathers had said: "Well, that is just the way it is"? They were anything but a homogeneous group of abstract idealists (in fact, each colony had its own agenda, and the Constitutional Convention was a nice example of pluralism in action[13]), but they were also willing to *change* the way it is. There is an important lesson about moral process here. Many of the participants in the Constitutional Convention, who were not abstract idealists to begin with, nonetheless seem to have been swept up by the process of moral debate. That is, the three-step process of (1) seeking reform, coupled with (2) constitutional debate between relatively free and equal participants, who were (3) motivated by the practical necessity to reach unanimous agreement on a body of ideals, probably took many of the Constitutional Convention members much further along the road toward idealistic changes than they ever meant to travel.

This is precisely the exciting point I wish to emphasize. The process of engaging in ethical reflection during open debates, while concerned about people and principles, and bounded by the need to reach agreement among free people, can take us far beyond "the way it is." Ethics is an exciting field of study primarily because it is never complete. We can always make the world a better place if we and other free people are willing to try. Applying theory to lived life increases both the quality of moral decisions and the excitement of living. To see this, we need to return to the practical side of normative ethics. How can we use the theories we have studied to attack ethical dilemmas in a pluralistic world? To answer this question we need to turn to THEORY OF IMPLEMENTATION in the next chapter.

■ STUDY QUESTIONS

1. What are the defining characteristics of an inalienable human right?
2. According to natural rights theory, what is the moral obligation of all conventional institutions?
3. What are some of the most common problems confronting a natural rights theory?
4. What is the intuitive ideal behind the social contract approach to ethics? Why does it have such a powerful appeal to individualists?
5. Why is the veil of ignorance supposed to give us more trustworthy intuitions about justice than we would expect to find in other contracts?
6. Why is accurate, complete information crucial to the legitimacy of a contract?
7. What are the two major kinds of criticisms that are leveled against Rawls's social contract theory?
8. What is Kant's major objection to the consequentialist approach to ethics?
9. Why must the categorical imperative be based on pure reason? What is the difference between a categorical and a conditional principle?
10. In what two ways can one fail the universalizability test when testing to see if an action is a moral duty?
11. In what sense does Kant's theory give both positive and negative duties?

■ NOTES

1. For a good, sophisticated introduction to human rights theory, see the anthology edited by Morton E. Winston, *The Philosophy of Human Rights* (Belmont, CA: Wadsworth Publishing Co., 1989).

2. See B. J. Diggs, *The State, Justice, and the Common Good* (Glenview, IL: Scott Foresman & Co., 1974), p. 33ff.

3. John Locke, "An Essay Concerning the True Original, Extent and End of Civil Government," in Ernest Barker, ed., *Social Contract* (London: Oxford University Press, 1968).

4. Robert Nozick, *Anarchy, State, and Utopia* (New York: Basic Books, 1974), p. 30.

5. David Hume, "Of the Original Contract," in Ernest Barker, ed., *Social Contract* (London: Oxford University Press, 1968), pp. 149, 154.

6. Ibid., pp. 150–151.

7. Jean-Jacques Rousseau, "The Social Contract," in Ernest Barker, ed., *Social Contract* (London: Oxford University Press, 1968), p. 171.

8. The material that follows is a summary of the points made in the landmark work on social contract theory by John Rawls, *A Theory of Justice* (Cambridge, MA: Harvard University Press, 1971), p. 132.

9. Rousseau, p. 190.

10. C. J. Wilentz, "New Jersey Supreme Court, In the Matter of Baby M.," in Tom Beauchamp and LeRoy Walters, eds., *Contemporary Issues in Bioethics* (Belmont, CA: Wadsworth Publishing Co., 1989), pp. 510–512.

11. Rawls, p. 60f.

12. Michael Sandel, *Liberalism and the Limits of Justice* (Cambridge: Cambridge University Press, 1982), p. 27ff.

13. John Rawls, "Justice as Fairness: Political Not Metaphysical," *Philosophy and Public Affairs*, **14**, 1985, p. 224ff.

14. Immanuel Kant, *Groundwork of the Metaphysics of Morals*, transl. by H. J. Paton (New York: Harper Torchbooks, 1964), pp. 68–69.

15. Ibid., p. 69.

16. Onora O'Neill, *Constructions of Reason: Explorations of Kant's Practical Philosophy* (Cambridge: Cambridge University Press, 1989).

17. Onora O'Neill, "The Moral Perplexities of Famine Relief," in Tom Regan, ed., *Matters of Life and Death*, (New York: Random House, 1980), p. 286.

18. Kant, p. 100f.

19. John Stuart Mill, "On Liberty," in R. A. Wasserstrom, ed., *Morality and the Law* (Belmont, CA: Wadsworth Publishing Co., 1971), p. 11.

20. See Garry Wills, *Inventing America* (New York: Vintage Books, 1979), chp. 3.

CHAPTER ELEVEN

Theory of Implementation: The Best Means

■ THE RELATIONSHIP BETWEEN MEANS AND ENDS

In applied ethics, we study ways to make theoretical goals real in concrete institutional structures. It is seldom the case that institutions are exactly the way we think they ought to be, so ethics will always draw our attention to the possibility for improvements. But, to talk ethically about changing institutions, we will have to develop a theory about how to choose ethical means to our goals. If we do not develop a sound theory of implementation before we undertake reforms, our attempts to create a better world by applying ideals may do more harm than good.

For instance, rather than blindly rebelling, the Zimbardo prisoners would have been better off to use the good reasons that justified their feelings of outrage to argue with the guards about the need for practical reforms. Remember this point. In ethics we focus on the reasons for making a change in the status quo, not the mere fact that people desire a change. The reasons used to justify an ideal theory will often also point us in the best direction for implementing changes. The process of reform is as important as the ideals that guide reform, and both should be justified with the same reasoning in order to avoid choosing self-defeating means or inadvertently embodying the wrong ends in our institutions. Thus, we will need a THEORY OF IMPLEMENTATION that can 'guide us toward the best means for achieving ideals'. One obvious goal is to find means for achieving our ends that will not corrupt us. If we use the wrong means, by the time we achieve our ideals we may no longer hold the high standards that started us on our moral journey.

The most obvious preliminary question is: "Which theoretical orientation should guide our theory of implementation?" Because it is not easy to answer this question, it would save considerable time if we could just bypass all the theoretical disagreements between the theories and go directly to concrete cases. Kohlberg tried something similar to this. After he finished his descriptive work, he recommended that agents use a fairly straightforward device of reason to analyze concrete value conflicts. He called his approach IDEAL ROLE-PLAYING and claimed the procedure could guide our conscience toward higher-stage solutions to

191

conflicts. If ideal role-playing can function as Kohlberg suggests, we can avoid having to choose among the five theories themselves. As a first step, then, we need to analyze whether ideal role-playing can serve as an overall implementation strategy.

■ *Ideal Role Playing*

To function at the highest stage of moral deliberation Kohlberg says we should use three steps. First, one should role-play by mentally stepping into each position in a situation (including one's own) in order to understand all the relevant claims that can be made. Second, one should be impartial. This means we should imagine we do not know who we are in a situation. We should ask, "If I could turn out to occupy the position of any of the parties (reverse positions with any of them), which claim would I intuit to be the strongest?" A totally impartial person is only interested in what is right. Since he has no personal stake, he should be able to reverse positions with anyone else and come to the same conclusion. The final step is to act in accordance with those claims that we can intuitively see are more deserving of satisfaction. To solve the Heinz dilemma (see Chapter Five) with this procedure, we ". . . must imagine whether the druggist could put himself in the wife's position and still maintain his claim and whether the wife could put herself in the druggist's position and still maintain her claim."[1] Kohlberg claims that intuitively we will feel the wife could, the druggist could not. Since only the wife's claim is completely reversible, she has the strongest right, and we should solve the dilemma in her favor.

On the surface it looks as though Kohlberg has made a significant contribution to normative philosophy. He has apparently made an empirical discovery that most people, because of developmental lag, hold popular theories that are inadequate according to advanced psychological and philosophical criteria. This is, indeed, a contribution if it clarifies some of our disagreements. But does it also indicate that we should abandon our attempts to resolve the disputes between the traditional consequentialist and nonconsequentialist approaches to ethics, and simply concentrate on sharpening ideal role playing as an ethical tool for implementing advanced intuitions? Of course not—the issues are not that simple.

Contemporary representatives of each of the five theories discussed in the last two chapters would argue that their theories would not lead moral agents into a state of ethical disequilibrium to any greater extent than would Kohlberg's own normative device of ideal role-playing. They would maintain that their theories are already stage six because they adequately integrate rights and duties and satisfy the metaethical criteria of universalizability, reversibility, consistency, and prescriptiveness. For example, contemporary utilitarians argue that we ought to calculate utility in the same manner as would an impartial benevolent spectator. Surely the impartiality of such a calculation will have the same substantive effect as using ideal role-playing. Also, social contract theory has been modified so as to guarantee autonomous universal judgments from behind a veil of ignorance, a constraint designed to ensure that principles chosen from a contractual position will satisfy the formal criteria just mentioned. Kohlberg would probably respond that the attempts of contemporary defenders to improve their traditional theories lend support to the notion that many early versions of traditional theories were defective from the moral point of view. But such a claim would only be of historical interest. If all of these theories now satisfy stage six criteria and yet are not synonymous theories, then the traditional problems between them remain. Merely studying moral development cannot tell us how to resolve disagreements between theories that are already at the same advanced level of abstraction. When theories all have the same developmental status, there are no developmental differences that can elevate one over the others.

■ Intuitionist Theories Are Incomplete

The main problem with ideal role-playing is that it represents an incomplete theory. The third step says to intuit who has the strongest claim. Which intuitions are correct? Even if a person claims to have stage six intuitions, she still needs to enunciate the principles behind her priorities. Would an ideal role-player empathize with all motives, or only those that were compatible with principles that follow from a well-thought-out moral theory? For example, an act utilitarian would argue that after putting yourself in the shoes of everyone involved you should add up the utilities and do the thing that will promote the greatest happiness for the greatest number. A social contract ideal role-player would have different intuitions, since she would be concerned with the ideal contractual context that ought to guide our current intuitions. That is, we cannot intuit which claim is strongest without first analyzing what ought to be the case in a just society.

Because different orientations will lead different ideal role-players to different intuitions, utilitarian and social contract theories seem preferable to ideal role-playing. They give us a wealth of background conceptions to focus on when we begin to ask questions about implementation. Ideal role-playing is just too silent about how to analyze background conditions. Is this device of reason a method for intuiting which principles apply in a given situation, or is it a method for guiding us toward merciful or benevolent intuitions in spite of the other principles that may apply? We cannot adequately answer this question, because ideal role-playing is only a procedure, not a principle with a background theory that can help us organize a complex world. Kohlberg treats it as though it were an example of pure procedural justice, which Rawls defines as "a correct or fair procedure such that the outcome is likewise correct or fair, whatever it is, provided that the procedure has been properly followed."[2] But how do we properly follow it?

Ideal role-playing seems attractive, but that is only because it is a restatement of the moral point of view found in all mainstream philosophical theories. They are all rationally based because they all express a concern about impartiality, universality, and respecting persons and principles. Because these theories are conceptually more detailed than ideal role-playing, however, they give us greater guidance about how to proceed with implementation. Thus, until metaethics shows us how to choose between them, we must respect the opinion of anyone who is seriously trying to use one of these theories to solve moral problems. The first question to ask when judging implementation strategies is not "Which theory are they using?" but "Are they using a theory that is morally responsible from the philosophical point of view?" If so, they will be less likely to be banal or make mistakes in the choice of means, and we should seriously consider their proposals.

■ Implementation and Moral Agents

Kohlberg's research also highlights a different implementation problem. How do we socialize an entire society so that its members have the broad-based reflective and emotional virtues needed to use an adequate ethical theory? It is helpful to consider Rawls's advice about how to implement his own ideal theory:

> Principles are to be universal in application. They must hold for everyone in virtue of their being moral persons. Thus, I assume that each can understand these principles and use them in his deliberations. This imposes an upper bound of sorts on how complex they can be, and on the kinds and number of distinctions they draw.[3]

How complex we make our principles will be a function of the level of understanding we expect the average moral agent to achieve. There are three broad alternatives available; each has different implications. First, advocates of an ethical theory can assume that people cannot understand anything more complex than a concrete rule. In this case, they will tell people to obey rules and just trust that rules have a principled justification. This strategy was used by the guards in the Zimbardo Prison Experiment. It may be appropriate for children, and it may be necessary in emergencies, but as a general policy it has serious ethical defects. People should be free to choose the rules and principles under which they must live, and freedom presupposes people understand what they are choosing. Surely, to socialize by rote alone is unacceptable in a society that wants people to be free, responsible moral agents.

A second alternative is to simplify principles and their justification, so that people who have trouble with abstract conceptions can understand and choose the simplified versions. This alternative requires authorities to present principles as slogans. Sloganeering underestimates both the importance and the complexity of the process of ethical debate. Simplification may be a necessary step early in an educational program or in the first stages of a debate, but it does not make sense for a society to remain at this level and bypass the process of complex educational debate that can promote greater understanding.

A third alternative, then, is best for the long run. Advocates of abstract theories should support social programs designed to help people develop the necessary competence for choosing and acting on abstract theories. Kohlberg's research on human development indicates that, other things being equal, people will naturally choose the conception of justice that correlates with their stage of cognitive development. If people have received intense exposure to the sophisticated debates and dialogues that allow them to understand abstract options, the advocates of the various theories can allow a process of cognitive and moral selection to run its course. If their theory is truly the best theoretical and practical alternative available, people who can understand it will choose it. If it is not the best available, it should not be chosen.

This option implies that the first step in any general theory of implementation is to distribute information and thinking skills as widely as possible. This will help us (1) place responsibility where it belongs—on moral agents themselves, (2) increase people's freedom of choice, and (3) hold one another responsible for our choices. If we have been introduced to the options and have the capacity to understand what we ought to choose, then ignorance is no excuse for our failure to choose properly.

■ Implementation of Particular Theories

Cognitive developmental theory can be helpful in trying to address the issue of how to implement theories. To give social allegiance and personal contingencies their proper moral weight we need the highly developed caring, rational objectivity that can make sense of formal theories, but Kohlberg's theory suggests that we are not stimulating this kind of development as well as we should. Too many real institutions imitate the model found in Zimbardo's prison. As Zimbardo said: "What vicarious learning takes place in prisons where power, authority, and control are the chief virtues to be modeled by prisoners [and guards]?" To counter this, institutions should encourage people to use fairly sophisticated decision procedures that will help them stay sensitive to the full range of moral variables. Of course, a decision procedure cannot do the job by itself, but it can help.

Earlier, I criticized ideal role-playing because it was an incomplete intuitionist approach that could not help us bypass theoretical considerations. However, I did not mean to imply that it is a mistake to encourage students to use this decision procedure. Because ideal role-playing emphasizes the moral point of view, I think it is a very useful tool for practicing some of the prerequisite skills needed in philosophical analysis. For example, William Penn reports[4] that he used ideal role-playing successfully in a Business Ethics class. He found that this simple decision procedure helped students reach a consensus about whether to use bribes when engaging in international business transactions. The students originally believed that it would be impossible to reach consensus on this issue, but when they used ideal role-playing, irrelevant personal differences were dropped from consideration. According to Kohlberg, one of the advantages of a higher stage of reasoning is its ability to help people reach a consensus; thus it is a mark in ideal role-playing's favor that Penn's students could reach agreement on a complex issue. However, Penn's results do not give ideal role-playing any "special" philosophical status as an implementation strategy. He might well have achieved the same results if he had his students use Rawls's veil of ignorance device or encouraged them to take the point of view of an impartial benevolent spectator. All of these impartiality devices will bring greater consensus since each encourages us to set aside irrelevant subjective differences.

Even if Kohlberg's research cannot tell us which stage six ethical theory is most adequate, it can help us understand some of the practical problems that come up in applied ethics. If ought implies can, then we cannot say that people ought to accept an abstract solution to a dilemma until they are capable of understanding what we are talking about. Can a well-designed decision procedure solve this problem? Not necessarily. Decision procedures make use of abstract principles. People at the lower stages may well make immoral decisions even when they are using a decision procedure like ideal role-playing, because they do not know how to calculate in the abstract manner required by that kind of procedure. Good principles can be easily abused by well-meaning people when they are blinded by an unsophisticated moral orientation. For instance, Eichmann claimed he was a Kantian; was he being disingenuous? Since a stage three person uses the rule of the peer group, he may well decide to go along with his group's illegitimate behavior rather than act autonomously as ideal theory demands. This means that an adequate decision procedure will have to be both fairly complex and fairly concrete. To add a further check on misuse of decision procedures, people must be encouraged to use them under conditions of critical public debate, and institutions themselves ought to be structured so as to welcome such methods into the boardrooms.

The seven-step procedure presented in Chapter Two is typical of the devices that are recommended by many ethicists to help people evaluate and solve concrete cases of value conflict. It is designed to help people avoid becoming either overwhelmed or overly simplistic. It is expected, of course, that people will need to go back and forth between the steps of such a decision procedure to make adjustments as the ethical deliberation progresses and becomes more complex, for instance, in order to add an important fact or an additional ethical assumption or principle that was not emphasized the first time through.

At this point it becomes clear how Kohlberg's research makes an important contribution to normative philosophy. It demonstrates forcefully why advanced normative theories must all agree on at least one substantive moral right. No matter what theory we favor, it must advocate giving people the educational experiences that are a prerequisite for properly using a decision procedure that emphasizes the moral point of view behind the theory. Rawls recognizes this fact explicitly when he states that "the moral education is an education for autonomy,"[5] where autonomy is defined as the ability to live according to principles that would be chosen from behind the veil of ignorance. If moral autonomy is to become an increasingly practical guide in our daily life, then, other things being equal, as many of our institutions as possible ought to be designed to promote this ideal or at least not inhibit it—especially those institutions that affect human development or create and disseminate information (e.g., family structures, day care centers, schools, universities, media agencies).

It is not enough to have a theory about where you would like to go; to have successful reforms you must also know how to build on the past. In his study of the failure of new settings (which were collective attempts to implement some ideal conception) Sarason found that the first step in any attempt at reform must be a historical study of the current setting. This requires us to consider conditions "before the beginning" of the "new" setting,[6] but unfortunately, whether the goal is self-transformation, a marriage, or the creation of a new society, this first step in implementation is often overlooked. Sarason says ". . . Consensus about values does not instruct one in how to create settings consistent with these values, and that is why the creation of settings is such an important problem" (p. 20). Time and time again, he found that people in agreement on values failed in their attempts at reforms because they were not aware of how much old forms structure the recommendations for reform itself. We must confront our history, build on it, and guard against it, if attempts at reform are not going to flounder. Sarason says:

> . . . Unless the compass that guides us has history built into it we will go in circles, feel lost, and conclude that the more things change the more they remain the same. . . . One can only sigh and say, "here we go again" when we see efforts to shape futures based on the rejection or ignorance of the past. . . . The creation of a modest setting proceeds (in the local sense) a-historically at its peril. (pp. 22–23)

Therefore, in advocating reforms we must begin with institutions that are already in place and then modify them in a judicious manner. Moral problems do not occur in a social vacuum; they occur on the job, at home, in schools, in a professional setting, and so forth. These institutions need to have the values that support moral autonomy built into them, but this will not be easy if the institutions do not have a history that favors autonomy. To get an idea about how to proceed, it will be instructive to evaluate a traditional institutional setting that is already governed by a code of ethics that advocates autonomy for its members. When an institution has such a code of ethics it should be consulted. It would be a mistake to ignore an institution's code of ethics and go right to a major theory to resolve conflicts, since such an approach would nullify the expectations developed in the ongoing institution. Since professions are well-established institutions in this sense (governed by national codes that advocate autonomous practice), let's consider how professionals ought to handle ethical problems.

■ PROFESSIONAL ETHICS AND AUTONOMY

PROFESSIONS occupy a very important place in society. They are "state-supported organizations that have been given monopoly control over the delivery of services essential for promoting vital social values." To practice medicine you must join the medical profession. To practice law you must become an officer of the court.

Society supports this system with protective laws that give individual professionals powerful advantages in the marketplace, considerable prestige, and fair job security. This special status is a privilege, however, and not a right.[7] If we abuse a privilege by using it purely to promote private ends, the privilege ought to be revoked. Most professionals are well aware of this point. They understand that in exchange for the privilege of monopoly power over delivery of an important service, society expects them to be extremely conscientious in carrying out professional duties. This background expectation is often ignored by students (and some professionals themselves), because they fail to consider the historical moral context that justifies professions.

There are several defining criteria that appear in almost all attempts to define professions.

1. Professions generally require their members to master the *esoteric knowledge* of the profession. This requires more than mere training in a skill. We hire professionals not just to perform skills for us, but also to diagnosis our situation and give us advice. To diagnosis properly, a professional needs background understanding of past practice and theories. Thus, states usually license professionals not only by requiring them to have higher education certificates, but also by having applicants pass state exams that have considerable theoretical content. A significant amount of professional education, then, emphasizes acquiring cognitive skills and theoretical knowledge that helps professionals function as autonomous experts in their field.

2. Professions also *serve social values* that are so important that society officially recognizes the professions' mission with laws and licensing procedures that give the professions the *privilege of exercising autonomous monopoly control* over the delivery of services.

3. Since professions exercise autonomy over an important social value, they need a way to standardize practice and communicate new techniques to one another. Professions each have a *national organization*, which sets standards of education, creates a *code of ethics* (that both regulates the client/professional relationship and defines the relationship between the profession and the society), investigates malpractice charges, encourages research to enhance the profession's ability to serve society, advises legislatures about the delivery of professional services, and so forth.

4. Finally, Paul Camenisch notes that professions claim in their codes of ethics that they have an *extra strong moral commitment* to serve the values to which each profession is dedicated.[8] That is, they maintain they are just as concerned about the delivery of ethical services as they are with their own self-interest. Every code that I have read asserts this extra strong commitment to professional values. As an example, consider the following statement from the International Federation of Accountants:

> . . . A distinguishing mark of a profession is acceptance of its responsibility to the public. The accountancy profession's public consists of clients, credit grantors, governments, employers, employees, investors, the business and financial community, and others who rely on the *objectivity* and integrity of professional accountants to maintain the orderly functioning of commerce.

> . . . A professional accountant's responsibility is not exclusively to satisfy the needs of an individual client or employer. The standards of the accountancy profession are heavily determined by the public interest.[9]

This high moral tone is found in all codes of ethics. I choose the accountant's code for an example, because many students seem to think that the business world is a place where ethics has no place. But those who do professional work in the business world would disagree. Most of them have a good understanding of how the entire system depends on ethical standards of objectivity and fair competition.

There is, then, a fairly explicit contract cited in codes of ethics. They tell society that a profession is not just an economic system out to further the financial interests of the professional. A code encourages society to trust a profession to look out for society's interests. Because it has the extra strong commitment and the necessary esoteric knowledge, society is also encouraged to give a profession the autonomy to govern and to police itself. All codes also point out that the relationship between a professional and a client is special. It is not only an economic relationship, it is a *fiduciary relationship*, which means it is "based on mutual trust." Together, client and professional are supposed to solve the client's problems within the boundaries set by the profession's code of ethics.

Being called a "professional," then, is an honor. It implies you are concerned about the standards of excellence needed to deliver a valuable service to society. We cannot respect a doctor who doesn't care about health care, or a lawyer who is not concerned about justice, or a teacher who does not care if students learn. Camenisch worries, however, that there are powerful forces at work that could undermine the strong fiduciary and moral commitment we expect from professionals.

> . . . Retaining this moral dimension even only as an expectation will not be easy in view of a general skepticism about the actual moral distinctiveness of the professions, a widespread doubt about the possibility of altruism in any human agent, and a supposedly pluralistic society in which the very existence of generally applicable moral standards is being questioned.
>
> [We should strive] . . . for retention in our view of the professions of a moral element in keeping with which members of the traditional professions claim to be prepared to enter into fiduciary relationships with their clients, to be trustworthy allies in the society's and in their clients' pursuit of certain highly valued goals, and to be prepared to subordinate their own self-interest to the needs of their clients to a degree not usually found among other economic agents. . . . (pp. 32–38)

For the sake of continued discussion, I will assume that the traditional moral commitment of the professions is on the rebound, especially since a series of scandals (like the involvement of so many lawyers in Watergate) have embarrassed professional organizations and schools by showing to what extent they have become lax in teaching new members about the type of commitment we expect from professionals. Certainly the codes of ethics of the various professions still claim that the professions as a whole have this extra strong commitment. Since they promise dedication, we should continue to hold them to the promise.

■ Professional Duties of Station

The fact that professions have their own codes of ethics creates an interesting problem. What if there is a conflict between professional duties of station and universal duties that fall on all moral agents? For example, everyone has a duty to maintain confidences, but a lawyer or a priest has accepted a professional station in life that gives them an extra strong duty with regard to this universal ethical value. Except in a few rare instances specified by their code of ethics itself, these professionals must not reveal a confidence of one of their clients at all, even in situations where we would expect an ordinary citizen to violate a confidence for the sake of the public good. For instance, what if an ordinary citizen promised someone in a bar that he would keep the person's secret. Then the person tells him that he has murdered a number of people. The ordinary citizen would be justified in overriding his agreement to keep the confidence; he should tell the police what he has heard. But a defense lawyer, or a priest in a confessional, are in a different situation. It may be unethical for them to go to the police with the same information. How can this be? Is there a separate system of ethics for professionals?

The question is: How should professionals correlate the duties established by their code of ethics with the universal duties that fall on all of us? If we treat codes of ethics as separate, independent moral systems, this means we have a concrete example of relativism. Professionals would be covered by two unrelated ethical systems, that is, the professional code and the universal principles that cover all of us. Since relativism leads to confusion, it would be better to correlate the ethical duties in a different way.

Most commentators do not accept the idea that there are two independent systems of ethics. Instead, codes of ethics are said to be SPECIFICATIONS of how particular institutions are trying to serve the same universal human values that apply to all of us. A code of ethics is subservient to general ethics because it is a specification of how a certain group of people who have accepted a professional duty of station are supposed to help implement one of the major values of the broader society (which itself ought to be governed by universal ethics). That is, society has decided that giving professionals extra strong duties and privileges with regard to certain values (such as confidentiality) is the best way to promote another higher universal value such as justice, health, or economic well-being. Professionals do not have an extra strong duty to confidentiality for its own sake; they have this duty because it is a necessary means for carrying out the first priority of the profession: to promote some higher value for the good of society. Because of these factors, it is clear that if a professional is involved in a moral dilemma, we must analyze how his duty of station under his code of ethics affects the situation, and also why the society allowed the profession to have such duties of station in the first place. For example, in order to protect due process rights that are fundamental to the justice system (which protects all of us), lawyers must keep confidences spoken by their client, not only for the client's personal benefit, but for the benefit of the system of justice that protects everyone. And in order to serve society's spiritual needs, we must allow professionals in the priesthood to keep their confidences with individuals.

This special privilege (or duty) creates dilemmas for individual professionals. There will be times when they feel conflicts between the universal level and the professional level of obligation. But, if the professional can be clear about how his professional duty of station is itself actually in the service of higher universal values, he may be able to work out some of these thorny conflicts without feeling like he is betraying one system or the other. For example, on the face of it, keeping the confidence of a killer does not seem to have much weight when compared to the public's interest in convicting him. But when we see keeping the confidence as a conflict between "the public's interest in protecting the universal value of justice as due process" and "the public's interest in catching this one person," then the weight we give to each of these interests seems to shift. Such complex cases create dilemmas precisely because they are not simply conflicts between higher and lower values. They are conflicts about how to implement competing universal values.

■ Professional Discretion

These considerations lead to another issue that often causes confusion in pluralistic cultures. How should a code deal with PROFESSIONAL DISCRETION? Codes of ethics cannot possibly cover every contingency that might arise in unique cases, thus professionals need autonomy or discretionary 'leeway to use esoteric knowledge to figure out the best means for carrying out the goals of their profession'. What exactly does the use of discretion allow? In a pluralistic world, unrestricted use of discretion would encourage arbitrary or relativistic judgments to enter professional life. Pollock-Byrne points out in *Ethics in Crime and Justice* that many people blame the use of discretion for unethical behavior in the criminal justice system:

> The very nature of policing necessarily involves some amount of discretion. Even courts have seemed to support police discretion over full enforcement. . . . This opens the door, however, for decision making outside the confines of legality. Unethical police behavior often arises directly from the power of discretion. Because police officers have the power to select and entrap suspects, they can also make that decision unethically, such as by taking a bribe in return for letting a suspect go. . . . Discretion is an important element in the criminal justice practitioner's role and plays a part in the creation of ethical dilemmas. Discretion in criminal justice has been attacked as contributing to injustice.[10]

One solution to this kind of concern is to narrow the definition of discretion. Discretion is supposed to be a professional call, not the substitution of personal preferences for professional principles. Thus, professionals should be able to discuss with others the reasoning behind their discretionary call. If you cannot give a responsible account for how you used your professional discretion, maybe you weren't making a professional decision at all. There is room for autonomy and individual initiative in professional life, but the initiative must make sense to others in the profession. Thus, Pollock-Byrne's example of taking bribes is not an example of abuse of discretion; it is an example of corruption.

A final point: What happens when professional values conflict with the larger values in a society? Other things being equal, society's values have priority. A profession's code of ethics defines the relationship that ought to exist between universal values, the society, the profession, and the professional. The code specifies how the profession and the individual professionals can best serve the higher values. Thus, to make certain that "The Code" prescribes proper goals and means, it needs to be evaluated not only by professionals but also by ethicists outside of the profession who will represent society's interests.

Since professions generally serve major human values, however, it is possible for a corrupt society to conflict with these values. For example, how can lawyers in a Nazi culture serve justice? Or doctors supervise the torture of prisoners? When this kind of special case arises, ethical people in a profession may have to rebel against their unjust society by giving allegiance directly to the universal values that would normally justify both the society and the profession.

A commitment to justice, health, education, or other universal values can be served in many ways. One way is to act as a citizen and lobby for laws that create institutions to promote human values such as justice, health, education, and so forth. Professions are these kinds of institutions. Another way is to take a further step and join one of the institutions that is dedicated to such values. Joining a profession or taking any other job is a moral choice. You are placing yourself in an institutional setting that will begin to socialize you. Therefore, as an aware moral agent you should review and judge the norms that your job or profession serves, and work for reforms when you think the code or rules are giving inadequate prescriptions.

■ APPLYING THEORY TO PRACTICE

To make the discussion of implementation concrete, I will end this introduction to applied philosophical ethics with an example of how one could use the decision model stated in Chapter Two to analyze a fairly typical conflict found in business practice. What follows is a short summary of a case discussed in Braybrooke's text, *Ethics in the World of Business*[11] (all quotations are taken from Braybrooke's account). The names of the people involved have been changed, but the facts are summarized as accurately as possible. The case went all the way up to the Florida

Appeals Court, but I will not use the court's reasoning in my analysis. While it is instructive to compare legal analysis with ethical analysis, it is not necessarily the best way to approach an ethical dilemma. Legal analysis presupposes prior legal contexts that may or may not themselves be ethical (but of course, if a legal context makes up part of the background in a case, it needs to be taken into consideration during an ethical analysis).

The discussion that follows illustrates how I have used the Chapter Two decision model to guide my deliberations about this particular ethical issue. The fact that I used the model does not mean that my solution to the case is obviously right. In ethics, we strive to do what is right, but there is no guarantee that we won't err. The questions addressed are complex, so it is possible for other reasonable professionals to disagree with my conclusions. I hope, however, that even the most severe critic of my position would acknowledge that I am genuinely striving to reach a decision in a manner that is morally responsible.

Mrs. Jones, "a widow of 51 years and without family, had a yen to be 'an accomplished dancer' with the hopes of finding 'new interest in life.' So on February 10, 1961" . . . (p. 68), she attended a promotional party at a dancing school where she was confronted with the school's accomplished sales technique. "Her grace and poise were elaborated upon and her rosy future as an 'excellent dancer' was painted for her in vivid and glowing colors" (p. 68). Eventually, for $14.50 cash, the school sold her eight half-hour dance lessons to be utilized within a month. This started her on a course of action that led to her buying fourteen "dance courses," which in less than sixteen months would add up to "2302 hours of dancing lessons for a total cash outlay of $31,090.45" (p. 68). All fourteen courses were agreed to in writing and paid for in advance, so there is apparently a series of legal contracts in this case. Each contract had the following addendum in heavy black print: "No one will be informed that you are taking dancing lessons. Your relations with us are held in strict confidence" (p. 68).

> From the time of her first contact with the dancing school in February 1961, . . .
> She was assured she had "grace and poise"; that she was "rapidly improving and developing in her dancing skill"; that the additional lessons would "make her a beautiful dancer, capable of dancing with the most accomplished dancers"; that she was "rapidly progressing in the development of her dancing skill and graceful-ness," etc., etc. She was given dance aptitude tests for the ostensible purpose of "determining" the number of remaining hours of instructions needed by her from time to time. . . . (pp. 68–69)

Her complaint to the court alleges that she has no dance aptitude and has trou-ble hearing the beat. She claims the dance instructors knew their statements were

> false and contrary to the plaintiff's true ability, [but] the truth was withheld from the plaintiff for the sole and specific intent to deceive and defraud the plaintiff and to induce her in the purchasing of additional hours of dance lessons. . . . In other words,

while she first exulted that she was entering the "spring of her life," she finally was awakened to the fact there was "spring" neither in her life nor in her feet. (p. 69)

Mrs. Jones asked the court to nullify the dance contracts, do an accounting of how much she owed for actual time spent in dance lessons, deduct that amount from the $31,090.45 paid, and return the balance not already used up by dance lessons. The dance school, on the other hand, argued that

contracts can only be rescinded for fraud or misrepresentation as to a material fact, rather than an opinion, prediction or expectation, and that the statements and representations set forth at length in the complaint were in the category of "trade puffing," within its legal orbit. (p. 69)

The defense attorneys were pointing out that reasonable consumers expect some flattery, so their behavior did not go beyond the limits expected in the business world and allowed by law. In addition, they argued that the instructors were only giving their opinion; they were not engaging in fraud by selling a material good that was in fact misrepresented. She was an adult consumer who voluntarily signed the agreements, and they wanted to keep the contracts made. The lower court found in the dance school's favor. It ruled that Mrs. Jones did not show cause why these contracts should be nullified. Mrs. Jones would not accept the ruling, so the case was appealed to a higher court. Would it be ethical for the appeals court to nullify this contract?

When analyzing a case, much of the preliminary work will be done on scratch pads, going back and forth between the steps in the decision model so that we can change our mind as we sharpen our understanding of the relevant variables. I am not going to show all of these intermediate steps here. Although I did spend some time thinking about the case on a scratch pad, at this point I'll go directly to the final stages of my analysis. Also, I am not interested only in rendering a decision, I am equally interested in formulating a set of ethical principles that can help me understand other similar cases in the future. Thus, my analysis may be more theoretical than a judge's decision needs to be.

The first step in the decision procedure asks us to provide a *background* context for the conflict. "What is the historical situation? Determine the empirical facts, list the significant stakeholders, and so forth." This dispute occurred in Florida, in a free enterprise economy, where sellers and consumers meet as individuals under conditions of fair competition. Transactions are governed by law, so practices such as fraud, coercion, theft, and misrepresentation are not considered to be legitimate business practices. We do not need to restate the facts that are presented by the parties in this dispute; we will simply assume that they are accurately stated. It might be useful to have more details, but often in ethics we do not have access to all the information we would like, and so we have to make decisions in a partial state of ignorance. We might, however, point out one additional psychological fact. Mrs. Jones is not a business woman engaged in a trading transaction. She is going through a period when she is emotionally vulnerable; she is alone, without family, and looking for a new beginning in life. Thus, the transaction involves more than an exchange of material commodities; it involves a person's fundamental hopes and dreams. Why is this relevant?

For one thing, when issues vital to our overall well-being are involved, we use higher standards of deliberation, that is, a rational man standard rather than a reasonable man standard. For another thing, it casts some light on how to characterize the background context. One approach to market transactions presupposes something called "trader's morality." Traders are assumed to be rational, autonomous agents voluntarily playing a financial game. "Trader's morality . . . [is] conceived of as ruling out force and outright fraud (for example, not delivering the goods specified), but as licensing both sides of a transaction to take advantage of the other's mistakes."[12] Two people engaged in a trading transaction should be wary, bargain tough, sign a contract, and then, no matter what the outcome, the agreement can be considered to be fair. All contracts are final, and people of good faith uphold them. We need to consider whether this case is appropriately covered by trader's morality.

Whether it seems appropriate to have a strong regulatory code in a particular system will depend on how we interpret the background for the system's institutions. Trader's morality assumes that business transactions are private undertakings between rational autonomous agents, thus any particular contract is not of public concern. That is, purely voluntary transactions in business that involve private profit do not involve the public good, so the public is not a stakeholder. Under this kind of background assumption, ethical codes may even seem rather irrelevant. If you are going to be honest or benevolent or kind, you do it because it contributes to your profit margin, not because you have public ethical duties as a business person. As a background context for the business world, trader's morality fosters the skepticism that leads to questions like: "Isn't the idea of business ethics an oxymoron?"*

"Trader's morality" or "buyer beware" represents one possible background from which to view this case, but it is not the only option. As discussed previously, professions illustrate a different context from which to view financial transactions. Professions are defined as institutions that serve social values and have codes of ethics. Professionals are supposed to be dedicated people who willingly submit to professional standards. When the relationship is not between traders but between professional and client, different expectations hold since profit is not the only value involved. But, what do we do with business institutions and practices that are not so clearly defined by a background professional code of ethics? For instance, what

---

* This skeptical point of view is captured in simple jokes like: "Dad, what is business ethics anyway?" "Well, son, it's like this. What if a little old lady comes into the store and inadvertently overpays by 100 dollars?" "Oh, I see, Dad. The ethical part has to do with the question: 'Should I tell her she made a mistake or should I keep the extra 100 dollars?' " "No, Son, that's not it. Business ethics is about whether or not to tell my partner about the sudden extra profit."

is the appropriate ethical background from which to view a dance studio's relationship with "clients"? Should we use the professional model, or the model of trader's morality?

As a moral agent affected by what goes on in the business world, why should I accept the view that business is only about private profit? Why not characterize business first as "an institution sanctioned by society to be the arena within which we meet the survival and economic needs of the people," and second as "a place where people can engage in fair exchange of commodities for their mutual advantage"? When characterized in this way, placing ethical boundaries on business transactions does not seem so inappropriate. Ethical theories do not assume that major institutional structures that affect all areas of life should exist outside of ethical boundaries. That is, even when issues of private profit are concerned, ethical theories judge all business practices. Often, societies decide that it is not ethical to allow practices in the business world like child labor, fraud, coercion, theft, deception, or taking unfair advantage of necessitous circumstances (e.g., gouging people during earthquakes, hurricanes, droughts, war, or emotional crises). I assume, therefore, that business practices are and ought to be covered by ethical norms.

This approach to business does not tell us exactly what kind of regulations to place on a market, but it does make the market a vital part of the public realm, and calls for public standards to guide ethical business practices. From this perspective it is possible to see many business transactions as similar to (but not synonymous with) professional transactions. That is, the system of business itself is considered to be in the service of broad human values. It asks participants to be dedicated to something beyond self-interest, and to voluntarily submit to codes of fair and just business practices for the good of the whole, and in ways that show respect for the individuals with whom they must deal.

Against this general background, we can pick out the following stakeholders in the case. First, there is Mrs. Jones and the dance school, who are in a contractual dispute. But other stakeholders include the members of the business world who have a vested interest in seeing contracts that are signed upheld (to them, the burden of proof is on Mrs. Jones to show cause why the court should overturn this contract), as well as the members of society who will be affected by general business practices.

Since this case has reached a state's appeals court, the state is an additional stakeholder that has an interest in having the case resolved in a way that will set the proper precedents for the future. What tone do we want to establish for business practices in general? Do we want policies that allow courts to enter into business transactions after the fact and reverse contracts that were signed by adults? What background standards do we want to establish for valid contracts between consumers and business persons, and between clients and those that provide a service? These considerations take us to the second stage of the decision procedure.

We need to isolate the principles and duties that make up our *ideal theory*. Is this a cold financial transaction where two parties (professional traders) simply have different interests, or are their special duties involved? Free enterprise is based on assumptions about rationality, autonomy, adequate information, and honest communication. Business people only sign contracts when they believe they have something to gain from the contract. Other things being equal, we expect an analysis of a contract to reveal how both parties to the contract expected to benefit.

As I stated at the end of Chapter Ten, I usually begin my own analysis of problems by asking Kantian questions. I see the business world as a subset of a larger world governed by the regulatory ideal of a kingdom of ends. Kant is clear that in an interdependent world we must use each other to get our needs met, but we should not use each other as a means only. The mere fact that there is a dispute does not mean that the parties are not respecting each other as ends. It is possible that both sides feel that they are within their rights, because they entered into the contract in good faith. We will have to return to this consideration in a moment.

Contracts are valid only between autonomous agents who are capable of looking out for their own interests (which is why children are not allowed to sign contracts). When voluntary consent is present, we usually assume all transactions are legitimate, since people do not consent to being harmed. Under these conditions, so long as there is no obvious coercion or fraud on the part of either party, we assume both parties have a legitimate claim to have a contract enforced as is. The lower court apparently saw the case in this light.

If we are going to have grounds to nullify this contract we have to call into question Mrs. Jones's capacity to give voluntary consent, question the honesty of the communication between the parties involved, find some special duty that is being violated by the contract, or argue that society has an overriding interest in forbidding contracts of this particular type. It is also possible for issues like benevolence and caring to enter into this kind of dispute, e.g., what if the contract will lead to abject misery for one of the parties? But in this case we do not have enough information to appeal to these two principles. We do not know how wealthy Mrs. Jones might be; perhaps $31,000 means little to her, and she is only disappointed because her dancing has not improved. We do not know how financially strapped the dance school might be; perhaps they will have to declare bankruptcy and lay off employees if they return the money. Without additional information, the best policy is to stay focused on the nature of the obligations that have been incurred as a result of this contract.

What is the nature of the contract? What duties are incurred as a result of this kind of business transaction? Let's return to the earlier discussion of professions in order to cast more light on the nature of the principles that might be involved.

The relationship that exists between a professional and a client is typically characterized as a fiduciary relationship, which means a relationship of mutual trust. The professional is in a position of having superior knowledge, and she has an obligation to use that superior position to serve the client, society, the profession, and herself. Thus, the contract between a professional and a client is not the kind of contract we find between typical traders in a marketplace. Traders do business "at arm's length,"[13] with a clear head, and no pretensions to intimacy or duties to watch out for the well-being of the other party. But professionals are serving vital human needs, and people come to them precisely because they are led to believe the professional can help them with those needs. The question is: Are there elements of a fiduciary relationship between Mrs. Jones and the dance school or is this a typical contract that we would expect to find between traders?

For the sake of brevity I will not list all the alternatives that are possible under the *Implementation* step. I'll simply go right to my major conclusion. I think that the practices of the dance school in the case are unethical. The dance school presented themselves in a professional light to a fairly vulnerable needy person who is not a normal "at arm's length" trader. There was a fiduciary relationship involving confidentiality (they promised her they would keep her lessons a secret). They presented themselves as being experts with the skills and esoteric knowledge to make her a dancer who would be able to dance "with the most accomplished dancers." Given that Mrs. Jones was hoping to develop a way of life around these accomplishments, she was not simply buying a luxury item. To her, this was a matter vital to the rest of her life. They were hired as experts to satisfy fundamental needs, so special obligations were created by this contract. She was not in a good position to judge her own progress, and the "experts" should have used their esoteric knowledge to give her sound advice on how bad her investment really was. Looking at the contract, if I assume she had been honestly dealt with, I cannot see how a reasonable consumer could have expected a sufficient return on the investment to have voluntarily signed such an agreement. Thus, I conclude Mrs. Jones was either deceived by puffery that went beyond what is legally permissible, or she was in a legally relevant condition of instability at the time she signed the contract. In short, I think the dance school took advantage of her necessitous circumstances, and the contract should not be allowed to stand. The dance school has a right to that portion of the payment that went for honest lessons, but the rest should be returned to Mrs. Jones.

As a citizen, I want to encourage the institutions in my society to be honest, fair, and not take advantage of vulnerable parties. There is still plenty of room for fair competition and dynamic business activities without letting businesses take advantage of people going through transitional crises. In this particular case, the findings of the Florida Appeals Court paralleled portions of my analysis. For similar legal reasons, they also nullified the contract.

■ THE PRACTICAL IMPACT OF A COURSE IN ETHICS

Habermas is surely correct when he argues that the knowledge gained through ethical reflection changes not only the way we see ethical events but also the type of event we are capable of considering. He makes the intriguing observation that inquiry into ethical theory ought to be at the same time self-reflective inquiry into how our own norms ought to be normed.[14] In an important sense, then, reflection about ethical theory is also historical self-reflection. There is a basic incompatibility between saying "I believe people are morally obligated to do X" and saying "I don't have to ever do X even if I do believe that people morally ought to." Ethical "ought" statements are not matters of taste. Once you understand them, you cannot choose to reject them for personal reasons without feeling obligated to give some kind of account that should make sense to other moral agents. If you refuse to try and act on what you claim is morally right, it will be hard for us to believe that you really care about doing the right thing. People who act in such a contradictory manner are either terribly confused or they are telling lies. Thus, we assume that if you learn anything important about what people ought to do, this knowledge will change you on a practical level.

The fact that ethics can have a practical impact explains why there is a certain danger to taking an ethics course. You may come to believe that some of the things you enjoy doing are not morally acceptable. If you do not know that a behavior is immoral, then doing it is not really immoral, it is amoral. You may be ignorant, but at least you are not evil. However, once you come to understand that an action is a violation of a norm you believe in, you can never again perform the behavior in an amoral fashion. With knowledge of good and bad comes the burden of guilt (the proverbial apple in the Garden of Eden). After an ethics course you will be even more accountable, for you will have ethical knowledge that you did not have before. On the other hand, you should also be in an improved position to give a theoretical justification for your moral behavior. The benefits of rational ethics far outweigh possible inconveniences, and improving one's ethical abilities is itself an ethical duty.

■ STUDY QUESTIONS

1. What is the proper relationship between means and ends?
2. Why are the five ethical theories preferable to Kohlberg's ideal role-playing?
3. Why is it going to be difficult to implement an abstract theory? What are the strengths of an approach that respects the ideal of moral autonomy?
4. Why do many ethicists recommend sophisticated decision procedures to aid practical ethical judgments?
5. Why is it as important to study our past as it is to have clear ideals before we begin the process of implementation?
6. Why does the status of a profession give its members special privileges and duties to society?
7. Why do professionals claim that society can trust their profession to look out for society's interests?
8. Why does the fact that there are codes of ethics for professions cause a potential for conflict with universal values? How can we solve this problem?
9. What do we mean by professional discretion? What kind of an account should a professional give?
10. Why is it easier to think of codes of ethics in a professional context than in the business world at large?

■ NOTES

1. Lawrence Kohlberg, "The Moral Adequacy of a Highest Stage of Moral Development," *The Journal of Philosophy*, 70, No. 18, Oct. 25, 1973, p. 643.

2. John Rawls, *A Theory of Justice* (Cambridge, MA: Harvard University Press, 1971), p. 86.

3. Ibid., p. 132.

4. William Penn, "Kohlberg and Professional Ethics," pp. 13–15. I was handed a photocopy of Penn's paper at the DePaul University conference on Business Ethics in 1984. As yet I have not been able to ascertain if it has been published.

5. Rawls, p. 516.

6. Seymour B. Sarason, *The Creation of Settings and the Future Societies* (Cambridge, MA: Brookline Books, 1972), p. xvii.

7. Michael D. Bayles, *Professional Ethics* (Belmont, CA: Wadsworth Publishing Co., 1981), p. 11.

8. Paul F. Camenisch, *Grounding Professional Ethics in a Pluralistic Society* (New York: Haven Publications, 1983) pp. 10, 33.

9. *Guideline on Ethics for Professional Accountants* (New York: International Federation of Accountants, 1991), p. 6.

10. Joycelyn M. Pollock-Byrne, *Ethics in Crime & Justice* (Pacific Grove, CA: Brooks/Cole Publishing Company, 1989), p. 84.

11. David Braybrooke, *Ethics in the World of Business* (Totowa, NJ: Rowman & Allanheld, 1983), pp. 68–70.

12. Ibid., pp. 70–71.

13. Ibid., p. 70. The Appeals Court in the Jones case made use of the idea that because the dance lessons were not conducted at arm's length, a special duty was incurred.

14. Jergen Habermas, *Communication and the Evolution of Society*, transl. by Thomas McCarthy (Boston: Beacon Press, 1976), p. 86.

Index